WASHINGTON ON FOOT

★ ★ ★ ★

23 WALKING TOURS AND MAPS OF WASHINGTON, DC,

OLD TOWN ALEXANDRIA, AND TAKOMA PARK

Edited by John J. Protopappas
and Alvin R. McNeal

Published in Association with
National Capital Area Chapter
American Planning Association

Smithsonian
Washing

Copy editor: Jennie Reinhardt
Production editor: Joanne Reams
Designer: Brian Barth

Library of Congress Cataloging-in-Publication Data
Washington on foot : 23 walking tours and maps of Washington, DC, Old Town Alexandria, and Takoma Park.—4th ed. / edited by John J. Protopappas and Alvin R. McNeal.
p. cm.
"Published in association with National Capital Area Chapter, American Planning Association."
ISBN 1-58834-115-1 (pbk. : alk. paper)
1. Walking—Washington (DC)—Guidebooks. 2. Walking—Maryland—Takoma Park—Guidebooks. 3. Walking—Virginia—Alexandria—Guidebooks. 4. Washington (DC)—Tours. 5. Takoma Park (md.)—Tours. 6. Alexandria (Va.)—Tours. I. Protopappas, John J. (John Joseph), 1946- II. McNeal, Alvin R. III. American Planning Association. National Capital Area Chapter.

F192.3.W335 2004
917.5304'42—dc22

2003070383

ISBN 13: 978-1-58834-115-0
British Library Cataloging-in-Publication Data available
Manufactured in the United States of America
10 09 08 2 3 4 5

∞ The paper used in this publication meets the minimum requirements of the American National Standard for Information Sciences Permanence of Paper for Printed Library Materials ANSI Z39.48-1992.

Contents

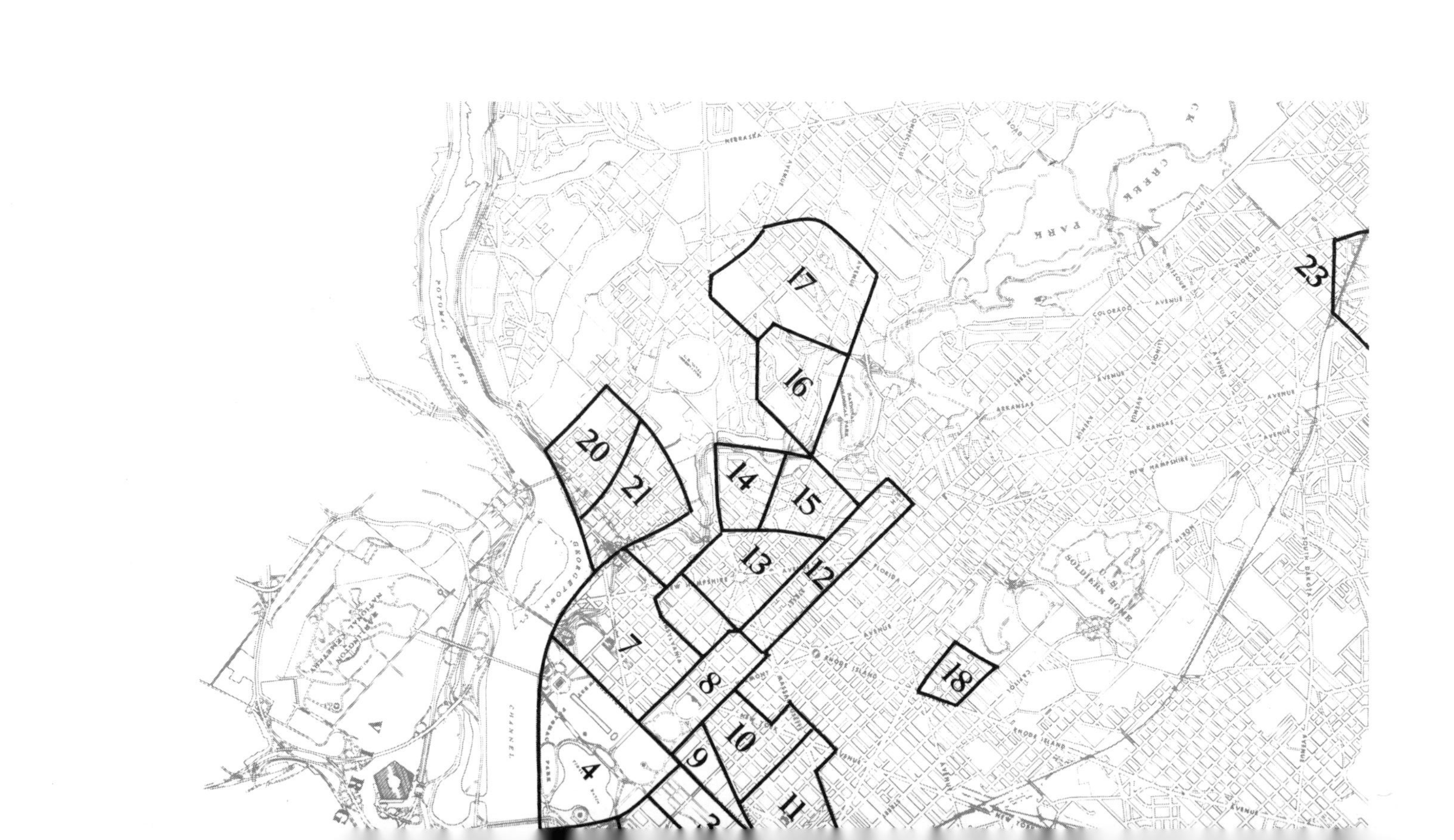
23
18
17
16
15
14
13
12
11
10
9
8
7
4
20
21
GEORGETOWN
CHANNEL
POTOMAC RIVER
CREEK
PARK
SOUTH DAKOTA
AVENUE
CONNECTICUT
NATIONAL ZOOLOGICAL PARK
ARLINGTON NATIONAL CEMETERY
U.S. SOLDIERS HOME

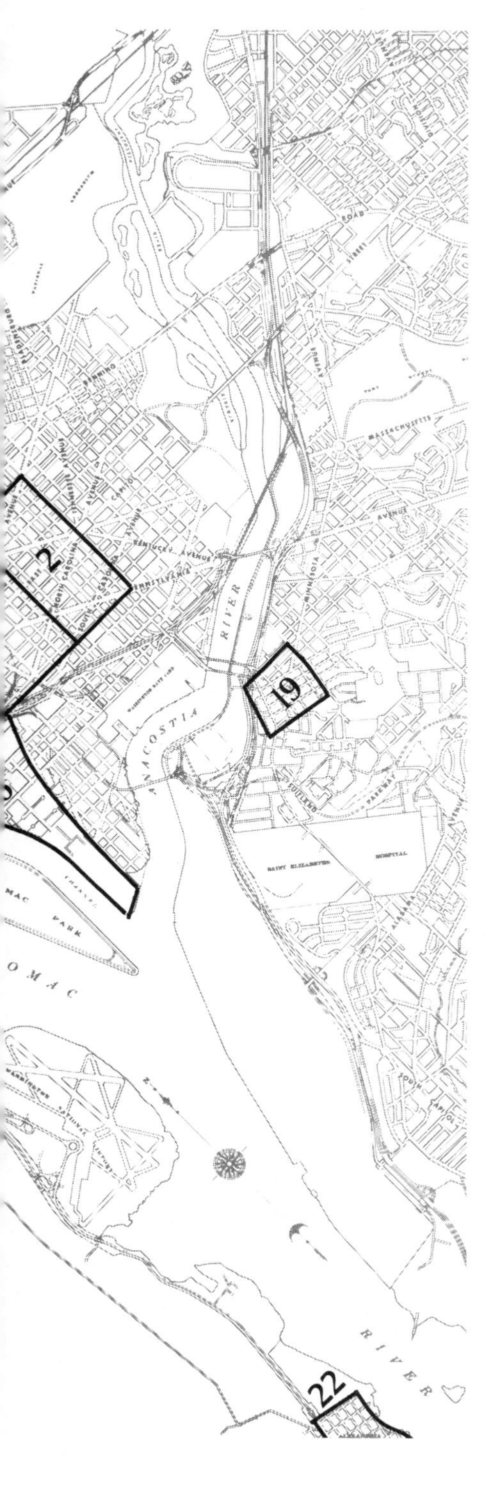

Tour Areas

1/Capitol Hill—West

2/Capitol Hill—East

3/The Mall—East

4/The Mall—West

5/Independence Avenue and L'Enfant Plaza

6/Southwest

7/Foggy Bottom

8/White House

9/Federal Triangle

10/Downtown—West of 9th Street

11/Downtown—East

12/16th Street/Meridian Hill

13/Dupont Circle

14/Kalorama

15/Adams-Morgan

16/Woodley Park and National Zoo

17/Cleveland Park and Washington Cathedral

18/LeDroit Park

19/Old Anacostia

20/Georgetown—West and Waterfront

21/Georgetown—East

22/Old Town Alexandria, Virginia

23/Takoma Park, Maryland

About Washington on Foot

Alvin R. McNeal

There are many ways to see cities, but for anyone desiring a sense of the history and the character of an urban place, the city is best seen on foot. A mosaic on a garden wall, the framed view of a church steeple from a narrow street, or the gleam of stained glass above a doorway—these are just a few of the visual rewards of a walking tour.

Washington on Foot is a guide to the neighborhoods as well as the monuments of the nation's capital. Twenty-three walking tours will steer you through the preserved colonial and federal quarters, the vital commercial districts, the distinguished residential neighborhoods, the revitalized urban-renewal areas, as well as the renowned memorials, public buildings, and museums of Washington. Two other tours will escort you through the 18th-century setting of Old Town Alexandria, Virginia, and Takoma Park, Maryland.

Originally published in 1976 for the National Planning Conference and updated periodically, *Washington on Foot* is used by thousands of visitors and residents interested in a close-up look at the historical, cultural, and architectural aspects of the Capital. Over the past 27 years, more than two dozen volunteers, including urban planners, architectural historians, and other urban professionals, have contributed to this publication; names of original authors and current updaters are provided at the introduction to each tour. More information about contributors can be found on page 231.

Washington on Foot is intended to serve the public as a guide to many of the significant features of the District of Columbia, Old Town Alexandria, Virginia, and Takoma Park, Maryland. The tours are designed for use by both pedestrians and bicyclists.

The Co-editors

John J. Protopappas is president of the Fraser Forbes Company, a major land development company in the Washington metropolitan area. Over the past 27 years he has practiced transportation and land-use planning in the United States and in Europe. He has been a guest lecturer on urban planning at the Catholic University of America and the University of Maryland. He has written for professional journals and was co-editor of the 1980 and 1992 editions of *Washington on Foot*. He is also a decorated veteran of the Vietnam conflict. Mr. Protopappas received a bachelor's degree from Niagara University and a master's degree from the Catholic University of America.

Alvin R. McNeal is president of the McNeal Group, a land-use planning and development firm based in Washington, DC. Until October 2003, he was manager of the Property Planning and Development Branch of the Washington Metropolitan Area Transit Authority (WMATA). This branch is responsible for WMATA's nationally recognized transit-oriented development program. He has been an urban planner in the Washington metropolitan area for over 25 years. Mr. McNeal received a bachelor's degree from North Carolina Central University and a master's degree from the University of Cincinnati. He has written for professional journals and was co-editor of the 1992 edition of *Washington on Foot*. He has been a part-time instructor in the Planning Department at the University of Virginia and has lectured at several universities. He is active in several planning and development organizations in the Washington Metropolitan area and elsewhere.

About the NCAC-APA

The National Capital Area Chapter (NCAC) of the American Planning Association (APA) is one of the oldest and largest chapters of the 30,000-member national organization. The chapter has more than 500 members in the District of Columbia and in Prince George's and Montgomery Counties, Maryland.

APA is the major organization in the country representing the interests of planning and planners. It was formed in 1978 by the merger of the American Institute of Planners and the American Society of Planning Officials. Members include practicing planners, local officials, architects, engineers, students, educators, and others interested in developing and maintaining well-planned urban and rural communities.

APA's member interests are represented through 44 chapters and 18 divisions concerned with areas of specialized practice. The various disciplines range from transportation and energy planning to law and environmental planning. For more information, contact APA's Washington, DC, office at 1776 Massachusetts Avenue NW, Washington, DC 20036, telephone (202) 872-0611 or www.planning.org. A subunit of APA, the American Institute of Certified Planners (AICP), fosters the professional development of APA members. It administers the certification exam for planners. AICP also is concerned with planning education and standards of planning practice.

Washington, DC

Washington, DC, has matured as a major national and international city. It is a city of considerable beauty and elegance. During its 200 years of history, it has developed into a center of international diplomacy and influence. Its numerous monuments are major tourist attractions. The White House, the Capitol, the Lincoln and Jefferson Memorials, and the Washington Monument are the nation's unique symbols of American democracy.

Washington is no longer thought of as a small town, even though its 10-mile-square size and more than half a million residents do not place it among those cities that are mentioned when one refers to large cities in the United States. The city's sphere of influence extends far beyond its geographic size and population. Washington is a capital city, a dynamic and vibrant metropolis that retains its small-town charm. The human scale of its buildings adds to the city's ambience.

Washington is the center and driving force of a sophisticated metropolitan region of over 4.7 million people in 2003, according to the Metropolitan Washington Council of Governments (WCOG). By the year 2010, this number is expected to increase to over 5 million, and jobs are projected to increase from 2.58 million in 2002 to over 3 million in 2010. According to WCOG, much of this new growth in population and employment will occur in the suburbs surrounding the city. The current population of the city is nearly 600,000. Jobs will continue to increase from a current level of over 700,000. Minority groups are well represented in Washington. Recent information from WCOG indicates that African Americans compose over 70 percent of the city's population. During the decades of the 1990s to the present, the size of the Hispanic and Asian populations has been steadily increasing in the city and throughout the Washington region. At the same time, Washington has experienced significant changes in total population, in the makeup of its households, and in its labor force and job base. The most dramatic shifts have occurred in the city's population and household constituency, reflecting changing social patterns. Prior to the 1970s, the city's households had been predominantly families with children. But the number of children in the city plummeted over the last three decades, as witnessed by the drop in school enrollments, and newer households are largely made up of singles or unrelated individuals.

Many of the new residents have relatively comfortable incomes, which permit them to enjoy the city's cultural amenities and restaurants and to purchase homes. These households have spurred much of the new residential construction and rehabilitation you will see as you visit the neighborhoods on your walking tours. These households have also fueled the escalation in the price of housing in the city.

The employment base of the city has changed from one consisting predominantly of federal government jobs to one made up largely of jobs in the private sector. Most of these jobs are in the service industry, a term generally associated with the finance, legal, health, real estate, and managerial professions. Increasingly, although the typical Washington worker is not employed by the federal government, he or she is likely to be employed by one of the businesses linked to the federal government. More indigenous to Washington are the thousands of journalists, lobbyists, and employees of the many trade associations headquartered in the city. The combination of residents, tourists, conventioneers, and workers gives the city high levels of daytime activity and a very busy nightlife at theaters, movies, hotels, nightclubs, bookstores, and restaurants.

Washington now rivals cities famous for their entertainment and cultural offerings. This change can be partly attributed to the opening of the John F. Kennedy Center for the Performing Arts in 1971. The Kennedy Center, with its imposing architectural styling, attracts performers and productions from all over the world. It has not only expanded the cultural offerings available in the city but also led to an increase in neighborhood and regional cultural institutions. The increasing number of theaters along 14th and 7th Streets NW, the refurbished Ford's Theatre on 10th Street NW, the National Theater and the restored Warner Theatre on Pennsylvania Avenue NW, and the Arena Stage in the southwest section of the city are important complements to the Kennedy Center. In fact, the city in 1990 established an arts zoning overlay along 14th and U Streets with density incentives to retain and attract additional theaters, art galleries, and other related functions to these areas. This action has resulted in attracting many bookstores, theaters, art galleries, and other arts-related functions to the areas. Art, entertainment, and cultural activities are also being developed throughout the city's downtown, particularly along 7th and E Streets, where a new theater is under construction and is slated to open in 2004 and at 7th and H Streets, where a major entertainment and retail complex is under construction with opening planned for December 2004.

The Smithsonian Institution's contribution to Washington's cultural resources as well as those of the nation is unsurpassed. It has one of the most impressive (and still expanding) arrays of museums and galleries in the world, a first-rate education program, and a distinguished performing arts program, all available to the public for free or for a modest fee. The core of the Smithsonian Institution is formed by the well-known museums centered on the Mall. The Mall is a large, open space linking the Capitol and the Lincoln Memorial that was designated in the earlier plans for the city but not formally landscaped until the 1930s. It is a well-used passive and active recreation area, popular with tourists and locals during the spring and summer and a showplace for museums, monuments, and memorials. And although debates are under way about the future of the Mall and the number of memorials that should be permitted, more museums and memorials are planned for the Mall.

Among the most notable of the Smithsonian's museums are the Arthur M. Sackler Gallery of Asian Art and the National Museum of African Art. Both are built partially underground and offer an exceptional collection of art treasures to the public. The very popular National Air and Space Museum, the National Museum of Natural History, and the Hirshhorn Museum and Sculpture Garden attract millions of visitors each year from the region and throughout the nation. The National Museum of the American Indian is slated to open to the public in 2004. In December 2003, the Smithsonian opened a new museum in Northern Virginia to display and preserve its collection of historic aviation and space artifacts. The 170-acre Steven F. Udvar-Hazy Center is near Dulles International

Airport, about 25 miles from the District of Columbia. The building contains over 750,000 square feet of exhibition, theater, restaurant, and classroom space. Vistors can walk among the engines, rockets, satellites, helicopters, airliners, and other flying machines on the floor or view hanging aircraft from elevated walkways. Public bus service is available between the National Air and Space Museum on the Mall and the new center. Call the center at (202) 357-2700 for opening hours and information on public transportation.

Visitors should not miss the National Gallery of Art, with its impressive collection of European and American paintings, sculptures, and exhibitions. You should also visit the new City Museum of Washington, DC, at Mount Vernon Square. It can be easily accessed via Metrorail or Metrobus. The museum, which opened in 2003, offers a multimedia journey through the history of the capital city and its many neighborhoods and profiles prominent individuals who have resided in the city.

The newly opened International Spy Museum explores the history, craft, practice, and contemporary role of espionage. It is located at 8th and F Streets NW in the heart of the emerging 7th Street Arts District. The Spy Museum is the first public museum in the United States dedicated solely to espionage, with the largest collection of international espionage artifacts ever on public display. A fee is charged to visit this museum.

Year round, more than 25 million tourists and conventioneers visit the other monuments and memorials scattered throughout the city. These visitors make a substantial contribution to the economic vitality of the city.

Washington is well endowed with public parks and memorials, many surrounded by large expanses of open space. Rock Creek Park—which includes the National Zoological Park, hiking and bicycling trails, the Carter Barron Amphitheatre, and many picnic and playground sites—extends from the city's northwest boundary with Maryland into the central business area anchored at the Potomac River by the Kennedy Center. In the very heart of the federal area are parks providing tennis courts, open spaces, walking areas, skating ponds, and other attractions. In recent years the District of Columbia has upgraded and redeveloped many of its neighborhood parks, including new buildings offering recreational activities.

Washington has been subject to almost continuous planning since its inception. Untold numbers of planners, architects, developers, and other visionaries have influenced the cityscape. Three of the most prominent were L'Enfant, Downing, and the McMillan Commission.

The core of Washington was largely developed as envisioned by Pierre Charles L'Enfant in his 1791 plan for the city, as modified by the McMillan Commission. L'Enfant focused on the siting of the major federal buildings and other symbols of the national government. His plan established the formal pattern of streets, avenues, squares, and circles that we see in the city today.

A second major plan, prepared in 1851 by Andrew Jackson Downing, was limited to the Mall area. It called for a natural landscape treatment of the Mall, deviating from the formalism of L'Enfant's plan. A third plan, which reinforced and extended L'Enfant's conception, was prepared by the McMillan Commission in 1902. This plan advanced a bold concept for development of the monumental core and formal federal areas of the city.

A casual walk along the Mall allows you to observe remnants of all of these earlier planning efforts. An excellent exhibit details the city's early planning history at the original Smithsonian building, known as "The Castle." Exhibits showing other aspects of the city's history were installed throughout the city to celebrate the bicentennial of its founding (1791–1991). Many of these are on permanent display at the National Building Museum, the National Museum of Natural History, and the new City Museum.

The original city planned by L'Enfant extended between the Potomac and Anacostia Rivers, south of Florida Avenue. This area encompasses the Downtown area as well as some of the city's most desirable neighborhoods. Downtown contains one major department store, hundreds of specialty shops and boutiques, restaurants, bars, theaters—and more than 80 million square feet of private and public office space. A major entertainment complex, containing a mix of housing, retail, and office space, is under construction at the Gallery Place Metrorail station. Business services, associations, and many of the city's innumerable lawyers and consultants occupy most of the private office buildings in the Downtown area. Washington's low skyline, most noticeable in the Downtown area, resulted from the congressionally mandated 1910 Height of Buildings Act, which limits the maximum height to 90–130 feet, depending upon location and zoning district. Only the north side of Pennsylvania Avenue, between 10th and 15th Streets NW, exceeds those limits, with some buildings reaching a height of 160 feet, owing to a special provision in the zoning regulations.

For over 150 years, Downtown Washington was the commercial and social center of the city and the surrounding region. Although this role was challenged somewhat from the 1950s to the 1970s as suburban retail centers emerged, Downtown still offers the greatest variety of goods and services to be found anywhere in the Washington metropolitan area. During the past three decades, plans and programs were initiated to revitalize Downtown. Some were very successful while others languished. Much of the development evident in Downtown today resulted from ideas formed during the last 30 years. Metrorail, the "old" and "new" convention centers, and the refurbished Pennsylvania Avenue and Union Station are notable examples.

The Washington Metrorail system ("Metro") opened in 1976. Together, the Metrorail and Metrobus systems carry more than 1.1 million riders a day. It was designed by Harry Weese and Associates and has won a number of architecture, design, and construction awards. The original 103-mile system was completed in

2001 and includes 83 stations; 41 stations are located in Washington, DC. The Metro system has stimulated substantial changes in land use and mobility patterns throughout the metropolitan area. Some estimates indicate that at least $25 billion in new development has occurred close to Metrorail stations. You will see evidence of this as you visit various neighborhoods in this publication. In addition, the combination of Metrorail and Metrobus trips has removed over 325,000 cars from the local road system.

The "old" Washington Convention Center, approximately 10 acres, dramatically affected its immediate environs as well as the convention business in the city. Several million visitors and conventioneers attended functions at the center each year. Within the immediate vicinity of the approximately 10-acre center, three large, convention-type hotels—the Ramada Renaissance, the Hyatt Regency, and the Crowne Plaza—were built. Several others were built elsewhere. The city's Chinatown is located immediately to the east of the Center, and several new restaurants, bars, and variety stores have opened in this area over the last few years. One of the longest Chinese arches in the United States was built along H Street NW, in the heart of Chinatown, in 1986.

The old Washington Convention Center was replaced by a new center, containing 2.3 million square feet, in March 2003. The old convention center site has been subject to an extensive planning and development process since 2002. A firm was selected to develop it in October 2003 with a mix of retail, housing, hotel, and cultural space. The new center is located north of Mount Vernon Square, two blocks north of the old center. A new convention hotel is to be developed immediately to the west of the structure.

Under the leadership of the now-defunct Pennsylvania Avenue Development Corporation, Pennsylvania Avenue underwent a major upgrading and has evolved into a showplace for the city. Several new office buildings with street-level retail shops are outstanding examples, including the Ronald Reagan Building and International Trade Center, the largest government building in the city, and a refurbished John Wilson Municipal Building, the home of the mayor and Council of the District of Columbia. The new office structures with their attractive retail components, along with residential buildings, landscaped public spaces, and urban parks, have given this thoroughfare the distinction of being the "Main Street" of the United States. The redevelopment of Pennsylvania Avenue will be completed under the auspices of the National Capital Planning Commission (NCPC). NCPC is the centeral planning agency for the federal government in the National Capital region. It has been responsible for coordination of all federal planning activities in the region since 1952. Before the passage of the Home Rule Act in 1973, NCPC also served as the local planning agency for the District of Columbia. The city and its residents are justifiably proud of this achievement. Pennsylvania Avenue is now a major tourist attraction and should be on any list of "must-see" areas in Washington, DC. A new Newseum, an interactive museum of news, has been planned for a site at 6th Street and Pennsylvania Avenue.

Union Station, designed by Daniel Burnham, was built as a train station in 1908. It underwent a complete renovation during the 1980s and has become a dazzling transportation, shopping, and restaurant site. The vaulted building contains over 200,000 square feet of retail, theater, restaurant, and entertainment space and 100,000 square feet of office space. It is a well-established multimodal transfer point for trips within the northeastern and southeastern corridors as a hub for Amtrak, the Maryland Commuter Rail system, and the Virginia Railway Express. A Metro station and several local bus routes serve the facility. Interstate bus service is available within a five-minute walk to the north of the station.

During your visit to Union Station, take time to view the surrounding area, which has been noticeably influenced by the revitalization of the station itself. You should note particularly the Postal Square Project to the west of the station, which has added the Smithsonian's National Postal Museum and a substantial amount of retail and office space to the area. The new Thurgood Marshall Federal Courts Building to the east is significant because of its architectural style, which reinterprets that of Union Station. Several buildings occupied by the United States Senate are also visible from the main entrance to Union Station on Massachusetts Avenue. Several new office buildings and new and renovated hotels of all types have been built in the area as well.

From August to May, Washington's resident population includes more than 90,000 students who attend the city's 20 universities and specialty schools. The city has seven major universities: George Washington University, Georgetown University, American University, the Catholic University of America, Howard University, the University of the District of Columbia, and the rapidly growing Southeastern University. Each campus has its own ambience, ranging from the Gothic architecture of several buildings on the campuses of Georgetown and Catholic Universities, to the city campus flair of Howard and George Washington Universities, to the highly contemporary facade of the University of the District of Columbia and the single contemporary building housing Southeastern University.

Washington's two great cathedrals are the Washington National Cathedral, in the Northwest section of the city, with magnificent landscaping and city vistas, and the National Shrine of the Immaculate Conception on the campus of the Catholic University of America in the Northeast. Their architecture and surroundings remain a vibrant part of the life of the entire region.

Outside the boundaries of the original city are more than 50 neighborhoods, largely developed during the 19th and 20th centuries. A few of the more notable ones are described in this book. Others are significant because of their historic locations along discontinued streetcar routes or the prominent persons who resided within their boundaries. A visit to any one of these areas will leave you with indelible images of a strong and lively neighborhood.

Many of Washington's neighborhoods are undergoing substantial housing redevelopment and other changes. However, some remain as they have been for generations. Most significant in all of these neighborhoods are the tree-lined streets, the varied architectural styles, and the diversity of the resident communities.

Washington has one of the country's most ambitious tree-planting programs. It was initiated in 1815, one year after the burning of the US Capitol. Many of the streets in the neighborhoods you will visit have trees that are more than 150 years old. Spend some time observing the interesting tree canopies for which Washington neighborhoods are famous. In 2002 the city received a $50 million grant from a private foundation for tree preservation.

Two prominent organizations that have had a great influence on the scale and urban design of many of the city's neighborhoods are the Commission of Fine Arts and the city's Historic Preservation Review Board (HPRB) and its predecessor organization, the Joint Committee on Landmarks. The Commission of Fine Arts was created in 1910 to carry forward the concepts of the McMillan Commission. The HPRB is a more contemporary preservation organization, charged with identifying and protecting historic resources in Washington and advising the city on preservation programs. Over 500 buildings, sites, and streets have been designated as historic landmarks. In addition, several of the neighborhoods you will visit are within one of the designated neighborhood historic districts in the city. These include Capitol Hill, LeDroit Park, Old Anacostia, Georgetown, Kalorama, Dupont Circle, and Mount Pleasant.

Before ending your tour of Washington, take time to attend one of the many free classical and pop concerts or seek out the city's vigorous network of neighborhood art museums and galleries or sample its chic restaurants and visit its varied neighborhood theaters. Whatever you decide to do while visiting the city and metropolitan area, enjoy yourself. The following pages we hope will help you in your discovery of Washington, DC, as a memorable "American Experience."

Old Town Alexandria

No visit to the nation's capital is complete without a trip to the nearby historic port city of Alexandria, Virginia, on the Potomac River. This colonial port city (along with Georgetown) is older than the District of Columbia itself. Today it bustles with active commercial life while retaining much of its 18th- and 19th-century residential atmosphere.

Takoma Park

Takoma Park, just over the District boundary in Maryland, is more than 150 years old. Its small-town ambience is a striking contrast to the more urban and suburban flavor of the surrounding areas. Many of its original buildings have been restored and provide an interesting backdrop for the unique open spaces and institutional buildings in the city. Its citizenry is a mix of several cultures. Many of the recently renovated storefronts along Piney Branch Road and Flower Avenue reflect the varied cultures in the city. A visit to Takoma Park should be a rewarding experience.

How to Use This Guide

Select any of the 23 tours listed here by the name of the area covered. For each, you'll find the walking distance and the time it takes to walk the route (not including visits to museums and historic houses). Public transit information to the starting point is provided (courtesy of the Washington Metropolitan Area Transit Authority). A map shows the route and locates the major sights by numbers keyed to the descriptive text. Sketches scattered throughout the book highlight some important sights. Please note that for several of the sites, the guide provides specific opening and tour times. However, since the terrorist events of September 11, 2001, and continuing security threats, many of the opening and tour times have changed. Please call for information before your visit.

Taking the Right Bus

The Washington Metropolitan Area Transit Authority (Metro) Information Service will tell you which Metrobus to take to any destination. Call (202) 637-7000 to obtain a bus timetable. This information is also available at Metrorail station kiosks and at www.wmata.com.

When you board your bus, you will be expected to pay the exact fare in passes, tokens, or cash. Metrobus operators do not carry change, nor do they sell passes. The basic fare is $1.20. Call (202) 637-1328 for any additional information on routes and fares.

If you need to change from one bus to another to reach your destination, you will be given a transfer at no additional cost. You must ask your bus operator for it when you pay your fare. Your transfer permits you to change to as many buses as required. Transfers are valid for two hours.

Route numbers and letters accompanying each tour in this guide refer to bus services available weekdays. These routes go to the beginning point of each tour or pass near it. *Note:* Special rush-hour and weekend Metrobus routings are not listed.

Using the Metro

The Metro is a pleasant and quick way to travel to and from the tour areas in the guide, particularly those in central Washington. Five Metro lines serve the Washington area. The Red Line provides service between Glenmont,

Maryland, and Shady Grove, Maryland, passing through Downtown Washington. The Blue Line links Franconia-Springfield in Virginia, and the Addison Road-Seat Pleasant station in Prince George's County, Maryland. The Yellow Line provides service from Mount Vernon Square/7th Street/Convention Center to Huntington Station in Fairfax County, Virginia. The Orange Line's terminals are at Vienna/Fairfax-GMU, in Virginia, and at New Carrollton, Maryland. The Orange and Blue Lines share tracks between Rosslyn and Stadium-Armory. (See the map of the Metrorail system.) The Green Line extends from Branch Avenue to Greenbelt; both segments are in Prince George's County. The Metro spans 103 miles, serving the outlying suburbs. Be sure to check the maps in each Metrorail station and car for information on extensions and new stations.

Three of the lines intersect at the Metro Center station in downtown Washington, facilitating transfers between the Red Line (upper level) and the Blue and Orange Lines (lower level). The Green, Yellow, and Red Lines intersect at Gallery Place. The Yellow and Green Lines also intersect with the Blue and Orange Lines at L'Enfant Plaza.

The name of the Metro station and the color of the line serving the beginning point of each walking tour are indicated in this guide. The "M" symbol on most tour maps identifies the locations of the station entrances. Hours of operation are as follows:

Monday through Thursday: 5:30 a.m.–midnight
Friday: 5:30 a.m.–3:00 a.m.
Saturday: 7:00 a.m.–3:00 a.m.
Sunday: 7:00 a.m.–midnight

The two-tier fare system is based on time and distance traveled. As of June 2003, the fares during rush hours (5:30 a.m.–9:30 a.m. and 3:00 p.m.–7:00 p.m. on weekdays) range between $1.20 and $3.60. The fare during nonrush hours ranges between $1.20 and $2.20, including all other times on weekdays as well as Saturdays, Sundays, and holidays. Farecards can be bought in any value from $1.20 to $30 and are good until used. Exit gates automatically deduct the fare and print the remaining value, if any, on the farecard. Check the charts in each station for the exact fare between stations on your route. The station attendant at the kiosk of each station can answer any questions.

WMATA is considering several changes to its policy that addresses transfers from the Metrorail system to Metrobuses. Interested readers should check with the Metrorail station managers or go to www.wmata.com to obtain the latest transfer policy.

On Not Getting Lost on Washington Streets

The city's quadrants (NW, SW, NE, SE) must be explained. The north–south axis through the Capitol, represented by North and South Capitol Streets, divides the eastern and western sections of the city. The east–west axis through the Capitol, represented by East Capitol Street and the center line of the Mall, separates the northern and southern sections. All streets within each of the quadrants bear the quadrant designation, and the quadrant describes its direction on the compass from the Capitol.

Street names generally ascend in alphabetical or numerical order; names of states are used for the diagonal avenues. Measuring north or south from the center line of the Mall, the parallel streets are designated by letters (A, B, C, and so on). Two-syllable names follow the letters from A to about W (such as Adams, Bryant, Channing). Beyond that, three-syllable names continue the pattern from A to about W (Albemarle, Brandywine, Chesapeake). Beyond that point, along the north–south line approximating 16th Street, the streets are named after trees and flowers, also in alphabetical order (Aspen, Butternut, Cedar). Running east and west from the line representing North and South Capitol Streets, the streets are numbered 1st, 2nd, 3rd, and 4th to somewhere in the 50s.

Numbering of addresses is also orderly. For example, between 1st Street and 2nd Street (on lettered and named streets), the house numbers are between 100 and 199; between 40th Street and 41st Street, the house numbers are between 4000 and 4099. To illustrate, nine blocks from A Street would be K Street: hence, 1000 15th Street would be the intersection of K and 15th Streets.

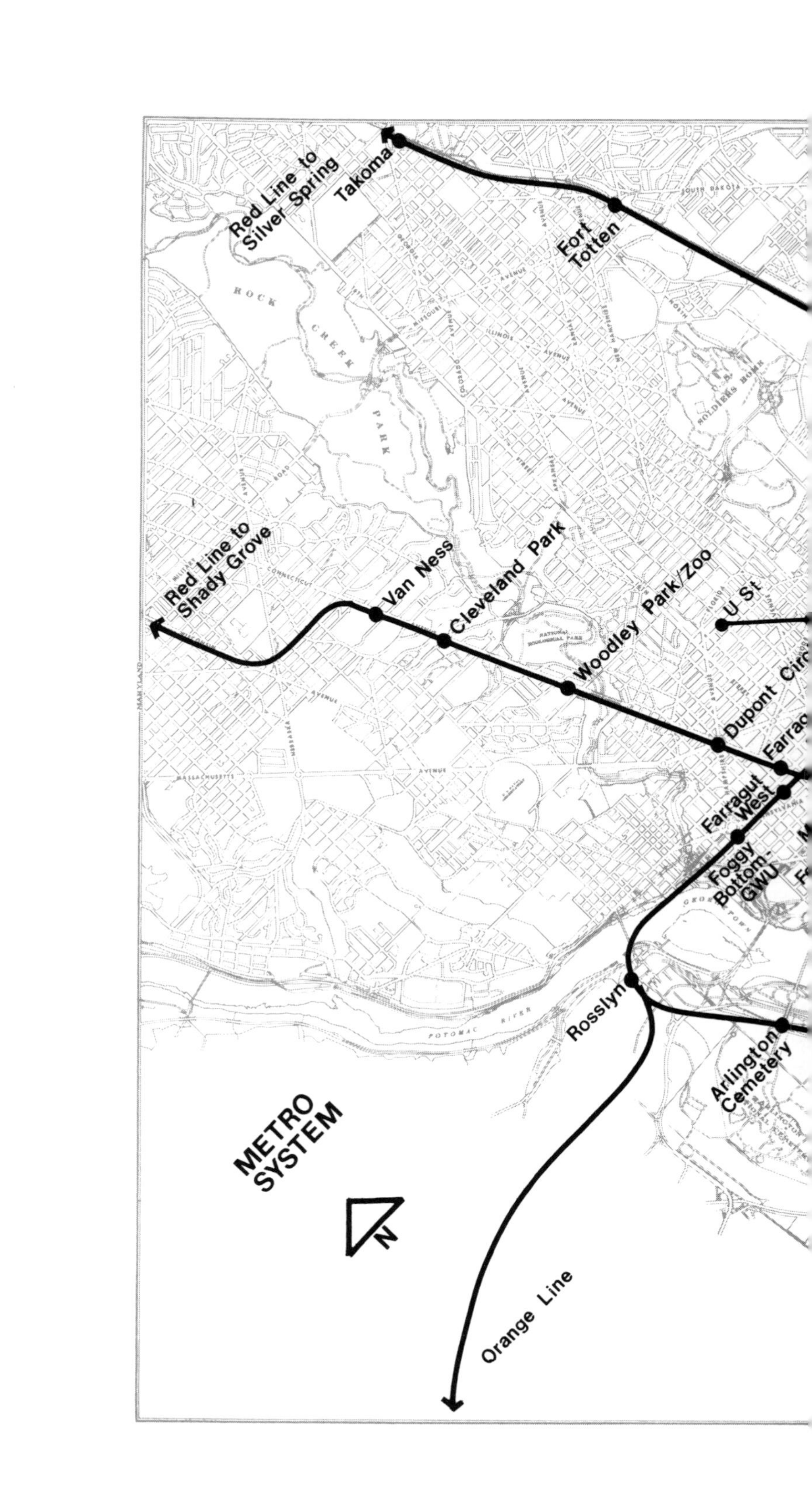

Red Line to Silver Spring
Takoma
Fort Totten
ROCK CREEK PARK
Red Line to Shady Grove
Van Ness
Cleveland Park
Woodley Park/Zoo
U St
Farragut West
Foggy Bottom-GWU
Rosslyn
POTOMAC RIVER
Arlington Cemetery
METRO SYSTEM
N
Orange Line

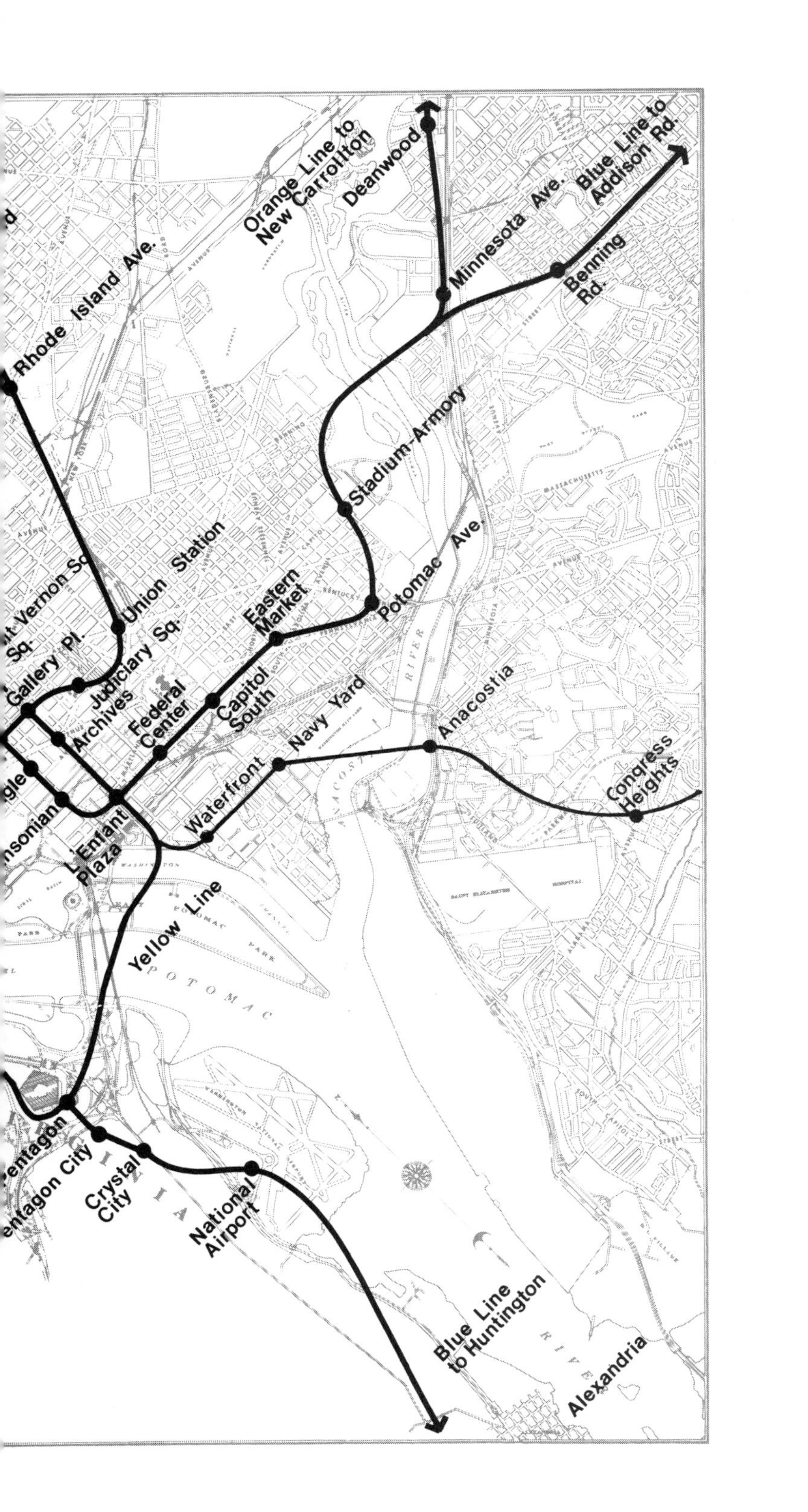
Orange Line to
New Carrollton
Deanwood
Blue Line to
Addison Rd.
Minnesota Ave.
Benning
Rd.
Rhode Island Ave.
Stadium-Armory
Union Station
Potomac Ave.
Eastern
Market
Judiciary Sq.
Gallery Pl.
Sq.
Archives
Federal
Center
Capitol
South
Navy Yard
Anacostia
Congress
Heights
Waterfront
L'Enfant
Plaza
Yellow Line
Crystal
City
National
Airport
Blue Line
to Huntington
Alexandria
POTOMAC
RIVER

L'Enfant's City

Capitol Hill—West

(Capitol complex; residential restoration area)

Clifford W. Moy, updated by Paul Douglass

Distance: 2 3/4 miles
Time: 1 1/4 hours
Bus: 13C, 13D, 40, 42, 80, 81, 96, D2, D4, D6, D8, X2, X4, and X8
Metro: Union Station (Red Line)

■ 1 The tour begins at **Union Station,** a multimodal transportation and shopping center about four blocks north of the Capitol at Massachusetts and Delaware Avenues NE. Architect Daniel H. Burnham designed Union Station to ensure that the two then-separate train terminals would be consolidated into one station. Since 1908, the station has also served as a monumental gateway into Washington, DC. The redesign of Union Station Plaza stresses "people orientation" (meaning a rechanneling of traffic) and the placement of flagpoles along the perimeter. An impressive structure in the center of the plaza is the **Columbus Memorial Fountain,** sculpted in 1912 by Lorado Taft.

In 1981 Congress passed the Union Station Redevelopment Act, providing for the development and restoration of Union Station. This act envisioned a "multimodal transportation center" concept. Today, the Union Station complex serves as a busy transportation hub, offering citywide, suburban, and interstate train services and access to local tour buses. It also includes a multilevel shopping center with specialty retail shops, an elongated food court, and many well-established restaurants and bars.

Just to the east of Union Station is the new Thurgood Marshall Federal Courts building.

To the north of Union Station is a new office building complex. Interstate bus service is available two blocks to the north via the Greyhound and Peter Pan bus services.

Immediately to the west of Union Station (2 Massachusetts Avenue NW) sits the former City Post Office Building, also designed by architect D. H. Burnham and completed in 1914. The building now houses the National Postal Museum (free) that features a stamp store for serious philatelists and traces the history of the US Mail Service. Guided tours are offered daily at 11:00 a.m. and 1:00 p.m.

Union Station

■ **2** This Capitol Hill **park** is one of the favorites of many congressional aides, particularly the younger set, who brown-bag their lunches. If you are here in the spring and summer you can see why. The many red oak trees and a sparkling water fountain are irresistible. To the west juts a concrete **monolith honoring Sen. Robert A. Taft** of Ohio. Designed by Douglass W. Orr in 1959, this memorial houses 27 bells that chime every quarter-hour.

■ **3** The **Capitol Grotto** (1879) is one of the best features of the Capitol grounds, designed by landscape architect Frederick Law Olmsted and originally conceived to tap fresh springwater.

■ **4** Also designed by Frederick Law Olmsted, the **Trolley Waiting Station** (about 1876) was originally served by horse-drawn trolley cars. Another waiting station is located at the southeast corner of the US Capitol.

■ **5** Asked by President George Washington to design a plan for the federal city, Major Pierre Charles L'Enfant, French engineer and architect, chose to position the **US Capitol** in one of two significant locations in the future city (the other was reserved for the president's house). Jenkins Hill, in L'Enfant's estimate, was like "a pedestal waiting for a monument." President Washington laid the cornerstone for the Capitol in 1793. After being partly destroyed by British troops in 1814, the Capitol was restored with the addition of a wooden dome. In 1857, two wings were added (providing expanded space for the Senate and the House of Representatives), and an iron dome replaced the wooden one in 1865. Atop the dome stands the Statue of Freedom. According to its sculptor, Thomas Crawford, the statue represents "Armed Liberty," her right hand grasping a sheathed sword while the other holds the wreath and shield. The Capitol is open to the public for guided tours only. Tours are available Monday through Saturday 9:00 a.m.–4:30 p.m.

U.S. Capitol

Free tour tickets must be obtained beginning at 9:00 a.m. at the Capital Guide Service kiosk located along the curving sidewalk near 1st Street SW and Independence Avenue. A new underground Capitol Visitors Center/Congressional Office Complex is expected to open in 2005.

■ 6 The **Sewall-Belmont House,** at 144 Constitution Avenue NE, was saved from demolition in 1974 by a special act of Congress and was subsequently entered into the National Register of Historic Places. Otherwise, the site would have been used for the Senate office building that now abuts the house. Robert Sewall, descended from an illustrious Maryland family, in 1800 built this three-story townhouse, which is characteristic of the federal period in style. His Capitol Hill home was leased to Albert Gallatin, secretary of the treasury (1801–13). In 1929 the National Women's Party purchased the house from Sen. Porter Dale. Some of the unusual furnishings include desks once owned by Henry Clay and Susan B. Anthony. Hours: weekdays 10:00 a.m.–2:00 p.m.; weekends and holidays 12:00–4:00 p.m.

■ 7 The **Hiram W. Johnson House** at 122 Maryland Avenue NE is also representative of the federal period and is listed in the National Register of Historic Places.

■ 8 Covered entirely in marble, the **Supreme Court Building** was completed in 1935. A spacious 100-foot-wide oval plaza lies at the foot of the main steps of the building. On the east front is a group of marble figures sculpted by Herman A. MacNeil, representing Confucius, Solon, and Moses. The building's renovation, scheduled for completion in 2008, will include a new visitors center.

■ 9 Created by an act of Congress in 1800, the **Library of Congress** housed its materials in the Capitol until 1896, when the Army Corps of Engineers built its main building (the Jefferson Building). The library serves not only the members of Congress but also government agencies and the general public. Outstanding collections of rare Chinese, Russian, and Japanese books are among its many treasures. A visit to the main reading room is a must. Public tours of the Great Hall are offered Monday through Friday at 11:30, 1:30, 2:30, and 3:30. Directly behind the Adams Building is a library annex. The **James Madison Memorial Library,** another annex on Independence Avenue between 1st and 2nd Streets, was opened in 1980.

■ 10 The **Folger Shakespeare Library** (1932—Paul Cret), at 201 East Capitol Street SE, is certainly a must for Shakespeare followers; especially noteworthy is the reproduction of an **Elizabethan Theater,** which is in active use all year.

■ 11 **Frederick Douglass's first Washington residence** was at 316 A Street NE. According to a Capitol Hill Restoration Society plaque, Douglass was the "precursor to the Civil Rights Movement . . . [and] resided in this building from 1871 to 1877."

■ 12 When it opened in this residential area in 1964, the **Museum of African Art** (318 A Street NE) was the first museum to house artifacts of and thereby promote the study of African heritage. The museum's collection has been

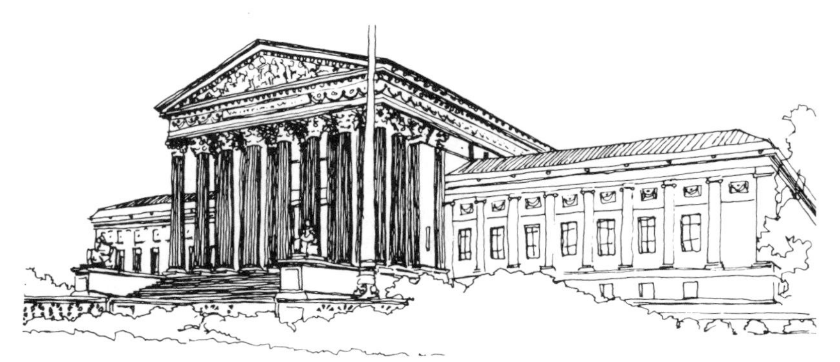

Supreme Court Building

moved to the Smithsonian's National Museum of African Art, located on the Mall at 950 Independence Avenue SW.

■ 13 The **townhouse on the corner of 4th and A Streets NE** is a converted store built around 1869. Compare this with the townhouse at 1100 Independence Avenue SE, located on the corner of Independence Avenue and 11th Street, which is in the same style but unrestored. (At this juncture, hardy walkers can test their stamina by detouring onto East Capitol Street into Tour 2. This tour will lead you back into Tour 1 at Pennsylvania Avenue and 4th Street.)

■ 14 The **Brumidi House,** at 324-326 A Street SE, was built about 1850. It was purportedly the home of Constantino Brumidi, an Italian artist, who at the age of 60 painted in 11 months the *Apotheosis of Washington* over 4,664 square feet in the Capitol dome. He was also responsible for the rotunda frescoes and other Capitol decorations.

■ 15 **St. Mark's Episcopal Church** (1888), located at 3rd and A Streets SE, is listed in the National Register of Historic Places. President Lyndon B. Johnson was a frequent visitor.

■ 16 The **townhouse at 120 4th Street SE** (built about 1876) is typical of the 1870s, with its flat facade, elaborate cornices, and lintels.

■ 17 The **Ebenezer United Methodist Church,** on 4th and D Streets SE, originally known as the Little Ebenezer Church, was constructed in 1838 and rebuilt in 1897. From March 1864 to May 1865, the church served as the first schoolhouse for blacks in Washington. The church is also the oldest black church on Capitol Hill, with a predominantly African American congregation.

■ 18 This vacant square is the site of the **old Providence Hospital**. It is now under the jurisdiction of the Architect of the Capitol as part of the "Capitol Grounds."

■ 19 This stretch of **North Carolina Avenue** is a fine example of the L'Enfant plan for the Federal City: the superimposition of bold, diagonal avenues over a standard grid pattern. The small, adjoining, triangular parks, particularly at E Street, have been the scene of many touch football games.

■ 20 This stretch of **New Jersey Avenue** frames a magnificent sight. The transition between residential and federal buildings, along with the view of the Capitol dome, is startling. Consequently, New Jersey Avenue residents have taken great pride in restoring their homes. The "Master Plan for Future Development of the Capitol Grounds and Related Areas" was completed in 1981 and remains largely unchanged. According to the "transition zone" classification, New Jersey Avenue will be able to retain its historic, residential character in the face of congressional growth.

■ 21 The **House Office Buildings** along Independence Avenue are, from west to east, the Sam Rayburn Building, the Nicholas Longworth Building, and the Joseph Cannon Building. You may want to stop by and visit your representative. (The subway between the Rayburn Building and the US Capitol generally runs when Congress is in session, weekdays 9:00 a.m.–8:00 p.m. and Saturday 9:00 a.m.–5:00 p.m. and when there is an evening session.)

■ 22 The **Bartholdi Fountain** (between Canal, also known as Washington Avenue, and 1st Streets on Independence Avenue) was designed by Frederic Auguste Bartholdi in 1876.

■ 23 The **US Botanic Garden** (Independence Avenue, Maryland Avenue, and 1st Street SW) was moved to its present location in 1933. The **Conservatory** was constructed during 1931–33. A multimillion-dollar renovation of the Conservatory was reopened in December 2001. The Conservatory houses permanent collections of plants from subtropical, tropical, and arid regions. Special exhibits showcase orchids and medicinal, economically significant, endangered, and primitive plants. It is definitely worth a visit.

■ 24 The **Ulysses S. Grant Memorial** (1922) is the largest and most expensive statuary grouping in Washington. The **Capitol Reflecting Pool** was designed by Skidmore, Owings & Merrill. Completed in 1970, the pool is directly over Interstate Highway 395, which underlies the Mall.

■ 25 The **National Museum of the American Indian,** under construction at press time, is expected to be completed in 2004. Its exhibits will showcase art, culture, and artifacts of American Indians.

■ 26 The tour ends at the steps of the west side of the US Capitol. The **view across the Mall** to the Washington Monument is memorable. In the words of Pierre L'Enfant, the site of the US Capitol is truly like "a pedestal waiting for a monument."

Capitol Hill—East

(Historic residential restoration area)

Clifford W. Moy, updated by Paul Douglass

Distance: 2 3/4 miles
Time: 1 1/4 hours
Bus: On East Capitol Street: 96; on 8th Street SE: 90 and 92
Metro: Eastern Market (Blue and Orange Lines)

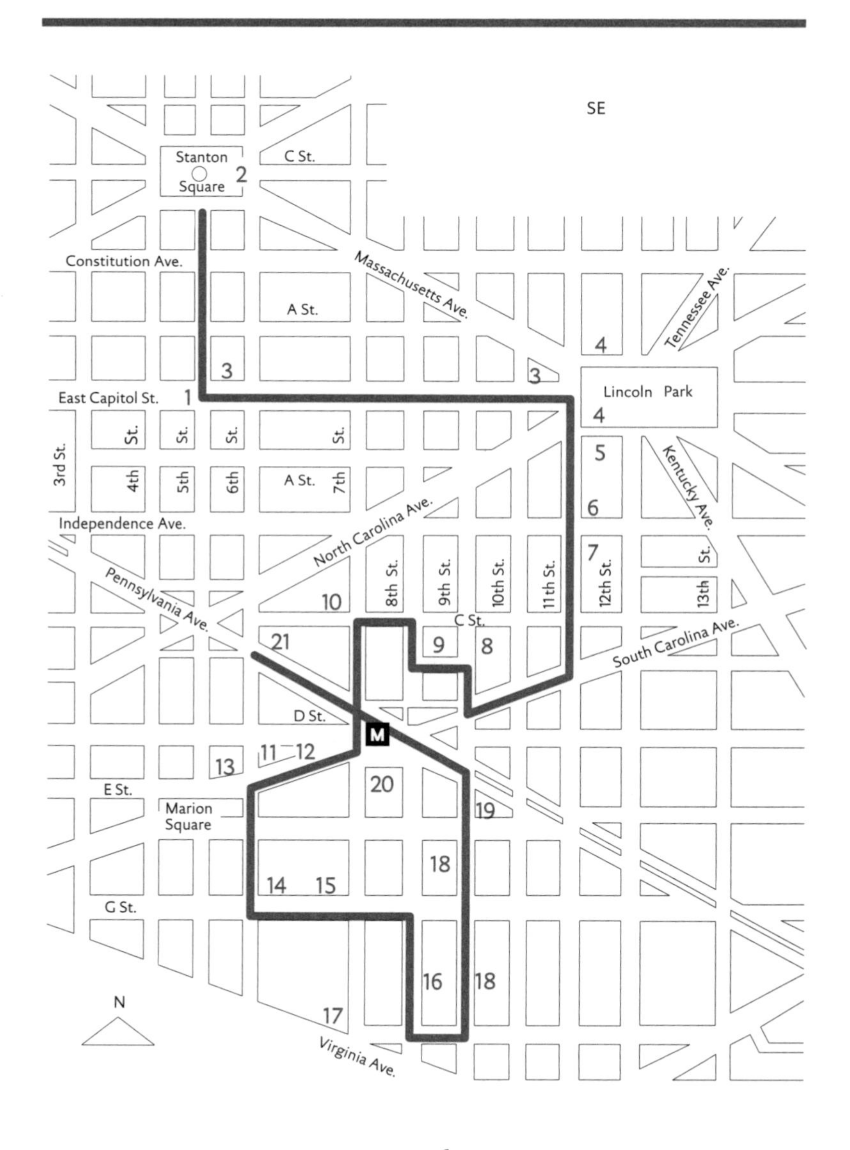

■ 1 The tour begins at 5th and East Capitol Streets SE. **East Capitol Street** is considered the "grand street" of the Capitol Hill community. It divides the northeast quadrant from the southeast quadrant of the city. The smaller scale of structures on adjacent streets north and south of East Capitol Street provides a sharp contrast. In 1974 Michael Franch prepared a report for the Joint Committee on Landmarks for the National Capital in which he found that "the general area of elite residence [for the years 1888, 1889, 1909, and 1918] was a diamond-shaped district between the Capitol and Lincoln Park, Stanton Park and Seward Square." As had been suspected, the heaviest concentration of elite residences was along East Capitol Street. The diversity of housing types and styles is tremendous. Everything from manor houses, federal townhouses, and brick row houses to more contemporary housing exists in the Capitol Hill area; it is a designated historic district. A community group, the Capitol Hill Restoration Society, has done much to encourage and to maintain the integrity of the Capitol Hill Historic District.

■ 2 There is an interesting **view from East Capitol Street,** looking north along 5th Street, which includes a statue of Maj. Gen. Nathaniel Greene on horseback in Stanton Square.

■ 3 The **townhouses at 512 and 514 East Capitol Street NE** (1879) are representative of the 1870s, with flat facades and elaborate cornices and lintels. Some of the townhouses, for instance those in the **1000 block of East Capitol Street NE** (1899), have balconies and/or roof decks.

■ 4 **Lincoln Park** and the **Emancipation Statue** (completed and dedicated in April 1876; President Ulysses S. Grant and Frederick Douglass were present at the ceremony) were constructed in memory of Abraham Lincoln. It was paid for by small donations from emancipated slaves. A more recent statue (dedicated in July

512 and 514 East Capitol Street

1974) at the east end of the park is in honor of **Mary McLeod Bethune,** a black educator and president and founder of Bethune-Cookman College in Daytona Beach, Florida. Hilliard Robinson, landscape architect, in conjunction with the National Park Service, designed the 7-acre park. The homes surrounding Lincoln Park are predominantly from 1890–95. Pay particular attention to the townhouse at **1125 East Capitol Street NE** (1892) near the northwest corner of Lincoln Park.

■ 5 The **granite row houses** with balconies (1111–19 East Capitol Street SE) were built in 1892.

■ 6 **Philadelphia Row** (124–154 11th Street SE) was built by James W. Gessford about 1866. He built 16 row houses in the style of Philadelphia to soothe his wife's homesickness for her native city.

■ 7 This **group of 15 row houses** (200–226 11th Street SE) was built by Charles Gessford in 1891, some 25 years after Philadelphia Row.

Philadelphia Row

■ 8 Constructed in 1967, the **Thomas Simmons House** (314–16 9th Street SE) is a fine example of the contemporary homes that are in keeping with the physical scale of the Capitol Hill Historic District. (Slip through the alley between nos. 321 and 319 9th Street; more cautious individuals may continue on 9th Street before turning onto C Street.)

■ 9 This set of **contemporary row houses** (801–19 C Street SE) was constructed in the mid-1960s.

■ **10** A walk through many of the alleys in the area will lead directly to **Eastern Market** on 7th and C Streets. The open-market activity will mesmerize even the most hardened tourist. Designed by Adolph Cluss and constructed in 1873, this market is the heart of the Capitol Hill community. Be sure to sample the cannoli at the bakery. Vendors offer fresh produce, flowers, and crafts; artists selling prints and other works of art surround more boutiques and shops lining 7th Street into Pennsylvania Avenue (weekends are especially busy).

Eastern Market

■ **11** The **Maples House,** now named the Friendship House Settlement, was built in 1795–1806 during the federal period by architect-builder William Lovering. Francis Scott Key was one of its many distinguished owners. The front entrance of the Maples House originally opened onto South Carolina Avenue, but today it goes by the 619 D Street SE address.

■ **12** This stretch of **South Carolina Avenue** provides a spacious and charming residential atmosphere that is typical of the Capitol Hill community.

■ **13** The **Carberry House,** at 423 6th Street SE, was built about 1813 reputedly of bricks that were used as ballast for navy ships and has been designated a historic site / structure by the Joint Committee on Landmarks. This stretch of 6th Street to G Street SE comprises some of the oldest houses on Capitol Hill, many built in the 1840s and 1850s.

■ **14** **Christ Church** (1806—Benjamin H. Latrobe). In the past, this church at 620 G Street SE served many individuals from the Navy Yard and Marine Barracks. It is believed to have been visited by Presidents Thomas Jefferson, James Madison, and James Monroe.

■ **15** The house at 636 G Street SE is the **birthplace of John Philip Sousa,** conductor, composer, and bandmaster of the US Marine Corps. The brightly painted residence was built in 1844.

■ **16** The **Marine Commandant's House** and the **Marine Barracks complex** occupy the entire square formed by 8th, 9th, G, and I Streets SE. Constructed in 1801–04 after George Hadfield's designs, the commandant's house is set apart by its physical scale from the nearby homes. The Marine Barracks surrounds an interior courtyard and parade ground, extremely well manicured in the traditional military style. The Marine Corps Band and the ceremonial units are housed at the Barracks. Along 8th Street, from Pennsylvania Avenue to the Southeast Freeway (also known as Barracks Row), commercial rejuvenation is very much in evidence.

■ **17** The **Ellen Wilson Townhomes** on Capitol Hill occupy a portion of land that was previously developed with the Ellen Wilson public housing complex. The Ellen Wilson complex was built in 1941 on a 5.3-acre site. The site was bisected by the construction of the Southwest Freeway into two parcels: to the south, the parcel contained several remaining public housing structures and to the north, the parcel was vacant. The northern parcel was reclaimed during the mid-1990s and used for construction of the Ellen Wilson Townhomes on Capitol Hill, a mixed-income complex of units that face away from the freeway. The complex is located between 6th and 7th and G and Virginia Avenue SE. In the immediate vicinity are several examples of former public school buildings that have been converted to upscale residences or other uses.

■ **18** Note the abrupt contrast of housing styles between the **contemporary and the older housing** in the 700 and 500 blocks on 9th Street.

■ **19** Constructed in 1865–66, the **Old Naval Hospital** on Pennsylvania Avenue between 9th and 10th Streets retains what may be the original cast-iron fence. Over the last few years, it has been occupied by various government agencies and community organizations. It is currently vacant and in need of rehabilitation.

■ **20** The square at Pennsylvania Avenue, between 7th and 8th Streets, is the entrance to the **Eastern Market Metro station.** Note the many buildings in the immediate vicinity of the square that have been upgraded, typical of this area of the city.

■ **21** The tour ends at the corner of Pennsylvania Avenue and 6th Street at the **National Permanent Building** (formerly named the Eastern Liberty Federal Building), built in 1975 and occupied in 1976. Designed by the architectural firm of Mills Petticord (now merged with HOK), the building features a metal mansard roof housing 90 solar collector panels designed to provide domestic hot water.

The Mall—East

(Major axis of monumental core, Smithsonian museums, art galleries)

Wilcomb Washburn and Kathryn Cousins, updated by Carol Truppi

Distance: 2 miles
Time: 1 hour minimum
Bus: On or near Independence Avenue: 13A, 32, 34, 35, 36, 52, 54, 70, and V7
Metro: Smithsonian (Blue and Orange Lines)

■ 1 The tour begins at the building popularly known as the **Castle** (1855—James Renwick), on Jefferson Drive between 9th and 11th Streets SW. In addition to two orientation theaters, the **Great Hall** contains an excellent exhibit on the history of the planning of Washington, DC. It introduces planning concepts to laypeople, as well as orienting the public to the city. Note particularly the innovative "perspective" models of the four major plans—those of L'Enfant (1791), Downing (1851), the McMillan Commission (1902), and the National Capital Planning Commission/Pennsylvania Avenue Development Corporation (1975). The original McMillan Commission models are also on display.

■ 2 Walk outside to the center of the **Mall.** You are midway on the major axis of the monumental core of the capital city as planned by L'Enfant. (The Mall was

Smithsonian Institution Building (The Castle)

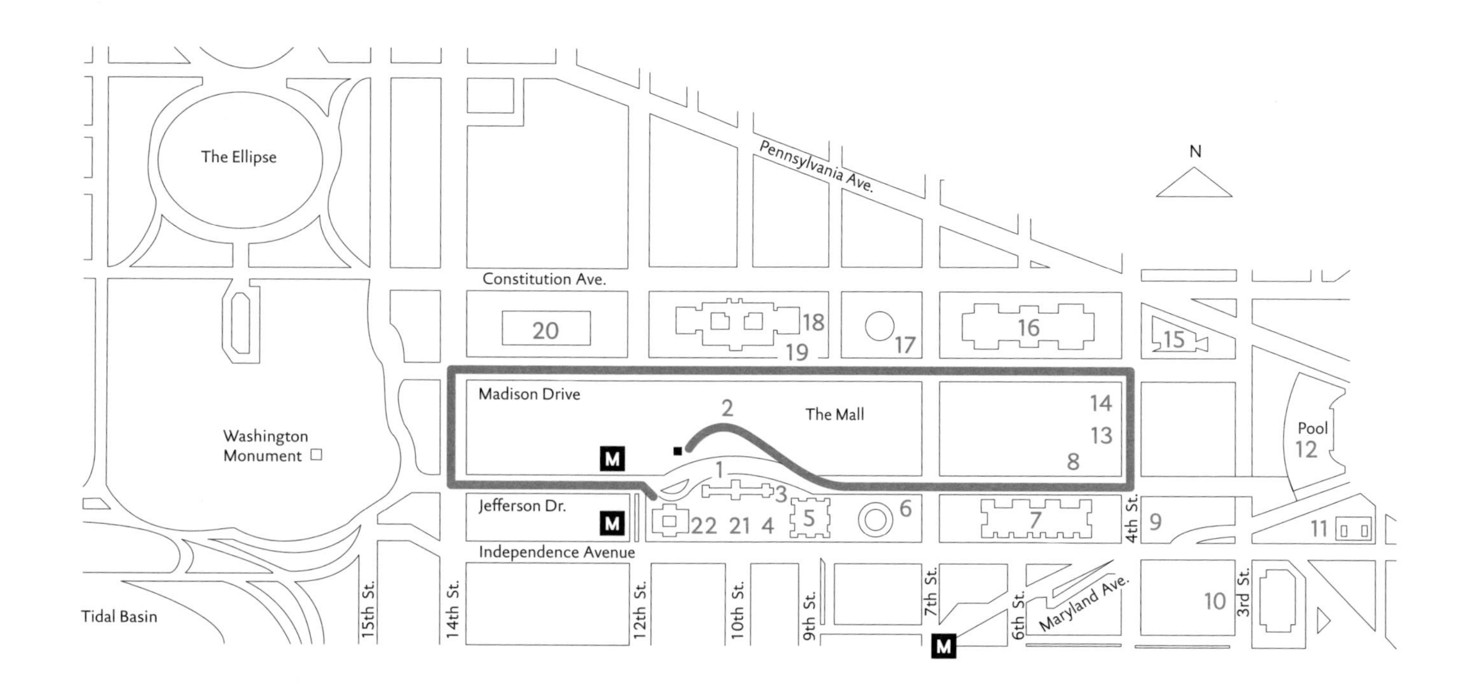
N
The Ellipse
Pennsylvania Ave.
Constitution Ave.
20
18
19
17
16
15
Madison Drive
2
The Mall
14
13
8
Pool
12
Washington
Monument
M
1
3
Jefferson Dr.
M
22
21
4
5
6
7
9
11
Independence Avenue
Tidal Basin
15th St.
14th St.
12th St.
10th St.
9th St.
7th St.
M
6th St.
Maryland Ave.
4th St.
10
3rd St.

extended beyond the Washington Monument to the Lincoln Memorial in the 20th century after the tidal flats and marshes west of the monument were filled in.) The greensward was planned by L'Enfant as a broad avenue, 400 feet wide, lined with grand residences. The Mall as it exists today represents a sensitive compromise between the monumental plans of L'Enfant and those of the McMillan Commission (executed without the broad central avenue L'Enfant had proposed), softened at the edges with humanistic touches suggestive of Downing (exemplified by the present-day ice rink, carousel, and Constitution Gardens, as well as numerous sports activities and the annual Festival of American Folklife). Debate continues about whether the proposed World War II Memorial, which will replace the rainbow pool at the Lincoln Memorial, will jeopardize the vista created by the L'Enfant and the McMillan Commission plans.

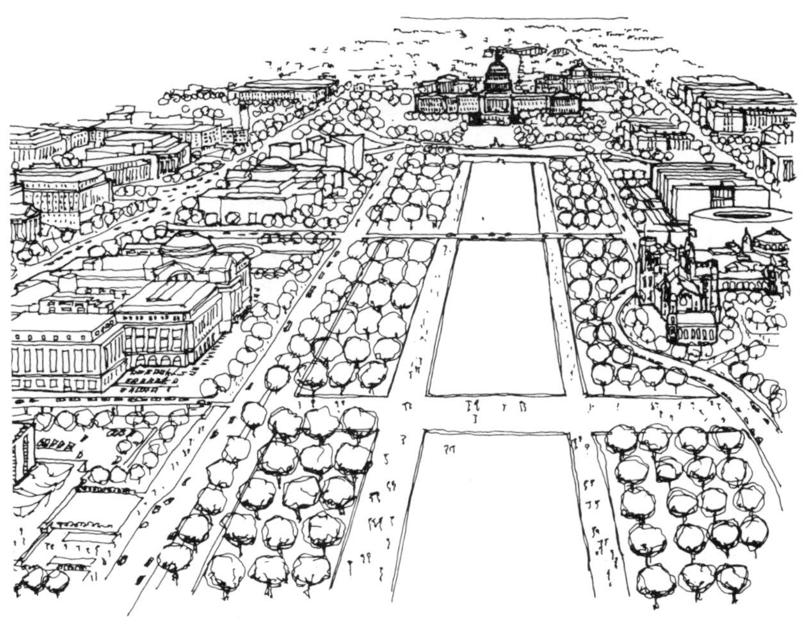

The Mall, looking east

■ **3** Behind the Smithsonian Building is the **Enid A. Haupt Garden,** a 4-acre Victorian-style garden that opened in 1987 as part of the redesigned Castle quadrangle. Protection of this welcome respite resulted in the designs for the National Museum of African Art, Arthur M. Sackler Gallery, and S. Dillon Ripley Center, which are almost entirely underground. Enid A. Haupt received the Liberty Hyde Bailey award from the American Horticultural Society for her extensive philanthropic contributions to horticulture.

■ **4** Directly east of the Smithsonian Building is an **urn commemorating Andrew Jackson Downing.** His plan for the Mall created the first landscaped American public park. In the 1930s, many of the mature trees planted in conformity with his plan were removed from the center of the Mall as it was "restored" to L'Enfant's more formal concept by the McMillan Commission.

■ 5 The **Arts and Industries Building** (1881—Cluss and Schulze, after plans by Montgomery Meigs), at Jefferson Drive and 9th Street, was originally the US National Museum and housed exhibits from the 1876 Centennial Exhibition held in Philadelphia. The exhibition spaces are closed for renovation, but the Discovery Theater remains open in 2004. The Kathrine Dulin Folger Rose Garden at the front entrance includes the numerous varieties of roses planted by the Smithsonian. The Mary Livingston Ripley Garden (1978—Hugh Newel Jacobsen) at the eastern border of the building is a place of informality and intimacy where a parking lot was once proposed. Six gardens have been installed and, although never part of the master plans for the National Mall, they do introduce seasonal interest that humanizes this monumental landscape without taking away from the classical formality of the plan. The gardens are small pockets of the picturesque whole envisioned by Andrew Jackson Downing.

■ 6 Continue east along Jefferson Drive to 7th Street, to the **Joseph H. Hirshhorn Museum and Sculpture Garden** (1974—Gordon Bunschaft of Skidmore, Owings & Merrill). Note the sunken outdoor sculpture garden north of Jefferson Drive, as well as the cylindrical building, which contains paintings and sculptures from the late 1800s to the present.

■ 7 Continue on Jefferson Drive across 7th Street to the **National Air and Space Museum** (1976—Gyo Obata of Helmuth, Obata and Kassabaum). Since its official opening on July 4, 1976, this has become the most popular Smithsonian museum—and the most heavily visited museum in the world.

National Air and Space Museum

■ 8 **The elms on the north side of Jefferson Drive** are part of a continuous band of trees on both sides of the Mall that emphasize the east–west axis. In winter, this allee of deciduous trees can appear cold and barren. Downing's argument that the Mall should be attractive above all in the winter, when

Congress is in session, has lost out to questionable arguments that evergreens are not tolerant of urban conditions, are messy, or present security problems.

■ **9** Across 4th Street from the National Air and Space Museum is the new **National Museum of the American Indian** (opening in 2004). The site is the last available space on the Mall and will be the centerpiece for Indian arts, history, and material culture. In consultation, collaboration, and cooperation with Native people and assistance from the architecture firm of Venturi, Scott Brown and Associates, the Smithsonian, and the National Museum of the American Indian, a guide called "The Way of the People" was compiled that documents the technical aspects of the architectural program and the philosophical approach in which the building respects and honors Native American cultures.

■ **10** At the corner of 4th Street and Jefferson Drive, you can view the **Hubert Humphrey Federal Office Building,** located at 3rd Street and Independence Avenue. It was designed by Marcel Breuer, who also designed the Housing and Urban Development Building (1968). The core of the building contains a 10-story exhaust shaft for Interstate Highway 395, which tunnels beneath the Mall.

Hubert Humphrey Federal Office Building

■ **11** The **US Botanic Garden Conservatory,** to the north of the Humphrey Building, is one of the oldest botanic gardens in North America. The first greenhouse was constructed in 1842, and a complete renovation and reconstruction of the 1933 Conservatory reopened in December 2001. Its exterior is largely unchanged, but an updated and modernized building system provides plumbing, electrical, and other architectural measures to support a living plant museum. New exhibits interpret the role of plants in supporting the earth's ecosystem and enriching human life. The Palm House reconstruction rises over 80 feet.

■ **12** Walk north on 4th Street. On your right are the **Ulysses S. Grant Memorial** and the **Capitol Reflecting Pool** (see Tour 1, Capitol Hill, no. 24), at 1st Street between Maryland and Pennsylvania Avenues.

■ **13** As you look **toward the Washington Monument,** it is interesting to realize that this impressive, open, grassy mall was not completed until 1975, when traffic and parking on the interior streets were replaced by pedestrian and bicycle paths. Between 1791 and 1972, the Mall had been the location of a cow pasture and slaughtering site, swamps, a Civil War hospital, a railroad station with numerous tracks, a trash-filled and stagnant canal, and "temporary" government buildings that existed from World War I to 1972. The railroad station was demolished after the opening of Union Station.

■ **14** This is a good site from which to note how the position of the **Smithsonian Institution Building** (the Castle) offended the sense of order of the monument-minded park planners of the 1900s. The McMillan Plan assumed the building would be removed, but the "defects" of Renwick's Norman "Castle," as seen by the formal eye of 1900, have become assets in the eyes of those accustomed to steel and glass monoliths. The warm, rusty colors that glow in the evening sun, the irregular dimensions, and the vertical and horizontal projections are a welcome change from the surrounding lackluster white sepulchers. Even its failure to stand back of the line prescribed by the turn-of-the-century planners appeals to our hidden rebelliousness.

■ **15** This striking building is the widely acclaimed **East Building of the National Gallery of Art** (I. M. Pei), which opened in 1978. Pei's building is an unabashedly modern solution to an awkward site. Yet its pink Tennessee marble echoes the material, if not the form, of the adjacent main building of the National Gallery of Art, to which it is connected by an underground passageway running under 4th Street. The East Building repeats its triangular theme throughout: in the ceiling designs and in the finely crafted walls whose sharp edges show wear from the admiring hands of many visitors. The museum-goer enters the building under a low ceiling and is then awed by a sunlit, four-story atrium around which the many galleries are grouped.

■ **16** Turn west on Madison to the **National Gallery of Art, Main Building** (1941—John Russell Pope). It contains the richest collection of fine arts in the city.

■ **17** Continue west to the **National Gallery of Art Sculpture Garden** between 7th and 9th Streets. Originally designed in 1974 by Skidmore, Owings & Merrill, this area includes a **pool and ice-skating rink.** This joint project of the National Park Service and the National Gallery of Art was redesigned and updated in 1999. The retention of the public fountain and skating rink (Olin Partnership with National Gallery staff) is a tribute to the success of the original design and the need for a year-round public space on the National Mall.

National Gallery of Art

■ **18** The **Butterfly Habitat Garden** is a slender but rich park alongside the Natural History Museum that supports plant species that attract eastern US butterflies. Plant labels provide the common and botanical names of the plants, region of origin, and life cycle they support. Habitats include the wetland, meadow, woods edge, and urban garden.

■ **19** In front of the **National Museum of Natural History** (1911—Hornblower and Marshall; 1965 wings—Mills, Petticord and Mills), between 9th and 12th Streets, you will see a few evergreens planted in conformity with Downing's 1851 Mall plan. The holly tree in the midst of the elms, slightly to the southeast of the building's steps, was scheduled for removal during the leveling process but was saved in the 1930s by Smithsonian Secretary Alexander Wetmore, an ornithologist, because it was the nesting place of his pet mockingbird. The museum is the home of the famous Hope Diamond, an IMAX theater, and an insect zoo.

■ **20** The **National Museum of American History** (1964—McKim, Mead and White), at Madison Drive between 12th and 14th Streets, is characteristic of the museums of the 1960s. Note the contrast with the lighter, more "open" Smithsonian museums of the 1970s. Popular exhibits include the original Star-Spangled Banner, Horatio Greenough's monumental sculpture of George Washington, and the First Ladies' gowns.

■ **21** Walk across the Mall to the **Freer Gallery of Art** (1923—Charles A. Platt), at 12th Street and Jefferson Drive. Built around a delightful interior court, the museum contains a small but choice collection of oriental art and the world's largest collection of James Abbott McNeil Whistler's works (including the famous Peacock Room).

■ **22** The tour ends at the **National Museum of African Art, the Arthur M. Sackler Gallery,** and the **S. Dillon Ripley Center.** Built mostly underground, they offer an exceptional collection of art treasures to the public.

The Mall—West

(National memorials)

Wilcomb Washburn and Kathryn Cousins, updated by Carol Truppi

Distance: 2 3/4 miles
Time: 2 hours
Bus: On Constitution Avenue: 13A, 13B; on 14th Street: 52
Metro: Federal Triangle or Smithsonian (Blue and Orange Lines)

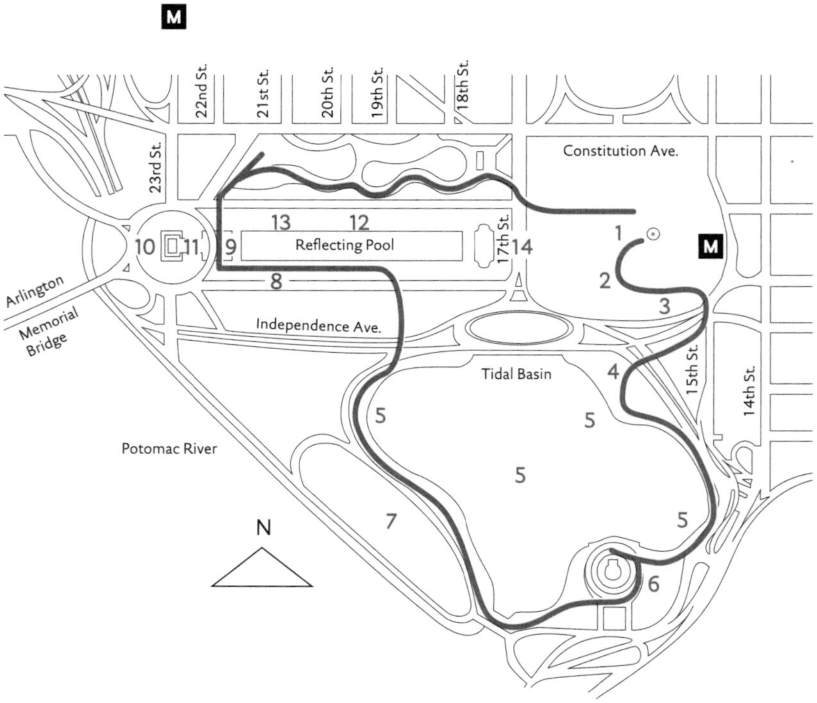

This tour includes the Washington, Jefferson, and Lincoln Memorials. Because of the tour length and inadequate parking, you may wish to buy a ticket for the Tourmobile, which enables you to see each site at your own pace. You can get on and off the Tourmobile at all major sites along the Mall for the entire day of purchase. Adult tickets can be purchased at major tourist spots on the Mall, including the three memorials on this tour. Call (202) 554-5100 for Tourmobile rates and information.

■ 1 The tour begins at the **Washington Monument** (1884—Robert Mills). Pierre L'Enfant chose this location for an equestrian statue that had been proposed by Congress, and George Washington approved the site. Because Congress failed to act decisively on the proposal, a group of private citizens, organized in 1833 as the Washington National Monument Society, offered a prize for the best design for a monument. Robert Mills's design for a 600-foot obelisk rising from a colonnaded base won; the society accepted the design minus the colonnaded base. Construction began in 1848, but funds ran out in 1855. Construction began again in 1876 after Congress had authorized the monument's completion at government expense. It was finally completed in 1885 by the US Army Corps of Engineers. If you look about one-quarter of the way up, you will see a distinct break in the color of the stone, marking the pause between construction phases.

L'Enfant's plan called for the monument to Washington to be located at the intersection of a north–south axis drawn south from the White House and an east–west axis drawn due west from the Capitol. The ground at that point, however, was at the time low and marshy, and when the monument was started early in the 19th century, it was placed on more solid ground 360 feet east and 120 feet south of the planned position. Down the hill to the northwest you will see the "Jefferson Pier," a stone monument placed there in 1810 to mark the true intersection of L'Enfant's proposed north–south and east–west axes. It was later removed but replaced in 1889. The Senate Park Commission planners sought to rectify the off-center position of the Washington Monument along the north–south axis by creating an elaborate sunken garden with a large circular pool to the west, but it was never built because engineers asserted that the monument's stability would be threatened. The planners also sought to rectify the off-center position of the monument along the east–west axis by slanting the Mall one degree south of its true east–west direction. At the time of this writing, the National Capital Planning Commission endorsed the design for stone walls that would ring the Washington Monument in concentric ovals. The walls and other landscaping would replace the concrete New Jersey barriers that were installed as a temporary security measure after 9/11. Visitors may take steps or elevators to the top of the monument to get a panoramic view of the District of Columbia and its suburbs. Tickets are required and may be reserved for a fee. Please call (202) 426-6841 for more information.

■ 2 Walk to the west of the Washington Monument and **look west toward the Lincoln Memorial.** All of the land toward the Potomac River was reclaimed from marsh and tidal land between the 1880s and the 1920s. Until then, the Potomac occasionally flooded right up to the south lawn of the White House. The McMillan Commission proposed extending the Mall from the Washington Monument to the proposed site for a Lincoln Memorial. The planners connected the two monuments with a reflecting pool and aligned the extension along the Senate Park Commission's new slanted east–west axis.

■ 3 Go south toward the Jefferson Memorial. The **Sylvan Theater,** at 15th Street and Independence Avenue, southeast of the Washington Monument, is the site of open-air summer musical, dramatic, and dance productions. Shakespearean plays are favorites.

■ **4** Continue south across Independence Avenue and walk west to East Basin Drive, near 17th Street, to the **Tulip Library.** This outdoor garden is planted with flowering annuals, which are well identified. The tulips in the spring are spectacular.

■ **5** The site of the **Tidal Basin** (1897—W. T. Twining), bordered by Independence Avenue and East Basin Drive, was originally part of the Potomac River. In 1882 the Tidal Basin was created as part of a plan to improve navigation on the Potomac and to reclaim some land for parks. The basin serves to flush the Washington Channel, as gates between the basin and channel are opened at low tide to release the Potomac waters that have filled the basin at high tide. The **cherry trees** surrounding the basin are among 3,000 given by Japan in 1912. The Cherry Blossom Festival—held each year in late March to early April—celebrates their short but enchanting blooming period.

■ **6** Continue along the Tidal Basin to the **Jefferson Memorial** (1943—John Russell Pope, architect; Rudulph Evans, sculptor). The McMillan Commission recommended a memorial in this location, but not specifically to Jefferson. There was considerable controversy on the design of the monument before its approval. It was criticized for combining outmoded classical architectural styles, being too similar to the Lincoln Memorial, and blocking the view of the Potomac from the White House. Defenders of the design said it was influenced by Jefferson's respect for classical styles, which he introduced to this country, and particularly by the Pantheon, which much of his own architecture resembled. The grounds are landscaped after designs of Frederick Law Olmsted. The site forms the south end of the major cross axis of the Mall with the White House at the north. (This axis is difficult to perceive on the ground because the Tidal Basin presents a barrier to direct access to the memorial from the north. It is readily apparent, however, on a map or from the air.)

■ **7** Continue around the Tidal Basin to the **Franklin Delano Roosevelt Memorial.** The entrance and visitor center are off Ohio Drive. However, you can also enter the memorial at the point closest to the Jefferson Memorial or at the middle. Designated in 1959, it was not dedicated until 1997 (Lawrence Halpern) and traces 12 years of American history. This monument to the era of FDR is actually a park with fountains, water features, and landscaping that create an attractive public space in which to view the memorial's statues, quotations, and history.

Take the Tourmobile to the Lincoln Memorial or walk northwest across West Potomac Park to Independence Avenue.

■ **8** The **Korean War Veterans Memorial** is at Independence Avenue and the Lincoln Memorial. It was built by the Korean War Veterans Memorial Advisory at a cost of $18 million in donated funds. It is on a 2.2-acre site adjacent to the Lincoln Memorial Reflecting Pool. It features a sculptured column of 19 foot soldiers arrayed for combat with the American flag. A 164-foot mural is inscribed "Freedom Is Not Free" and is etched with 2,500 photographic images of nurses,

Jefferson Memorial

chaplains, crew chiefs, mechanics, and other support personnel to symbolize the vast effort that sustained the military operation.

■ 9 The site of the **Lincoln Memorial** (1922—Henry Bacon, architect; Daniel Chester French, sculptor) had been debated since 1867. Many early proposals stressed commemorating Abraham Lincoln as a war hero rather than as a humanitarian. Alternatives considered were a Lincoln Highway between Gettysburg and Washington and sites near Union Station and the Capitol. In 1911 the decision was made to locate the memorial here on the continuation of the axis of the Capitol and Washington Monument, as called for in the McMillan Plan, despite objections that the land was swampy and inaccessible. Following a design derived from a Greek temple, the columns are tilted slightly inward to prevent the optical illusion of a bulging top. Many motifs representing Lincoln and America are incorporated into the monument, including the 36 columns that symbolize the 36 states that made up the Union while Lincoln was president. Although some people questioned a design based on a Greek temple to commemorate someone who was born in a log cabin and who proudly acknowledged that heritage, Daniel French said, "The Greeks alone were best able to express in their building . . . the highest attributes and the greatest beauty known to man." The Gettysburg Address and Lincoln's second inaugural speech are inscribed on the walls. Site of Martin Luther King Jr.'s "I Have a Dream" speech of 1963, a portion of which is inscribed on a plaque, the memorial pays homage to Lincoln's "simplicity, his grandeur, and his power."

Lincolin Memorial

■ **10** Walk around the Lincoln Memorial to the rear, or west side, for the **view across the Potomac.** The **Arlington Memorial Bridge** (McKim, Mead and White, architects; Leo Friedlander, sculptor) is considered one of the finest bridges in the country. Designed with the intent of symbolically reuniting the North and South, it was recommended by the McMillan Commission and built in the 1920s. The bridge, which contains an operable (though rarely used) draw span cleverly concealed in the center section, provides access to the **Arlington National Cemetery.** About halfway up the hill straight ahead of the bridge is the **grave of John F. Kennedy,** where the eternal flame can be seen at night. Farther up the hill is **Arlington House** (the Custis-Lee Mansion), home of Robert E. Lee.

■ **11** Walk around the Lincoln Memorial to the entrance and look toward the Capitol. The truly spectacular **view** is one of the most photographed in Washington. It is here that the current design policy of maintaining a formal treatment at the center of the Mall and a more people-oriented treatment at its edges is most apparent. The **Reflecting Pool** is designed to mirror, and to link in a formal and inspiring setting, the monuments at either end. When an artificial ice-skating facility was proposed for the pool in the 1960s, it was turned down by the National Park Service as not in keeping with the dignity of the Mall. Such a facility has been installed in the area between the National Gallery of Art and the National Museum of Natural History (see Tour 3, The Mall—East, no. 17).

■ **12** To the north (formerly the site of "Main Navy"—temporary buildings from World War I that outlasted World War II) is the site of **Constitution Gardens** (Skidmore, Owings & Merrill). Originally planned as a vibrant, day- and nighttime attraction (modeled on the Tivoli Gardens in Copenhagen), the proposed concessionary activities were almost entirely eliminated in order to reduce initial costs. Since their opening in 1976, the gardens have failed to attract the crowds expected. An irregularly shaped lake forms the center of the park. Note the total absence of evergreens, which makes the landscape barren in winter (see Tour 3, The Mall—East, no. 8).

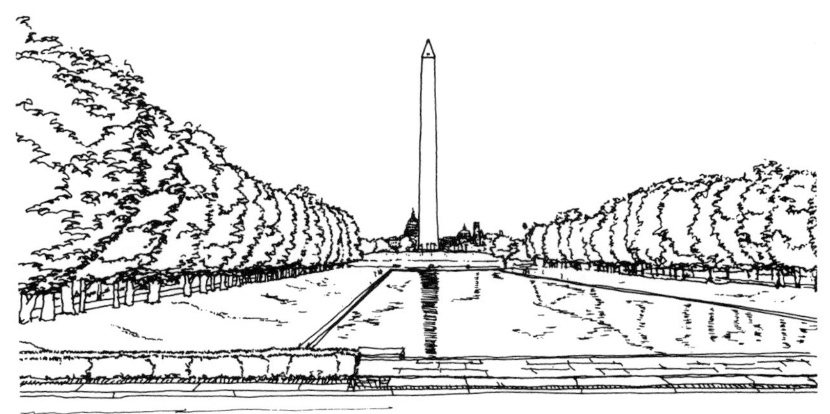

Washington Monument / Reflecting Pool

■ **13** The **Vietnam Veterans Memorial,** dedicated in 1982, is one of Washington's most unusual monuments, both in its design and in the manner of its creation. Initiated by private citizens who had fought in Vietnam, it was built without public funds, and its winning design—by a young Chinese-American student at Yale University, Maya Lin—was the product of an open architectural competition. The monument forms an open V-shaped slash in the ground, the ends of which point to the Washington Monument on one side and the Lincoln Memorial on the other. On its polished black marble panels are inscribed, chronologically in order of their deaths, the names of the more than 50,000 Americans killed during the US involvement in Vietnam. The monument has attracted great numbers of visitors, who move reverently past the panels, leaving small tokens of remembrance—flowers, pictures, flags—for those lost in the war. The final judgment on the memorial has yet to be written; indeed, a flagpole and a representational sculpture of these servicemen have been added to meet the criticisms of those who assert that the monument is too funereal and not sufficiently celebratory in character. Yet it can be said that the memorial is a moving work of art that rises above the controversial character of the Vietnam War.

■ **14** As you return to the Washington Monument, you will pass by the **National World War II Memorial** (2004—design team includes Friedr Florian, Leo A. Daly, Hartman-Cox, Oehme Van Sweden, and Ray Kaskey working with the American Battle Monuments Commission and the National Capital Planning Commission). It replaces the Rainbow Pool. For many people, the memorial has altered the historic integrity of the National Mall as envisioned by Pierre L'Enfant and the McMillan Plan, including the vista between the Lincoln Memorial and the Washington Monument. Pressure from Congress and special interest groups has led to a movement to create protective legislation and agency directives for the Mall that can help to retain the integrity of this nationally significant landscape.

Independence Avenue and L'Enfant Plaza

(Federal office buildings, large commercial urban redevelopment project)

Charity Vanderbilt Davidson, updated by John J. Protopappas
and Stephanie L. Protopappas

Distance: 3/4 mile
Time: 1 1/4 hours
Bus: Along Independence Avenue: 32, 34, 35, 36, P2, P6, and W12
Metro: Federal Center/Southwest (Blue and Orange Lines)

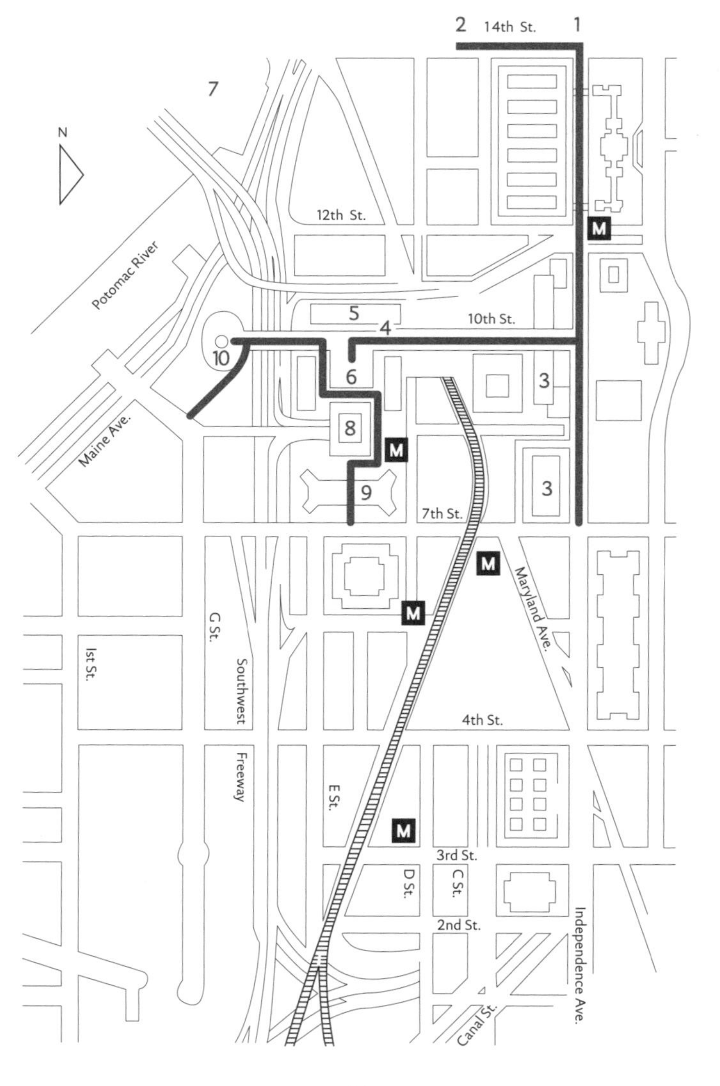

The Independence Avenue/L'Enfant Plaza area is the northern edge of Washington's Southwest quadrant. During the first half of the 19th century, it was a very desirable residential area. Only a few commercial structures (including the most famous of the city's slave pens) were in evidence. After the Baltimore and Potomac Railroad laid tracks along Maryland and Virginia Avenues in 1873, the western end of the area between B Street (Independence Avenue) and the waterfront became a vast railroad yard, and the desirability of nearby areas as residential neighborhoods diminished.

Prior to 1900 the only government agencies with a strong interest in the area were the Department of Agriculture, with buildings along B Street, and the Bureau of Engraving and Printing, on 14th Street (making use of railroad for freight service). Federal interest in the northern fringes of the Southwest increased during the first decades of the 20th century, with the erection of some additional buildings for Agriculture and Engraving and Printing offices, but in general the area retained much of its 19th-century appearance because government departments preferred to rent space in existing structures.

During World War I, the federal bureaucracy mushroomed, and it became all too apparent that the federal government could no longer make do with offices scattered all over the city. The Independence Avenue/L'Enfant Plaza area was included in the kite-shaped monumental core proposed by the Senate Park Commission in 1902, but its use was undefined and little action was taken. By the 1920s, a new building program had become a necessity. Most of the attention was focused on the Federal Triangle between Pennsylvania Avenue NW and the Mall. But by the 1930s, the newly created National Capital Park and Planning Commission (today the National Capital Planning Commission [NCPC]) was drawing up plans for similar developments in other parts of the city. One of the areas proposed was the Southwest Rectangle, bounded by B Street (later given the more pretentious name of Independence Avenue), 14th Street, the current right of way of the Southwest Freeway, and 2nd Street.

Nothing further was done until the 1950s, when plans for the redevelopment of the entire Southwest were drawn up. Although an area roughly the same as the old Southwest Rectangle was set aside for development as government offices, no plan specified the location of any of the proposed buildings or their spatial relationship to one another. The awkward positioning of many of the offices in the redeveloped federal area is a result of this omission from the recent plans.

This tour begins at the westernmost entrance to the Smithsonian Metro station, located at 12th and Independence Avenue SW at the northeast corner of the **Department of Agriculture (South Building).** The concentration of buildings, which constitutes the headquarters of the Department of Agriculture, covers three city blocks. Several of these buildings were completed during the 1930s as part of the Southwest Rectangle project. As you exit the Metro station, walk west for one block along C Street SW to 14th Street SW. Tour sites no.1 and no.2 are located on the west side of 14th Street.

■ **1** The **US Holocaust Memorial Museum** is south of the Sidney R. Yates Federal Building, at 14th Street SW and Raoul Wallenberg Place SW. It was dedicated on April 22, 1993. Planning for the museum started during the presidency of Jimmy Carter. In November 1978, President Carter established the President's Commission on the Holocaust and charged it with issuing a report on the state of Holocaust remembrance and education in the United States. In September 1979, the President's Commission presented its recommendation, to "establish a living memorial to honor the victims and survivors of the Holocaust and to ensure that the lessons of the Holocaust will be taught in perpetuity." Pei Cobb Freed & Partners designed the museum, a multistoried complex that provides classrooms, theaters, auditoriums, meeting spaces, a variety of interactive learning activities, permanent exhibitions, and a Hall of Remembrance. It also includes the Anne Frank Writer Exhibition. No pass is necessary for entering the museum building and the interactive exhibitions; however, a pass is needed to view the permanent exhibition. You should allow extra time when you visit the museum to pass though the entry line. The permanent exhibition is highly recommended.

■ **2** The **Bureau of Engraving and Printing** Building complex is located on both sides of 14th Street SW, but the public entrance for tours of the building is to the south of the Holocaust Memorial Museum. A second public entrance on Raoul Wallenberg Place provides access to the bookstore and gift shop. The Bureau of Engraving and Printing is where millions of dollars, as well as stamps and other official documents, are printed every day. It is open to the public daily 8:00 a.m.–2:00 p.m. except Saturday, Sunday, and holidays.

■ **3** The **James Forrestal Building (FOB No. 5),** at Independence Avenue and 10th Street (1970—Curtis & Davis), the one federal office building to have both a name and a number, is probably the most special of the "universal" buildings. It actually consists of three structures: the 660-foot-long main building fronting on Independence Avenue, a taller office annex behind, and a separate cafeteria building. The large horizontal building originally was conceived as two of the General Services Administration's "universal office buildings," one on each side of 10th Street. However, the Department of Defense convinced Congress that the specialized nature of the department's activities required that the majority of its facilities on this site be contained in a single structure. Congress then approved the concept of a single building spanning 10th Street. It finally was agreed that the first floor of the horizontal building would be lifted 30 feet above street level to avoid blocking the 10th Street vista of the Smithsonian Castle tower. It was felt that the sense of space created by the horizontal opening between the plaza and the first floor more than compensated for the loss of the narrow view up 10th Street. The feeling of unity between the Forrestal Building and the developing 10th Street Mall/L'Enfant Plaza complex to the south was reinforced by the use of coordinated paving materials on all three projects. The presence of the surface railroad on Maryland Avenue required that the two building complexes be on different levels. A lower-level passage serves as a circulation system for the three parts of the building and as a boarding area for commuter buses.

■ 4 The **10th Street Mall** and L'Enfant Plaza (1965—10th Street Mall, Wright & Gane, architects; 1965—10th Street Overlook, office of Dan Kiley, landscape architect; 1965—L'Enfant Plaza, North and South Buildings and Plaza, I. M. Pei & Associates; 1970–73—L'Enfant Plaza Hotel, Vlastimil Koubek). Original development plans for 10th Street envisioned it as an esplanade lined with structures restricted to commercial and residential uses. A slightly later plan proposed that 10th Street be widened and serve as a throughway between downtown Washington and the Southwest Freeway.

L'Enfant Plaza and 10th Street Mall

Early in 1954, Webb & Knapp, the New York developers, proposed a renewal plan for the entire Southwest, including 10th Street and L'Enfant Plaza. As originally worked out by William Zeckendorf of Webb & Knapp and I. M. Pei, this proposal called for widening 10th Street and developing it as a 1,200-foot-long mall. This mall was to be flanked with public and semipublic office buildings. L'Enfant Plaza, originally planned to be farther east of 10th Street, was to be an enclosed square surrounded by private office buildings. It was also expected to develop as a cultural and entertainment / convention center, with a hotel, performance hall, theater, and outdoor cafes. The mall itself was to terminate in a semicircular reflecting pool and waterfront park on the Washington Channel, balancing another large fountain treatment in the Smithsonian yard.

By the time construction began, significant changes had been made in the plan. In 1960 urban designer Willow von Molke proposed the development of the 10th Street axis as a waterfront overlook. I. M. Pei & Associates drew up a master plan for the mall and plaza that brought the plaza west to its present location; after public hearings, this master plan was incorporated into the official renewal plan approved by the NCPC. By then Webb & Knapp had withdrawn and the project had been taken over by the L'Enfant Plaza Corporation.

■ **5–6** Walk up the west side of the 10th Street Mall past the **Postal Service Building** to **L'Enfant Plaza (6).** Note that the mall bridges the railroad tracks that cut through the site and that nothing has been done to develop the Maryland Avenue vista toward the Capitol. The Pei proposal had included a major focal sculpture for the plaza, but this too was eliminated. The paving for both the mall and L'Enfant Plaza is Hastings block inlaid with red granite. No effort has been made to differentiate visually between public and private property along the mall or in the plaza. The center strip down the mall was intended to be a cascade of water flowing toward Independence Avenue, but it leaked and was drained.

■ **7** To the west is **East Potomac Park,** created by the Army Corps of Engineers during dredging operations along the Potomac in the 1880s. Among its recreation facilities is one of three public golf courses in the city.

■ **8** The buildings to the north and south of the plaza are office towers; the one to the east is the **L'Enfant Plaza Hotel.** There is parking for 1,300 cars under the plaza, with direct ramps on and off the nearby expressway. There is also direct access to the Metro subway system.

Proceed across 10th Street and down the stairs on either side of the fountain. These lead to the 100,000-square-foot underground shopping mall. As with the plaza above, this retail facility gets intensive use by workers from the surrounding buildings. Once the shopping mall has been explored, continue east along the main corridor of the shopping arcade to the exit to the curvilinear HUD Building.

■ **9 Department of Housing and Urban Development** (1968—Marcel Breuer and Herbert Beckhard), 451 7th Street SW. Walk through the HUD Building to the 7th Street entrance and plaza. Commissioned in 1963, when HUD was still the Housing and Home Finance Agency, this was one of the first buildings constructed after President Kennedy issued his directive on "Guiding Principles for Federal Architecture." To raise the aesthetic standards of federal buildings, the General Services Administration provided that a percentage of the construction costs be devoted to artistic embellishments (such as plazas and sculpture).

Breuer became involved with curvilinear structures while designing a building for UNESCO and a research lab for IBM at LaGaude, France. The French favor such buildings because they permit a maximum amount of natural light in a maximum number of offices (thereby reducing the amount of electricity required), while keeping the distance between offices to a minimum. The architect selected a curvilinear shape for the HUD Building partly because it would yield the best window-distance ratio in a large structure on a restricted site and partly because its lines would be sympathetic to the curves of the Southwest Freeway adjacent to it. The building is a double Y, with each wing touching the property lines only at the corners. It provides office space for more than 6,000 employees and has three levels of parking under the plaza. The plaza itself is also an effort to relate the 7th Street connection to the Mall.

The rectangular white building (Edward Durell Stone, architect) directly across 7th Street was privately built but is occupied by the Department of Transportation. Return to the underground arcade and follow the overhead signs to the L'Enfant Plaza Hotel lobby. Exit from the lobby via the south doors in order to walk around the hotel's terrace. The section of terrace just south of the hotel is provided with umbrella-shaded tables, available to anyone wishing to use them; additional seating is provided elsewhere around the terrace.

Walk along the terrace in a counterclockwise direction. Note the small, walled, grassy space that separates the hotel from the HUD Building; small as it is, this open space also is used intensively.

This juxtaposition of buildings results from the lack of a single design plan for the section of the redevelopment area designated for office use; each building was developed without direct coordination with its neighbors.

Continuing along the terrace, the railroad track barrier is once again very evident. The north side of the terrace provides an excellent **view** of the Arts and Industries Building and the downtown skyline beyond the Mall.

■ **10** Now walk back to the front of the hotel, across the plaza, and back to the 10th Street Mall. Continue south along the mall to the **Benjamin Banneker Circle and Fountain,** where it terminates. This overlook provides a **panoramic view** of the Washington Channel and the redeveloped Southwest. Moving counterclockwise around the overlook, you can see townhouses constructed by local development company Eakin Youngentob and Associates.

Southwest

(Established residential areas, regional theater, and waterfront)

Charity Vanderbilt Davidson, updated by Stephanie L. Protopappas

Distance: 2 miles
Time: 1 1/2 hours
Bus: To 7th and I (Eye) Streets: 70, M8, V4, and V6
Metro: L'Enfant Plaza (Blue and Orange Lines), exiting at 7th Street; Waterfront/SE University Station (Green Line) at 4th and M Streets

When the Federal City was laid out in 1791–92, it was expected that the Southwest quadrant would develop as a mixed residential/commercial center. During the last decade of the 18th century, wealthy citizens built homes in the area and a real estate syndicate built several rows of substantial brick dwellings for speculative purposes. Unfortunately, the Southwest's commercial dreams were never realized. It was hoped that the City Canal would enable the area to attract some of Georgetown's trade, but the mismanaged, decaying canal proved to be a barrier that isolated the Southwest from the rest of the developing city, rather than a commercial link.

Early in 1952, two plans were offered for the redevelopment of 427 acres in the Southwest. The first plan, prepared by Elbert Peets for the NCPC, called for the rehabilitation of many of the residential structures, but it was rejected as socially and financially impossible. The second plan, commissioned by the District of Columbia Redevelopment Land Agency (RLA, today part of the National Capital Revitalization Corporation), was prepared by the St. Louis planning firm of Harland Bartholomew and Associates and by two Washington architects, Louis Justement and Chloethiel Woodard Smith. The Smith-Justement plan called for the demolition of nearly all existing structures and the erection of approximately 5,000 new dwelling units. The NCPC then prepared a third plan, stressing redevelopment rather than rehabilitation. The RLA began to accept bids for Area B, the section east of Canal Street and Delaware Avenue, reserved for public housing.

In 1953 President Eisenhower persuaded the New York development firm of Webb & Knapp to prepare a plan for 440 acres, which had been set aside for private development. Prepared by Webb & Knapp's architectural and planning staff, headed by I. M. Pei, and Chicago architect Harry Weese, the plan was unveiled early in 1954. The area south of the freeway was to be residential, with high-rise apartment towers interspersed among clusters of townhouses; this proposal for mixed building types was innovative for its time, as developers had previously segregated high-rise and low-rise structures. The plans prepared by Peets and Smith and Justement had called for rebuilding the retail commercial streets. However,

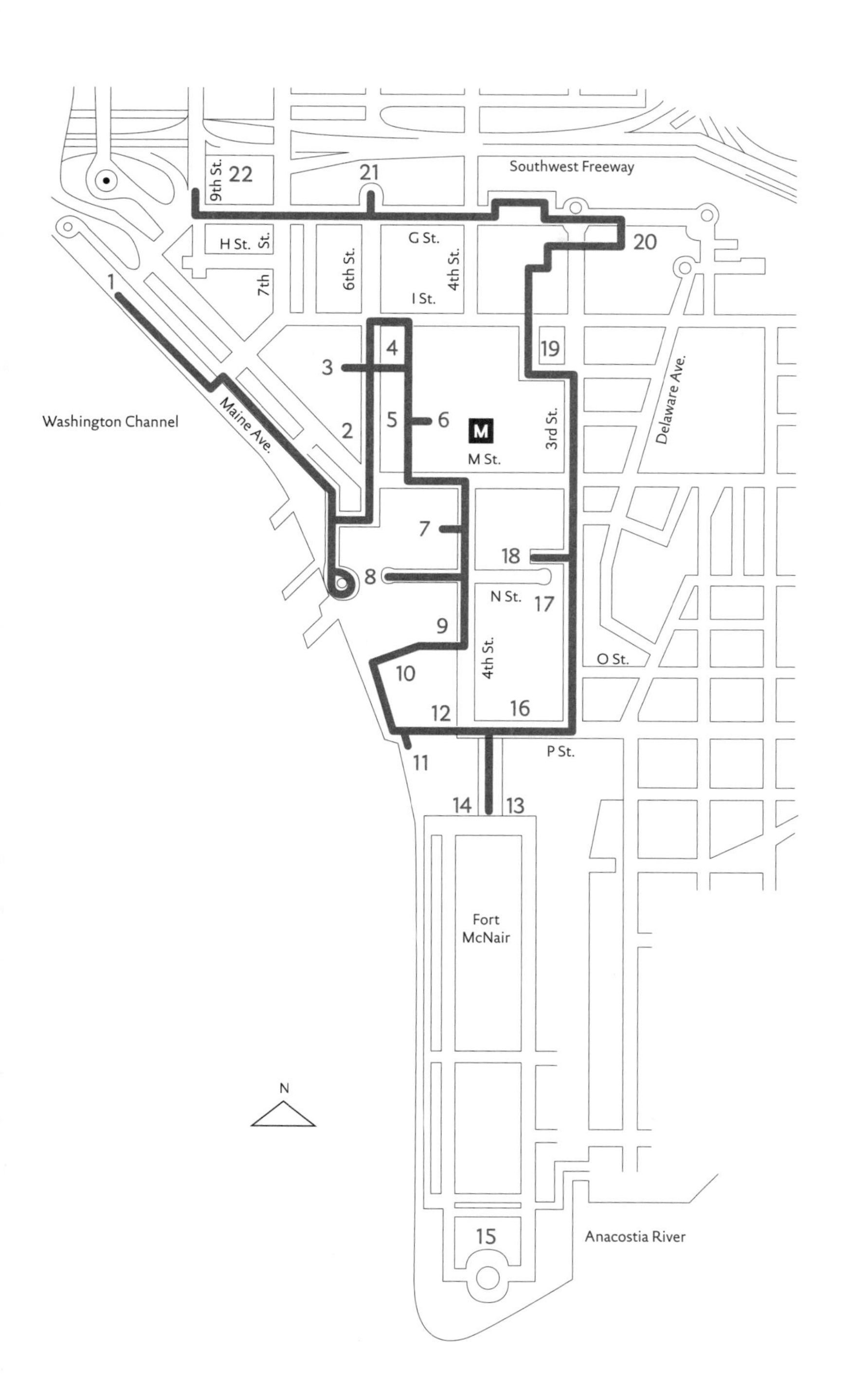

Southwest Freeway
9th St.
22
21
20
H St.
St.
G St.
6th St.
4th St.
I St.
7th
1
19
4
3
Washington Channel
Maine Ave.
2
5
6
M
M St.
3rd St.
Delaware Ave.
7
18
8
N St.
17
9
4th St.
O St.
10
12
16
11
P St.
14
13
Fort McNair
N
15
Anacostia River

the new plan included a town center, or shopping mall, to serve the entire Southwest, and the waterfront was to be completely redeveloped. In exchange for formulating the plan, Webb & Knapp was given a choice of areas to develop; the firm chose the area of the town center—what is today L'Enfant Plaza (see Tour 5, Independence Avenue and L'Enfant Plaza) and the residential section north of M Street. The basic concepts of the Webb & Knapp plan (sometimes also referred to as the Zeckendorf-Pei plan) were finally adopted by the NCPC in 1956, but many of the details were altered. Webb & Knapp began work on its portion of the project but was forced to withdraw later for financial reasons.

The Peets plan of 1952 had tried to work with the original street plan, but subsequent development plans called for substantial changes, such as the creation of "super blocks" by closing many of the streets. One of the recurring themes in the redevelopment area is the variety of ways in which different developers have used the old street spaces.

■ 1 The **Southwest Waterfront** has had a mixed development history. Prior to the early 1950s, much of the area was occupied by freestanding commercial establishments, dilapidated warehouses, railroad yards, and wooden building piers that were in varying stages of disrepair. The Washington architectural firm of Saherlee and Smith prepared a tentative renewal plan for the waterfront. However, this plan was rejected by the NCPC as not being sensitive to the treatment of the water's edge. The NCPC drew up an alternate set of objectives that emphasized low-scale buildings with well-landscaped, open areas, and the waterfront was largely developed as envisioned. The few buildings that were built along the waterfront have been kept low so that the view of the canal would be enjoyed by residents throughout the Southwest Waterfront area. Public parking was mostly contained in structures. From west to east, the waterfront until recently offered an interesting array of restaurants and other activities. Today the buildings along the waterfront areas show signs of deterioration, the public spaces need upgrading, and the once-vibrant public amenity suffers from a lack of public and private investment in its infrastructure. A revitalization plan proposing a mix of housing, retail, entertainment, and open spaces has been developed by the District's Office of Planning. A public-private development entity has been proposed to implement the plan a 25-year period.

The waterfront offers several seafood restaurants, nightclubs, and a motel. Highlights of the waterfront include:

Washington Marina is a one-story building that provides services to boating enthusiasts. You may purchase, dock, or rent a boat or have one repaired at this shop.

Fish Wharf is one of the most colorful spots along the waterfront. Initially a depot from which local fishermen could sell their daily catch to the public, the wharf is now home to a series of permanently docked flatboats that have been converted into retail seafood shops. Most of the products sold by the retailers today are brought in by refrigerated trucks. This area attracts patrons from throughout the Washington metropolitan area. It has become well known for its supply of Maryland blue crabs and a wide variety of fresh and prepared seafood.

The **Capital Yacht Club,** in the somewhat nondescript building adjacent to the Fish Wharf, is one of several such establishments along the Potomac River.

The ***Spirit of Washington*** tour office books water-related activities on cruise vessels, ranging from day and night dining cruises along the Potomac River to sightseeing excursions to Mount Vernon, the home of George Washington. During each tour, the guests can enjoy a lavish buffet meal and be entertained by an on-board group of local singers and dancers.

The **District of Columbia Police's fire and harbor patrols** occupy a building at the easternmost extent of Maine Avenue. Water rescue teams of officers are housed here, too. Several water rescue training programs are conducted from this facility weekly. It is possible to tour this building if reservations are made in advance.

■ **2 Arena Stage** (1961) and the **Kreeger Theater** (1970—Harry Weese and Associates), 6th and M Streets. Arena Stage's company was a pioneer of theater-in-the-round in America. One of the best resident theater companies in the country today, it was the first theater company outside of New York to win a Tony Award. The polygonal theater building, which seats 750, is separate from but connected to the elongated administration building that houses the supporting facilities.

Arena Stage

The three-story Kreeger Theater wraps around one corner of this administration wing. It seats 500 and allows the company to expand its program of experimental plays, children's theater, and teaching. Unlike Arena Stage, which is truly theater-in-the-round, the Kreeger's stage is fan shaped.

The exterior materials of both buildings are identical, making the two buildings "an aesthetic, functional whole," according to architect Weese.

■ 3 **Waterside Towers,** 901–47 6th Street SW (1970—Chloethiel Woodard Smith & Associated Architects). This complex of townhouses and high-rise apartments can be entered by walking down the driveway entrance. The townhouses serve as a wall around a large, landscaped interior courtyard that covers the underground parking facility. The uninterrupted openness of this courtyard contrasts with the courtyard treatments in other developments in the area.

■ 4 The **park** with the pond was designed by Ian McHarg, a nationally recognized landscape architect.

■ 5 **Town Center Plaza,** 1100 block of 6th Street (1961–62—I. M. Pei & Associates). Built in two phases, these apartments won a Federal Housing Administration honor award and are significant because they demonstrate that good residential architecture can be produced within the financial constraints set by developers. They are the only apartments in the redevelopment area that do not have balconies and are not accompanied by townhouses. Their courtyards have been created from the old street space and trees of L Street.

■ 6 **Waterside Mall,** 400 M Street SW (1972—Chloethiel Woodard Smith & Associated Architects). The large office tower is part of the office and retail development known as Waterside Mall. This project is being transformed by the Forest Cities Group into a mixed-use development of 100,000 square feet of retail, 2 million square feet of office, and 400 residential units—a town center, as envisioned by the original designers. Initially designed along the lines of a suburban shopping center, the mall was redesigned when it was determined that a facility containing more neighborhood service functions (restaurants, medical offices, shops) was needed. This concept was not successful at the time, for many of the original shops closed, and the developers were reluctant to complete the structure. But times and market conditions change, and it appears that Forest Cities is going to have a very successful project.

■ 7 **Tiber Island,** bounded by M, N, and 4th Streets and the waterfront (1965—Keyes, Lethbridge and Condon), was the winner of the first RLA design competition and of a 1961 AIA Honor Award. It consists of four eight-story apartment towers (368 units) and 85 two-to-three-story townhouses. It is especially interesting because of the spatial relationship between its high-rise and low-rise elements and the way in which the District of Columbia zoning code was interpreted to permit the design's implementation.

■ 8 The **Thomas Law House,** also known as the Honeymoon House, is located at 1252 6th Street SW, in the southeast corner of Tiber Island. Law was a major promoter of south Washington development. His federal-style house, built between 1794 and 1796, is among Washington's oldest extant structures and is

Tiber Island

listed on the National Register of Historic Places. It was rehabilitated in 1965 to serve as a community center for residents of Tiber Island and Carrollsburg Square (see this tour, no. 18).

■ 9 **Harbour Square,** bound by 4th, N, and O Streets and the waterfront (1966—Chloethiel Woodard Smith & Associated Architects). This complex not only includes high-rise apartments and townhouses but also has incorporated three of the late-18th- to early-19th-century structures that survived the extensive demolition carried out in the renewal area:

The **Edward Simon Lewis House,** at 456 N Street SW, was built about 1817 and is typical of the early-19th-century brick houses in Washington. Originally built as a single-family house, the structure was converted into apartments in the 1920s; during the 1930s, its tenants included journalists Lewis J. Heath and Ernie Pyle. After rehabilitation in 1964–66, the house was included in Harbour Square as a single-family townhouse.

The **Duncanson Cranch House,** 468–70 N Street SW, like Wheat Row (below), was built about 1794 by the real estate syndicate of James Greenleaf (a former American consul in Amsterdam), Robert Morris (a Philadelphia financier), and John Nicholson (also of Philadelphia). It comprises two townhouses in Harbour Square.

Wheat Row, at 1315–21 4th Street SW, is an important example of the conservative, vernacular domestic architecture constructed during the federal period. Built in 1794, it is believed to be the first speculative housing built in the City of Washington by the Greenleaf syndicate. It was rehabilitated in 1964–66 and included in Harbour Square as four townhouses.

■ 10 The **Water Garden** in the center of the Harbour Square complex is the dominant element in the development's pedestrian square. It includes sculptured forms, platforms, walks, and seating. Planting includes flowering water plants and willow trees. It is inoperative during the colder months of the year.

Wheat Row in Harbour Square

■ 11 **Waterside Park** (1967–68—Sasaki, Dawson and Demay). Walk around this park near a grove of willow trees and southwest along the seawall to the Titanic Memorial.

■ 12 **Riverside, Edgewater,** and **1401–15 4th Street** (formerly the J. Finley House and Chalk House), bounded by 4th, O, and P Streets and the waterfront (1966—Morris Lapidus Associates). These apartments and townhouses were originally a single development. The Riverside and Edgewater have been converted to condominiums; 1401–15 4th Street are now fee-simple townhouses. This complex won the third RLA design competition. Note the use of old street space for a greenway along O Street.

■ 13 **Fort Leslie J. McNair** (1903—McKim, Mead and White) was established in 1794 as the Washington Arsenal. A feature of the L'Enfant plan, Fort McNair has been known by a variety of names (Washington Arsenal, US Arsenal at Greenleaf Point, Washington Barracks). The first fortifications were erected in 1791 and the first arsenal buildings in 1803–4. It was one of the earliest employers in Washington. All of the original buildings were destroyed by an explosion during the British occupation of Washington in August 1814. The arsenal buildings were rebuilt and served as a distribution center for arms.

■ 14 The first **US Penitentiary,** opened on the northern end of the arsenal grounds in 1826, is best known as the site of the trial and execution of four of the Lincoln conspirators and of the commandant of the Confederate prison at Andersonville, Georgia. Most of the penitentiary buildings were razed in

1869, but a portion of the complex remains in the center of the greensward. The arsenal grounds were used for storage by the Quartermaster Corps after 1881. Between 1898 and 1909, the general hospital on the grounds was the site of many of Maj. Walter Reed's experiments with yellow fever.

■ **15** In 1903 the New York architectural firm of McKim, Mead and White was retained to design a building for the new **National War College** and to develop a master plan for the entire installation. Most of the firm's plan (which called for a long mall, flanked by white-columned officers' houses, with the War College at the end as the focal point) was implemented. An unconfirmed story relates that the designer was so angry when he learned that the War Department had refused to tear down the few remaining arsenal and penitentiary buildings in the middle of the proposed mall (thereby blocking the vista to the War College) that he refused to set foot on the site again. To this day the vista is still blocked, and to view the War College it is necessary to walk half the length of the mall, beyond the old penitentiary and arsenal buildings. Since 9/11, the college and Fort McNair have been closed to the public.

■ **16 Channel Square,** 325 P Street SW (1968—Harry Weese and Associates), consists of tan-colored townhouses and an apartment tower, designed as middle-income housing under Section 221 D3 of the Housing Act of 1949. This section of the act subsidized the developer's interest rate, and, in turn, rents have been kept well below existing market rates.

■ **17 River Park Mutual Homes Cooperative,** bounded by 4th, O, N, and 3rd Streets (1962—Charles M. Goodman Associates), was the first owner-occupied development in the new Southwest. It includes 134 townhouses and 384 adjacent apartments. The apartment building was designed to serve as a barrier between the development's barrel-vaulted townhouses and the public housing across Delaware Avenue.

This wall-like quality can best be experienced by walking north between the apartment building and the townhouses. The former street spaces in the complex have been landscaped and terminate in cul-de-sacs.

■ **18 Carrollsburg Square,** bounded by M, N, 4th, and 3rd Streets (1965—Keyes, Lethbridge and Condon, architects; Eric Paepcke, landscape architect), was the winner of the second RLA design competition. Like Tiber Island, Carrollsburg Square has a central pedestrian area over an underground garage, but here the plaza has been divided into more small residential courts. Here again, each court has been given its own character by means of variations in landscaping and architectural detail. Carrollsburg Square was intended as a transition between Tiber Island and the public housing immediately to the east.

■ **19** Note the **park** by landscape designer Ian McHarg that occupies the northern half of the square along the north side of the Town Center. Walk west through the **elongated park** (also by McHarg) to the central plaza. These were intended as low-maintenance parks, but a great deal of work is still required. A variety of community facilities (library, churches, public transportation) are concentrated in this area. The large-scale dislocation of people caused by the renewal raised particular problems for local churches. The National Council of Churches worked with the congregations in Southwest to determine which churches would remain in the area, which would combine facilities, if not congregations, and which would relocate. Two of the remaining churches flank the park.

■ 20 **Capitol Park apartments and townhouses,** bounded by 3rd and I Streets, Delaware Avenue, and the Southwest Freeway (1959—Satterlee and Smith; 1963—Smith and Associates). Built on the site of Dixon's Court, one of Washington's largest and most infamous inhabited alleys, Capitol Park was the first of the new projects erected in the Southwest. It was given an AIA merit award in 1960. The apartment tower at 800 4th Street SW was the first building (402 units) of a group that was ultimately intended to contain 1,600 units. Although built in stages, the complex was designed as a unified whole. The accompanying townhouses are FHA Honor Award winners. The development is best known for its parklike atmosphere. The feeling of openness that pervades Capitol Park, with its use of glass, contrasts sharply with the feeling of containment present in other, later Southwest developments.

■ 21 After exploring Capitol Park, cross 4th Street and walk west along G Street past the townhouses (1966–69—Walter Pater) to the **park** at the end of 6th Street. Walk north across the park to the retaining wall on the far side of the parking lot for one of the most spectacular **views** of the Southwest Freeway, which is a major physical barrier in the neighborhood. It effectively eliminates the residential part of Southwest from the office-development areas. The townhouses are interesting because they are grouped around **common greens** that are maintained and owned by the homeowners.

■ 22 Near the corner of G and 7th Streets the tract (Parcel 76) has been transformed into an **upscale townhouse site** by Eakin Youngentob, a well-established townhouse builder in the Washington area.

Foggy Bottom

(Historic residential neighborhood, Watergate complex, Kennedy Center, George Washington University, State Department, Constitution Avenue)

Zachary Domike, updated by John J. Protopappas

Distance: 2 3/4 miles
Time: 2 hours
Bus: Along Pennsylvania Avenue: 32, 34, 35, 36, 42 and 80
Metro: Farragut West (Blue and Orange Lines)

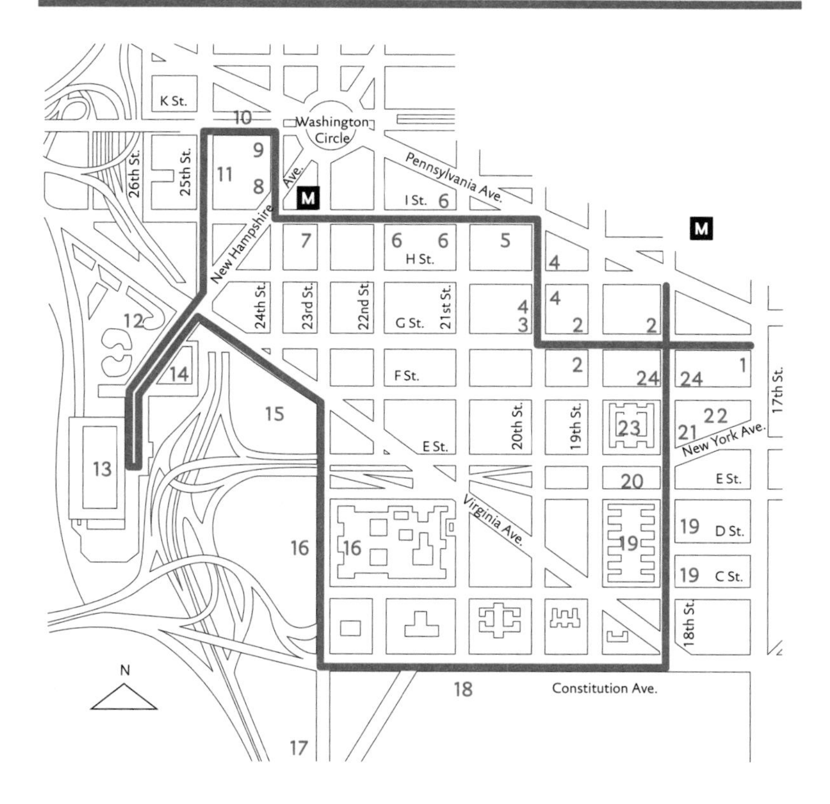

Foggy Bottom presents one of the most complex tapestries of urban growth and change to be found in Washington, DC.

The history of Foggy Bottom can be traced back to the mid-17th century, when it was part of the land grant known as the Widow's Mite. In 1763 Jacob Funk purchased a tract of 130 acres, located generally between what is now 19th and 24th Streets, H Street, and the Potomac River, and laid out the town of

Hamburg. Also known as Funkstown, the area was one of a series of port towns situated along the Potomac in the mid-18th century, of which Georgetown and Alexandria were the most successful. Throughout the remainder of the century, little development occurred in Hamburg, and the area did not pose an obstacle to Pierre L'Enfant's street plan, which covered the Maryland side of the Potomac River as far north as Boundary Street (now Florida Avenue).

L'Enfant's plan set forth Washington Circle as the focus for growth in the Foggy Bottom area. The grid of numbered and lettered streets was cut through by radial avenues that tied the area to other focal points throughout the city. Market structures reinforced the growth plan, as did the residential and commercial development that clustered close to the president's house and along Pennsylvania Avenue.

In the 19th century, a thriving waterside settlement developed along the Potomac River and Rock Creek. On the high ground of Foggy Bottom, north of E Street and east of 23rd Street, substantial residences were built to house the fashionable scientific and military communities and the diplomatic corps. On the low ground, south of E Street and west of 23rd Street, modest dwellings were built to accommodate workers who toiled in the nearby glassworks, breweries, cement company, and gas works. The ill-built and much-polluted City Canal (along what is now Constitution Avenue) and the marshy lands merging into the Potomac underscored the undesirable nature of the lowlands. In fact, the desolate character of this section is said to have given rise to Foggy Bottom's name.

The filling-in of the City Canal and the reclamation of the "Potomac Flats" in the late 19th century transformed the lowland area and created a large swath of land available for development. This canvas stood ready for the grand plans of the McMillan Commission of 1902 as it recommended sites for public buildings and parks. The departure of the affluent residents to more fashionable neighborhoods elsewhere in the District, and a new appreciation of the proximity of the area to the White House and Downtown, changed the residential character of Foggy Bottom. Apartment buildings were wedged in between townhouses. Remaining townhouses were adapted to institutional use, as exemplified by the removal of George Washington University from 15th and I Streets to 2023 G Street NW in 1912.

Throughout much of the 20th century, the area has served as the battleground between proponents of high-density development and defenders of the surviving townhouses, and between residents who prize Foggy Bottom's neighborly qualities and institutions that wish to expand their operations into office structures occupied only from nine to five. Foggy Bottom has also served as the stage for post–World War II urban renewal and highway plans, of which some were carried out and others were aborted. The area has been further transformed by luxury condominiums, cooperatives, and rental apartment buildings in the Watergate complex, including the extensive rehabilitation of the row houses throughout the neighborhood.

■ **1** Begin the tour at 17th and G Streets. Heading west, you see on the left the offices of the **Federal Home Loan Bank Board.** Completed in 1978 after the designs of Max Urbahn, this lively office complex presents a small-scale version of New York City's Rockefeller Center, complete with skating rink, restaurants, and shops.

■ **2** At 18th and G Streets and 20th and G Streets are buildings occupied by the **World Bank** (International Bank for Reconstruction and Development) and the **International Monetary Fund.** The addition to the complex on the north side of the block between 19th and 20th Streets has a spectacular enclosed interior courtyard. The Mexican Embassy is located at 1911 Pennsylvania Avenue NW. On the south side of the block, the most recent building stands on the site of the early-19th-century **Lenthall Houses,** which were moved by George Washington University to 21st Street, between F and G Streets, as part of a preservation compromise with the community. The block also retains the **F Street Club** (about 1853) and a portion of its garden at the northeast corner of 20th and F Streets. On the same block, at the southeast corner of 20th and G Streets, stands the **United Church of Christ-United Methodist,** a combined German Lutheran and Methodist congregation. Originally built as the Concordia Lutheran Evangelical Church, it is a reminder of the former German settlement in Foggy Bottom. Services in German are still offered.

■ **3** The cross streets of 20th and G form one of the major entrances to **George Washington University.** Founded in 1821, the university was first located on College Hill in the area now known as Columbia Heights. In the early 1880s, the university moved to 15th and H Streets and later spread into other locations throughout the Downtown area. In 1912 it secured its first foothold in Foggy Bottom by purchasing a townhouse at 2023 G Street NW. Over the next 79 years, the university increased its land holdings many times over, until it, along with the federal government, constituted the largest institutional presence in Foggy Bottom.

In the early years of its growth and expansion in Foggy Bottom, George Washington University constructed a quadrangle of Georgian-style buildings on the block bounded by 20th, G, 21st, and H Streets. During the Great Depression, the university buildings became more spartan in design. In the post–World War II period, several limestone-faced buildings were constructed. The university has constructed a variety of academic buildings; many appear to replicate the office structures found elsewhere along K Street.

The university's growth and expansion has frequently brought it into conflict with the residents. The university has entered into a number of compromises with the District of Columbia and the community to limit the expansion of the campus into the residential areas of the Foggy Bottom community.

■ **4** Moving north along 20th Street, you can see the university's **Law School Complex** on the left and the **World Bank Complex** on the right.

■ **5** After you turn left at 20th and I Streets, the **2000 Pennsylvania Avenue Complex** comes into view. One of the most controversial preservation compromises struck between the university and the community, this assemblage attempts to preserve the front sections of a strip of 19th-century buildings referred to as the Red Lion Row, named after a popular eatery that formerly occupied one of the buildings. Behind the line of older buildings, a high-rise office structure looms, in much the same way that the New Executive Office Building stands as a backdrop to the residential-scale buildings along Jackson Place, facing Lafayette Square. Critics have decried this preservation solution as only "facade deep" and one that does little to improve the quality of design of the larger office structure. The architectural firm associated with the Lafayette Square project, John Carl Warnecke Associates, was also involved in the design of the 2000 Pennsylvania Avenue project, along with the firm of Hellmuth, Obata and Kassabaum.

■ 6 Continuing along I Street, you will pass the side of the **Marvin Center,** the student union of George Washington University. At the southeast corner of 22nd and I Streets, the **Academic Cluster** represents a new architectural style for the university. Sheathed in glass, this building suggests a lighter touch to large buildings and, one might hope, a more creative era for the university's construction program.

■ 7 At 23rd and I Streets is another **entrance to the university.** The Foggy Bottom/GWU Metro stop is located here, at the conjunction of the new George Washington University Hospital and the university's School of Medicine and Health Services. The old hospital building, to the west of the new hospital, was

St. Mary's Church

demolished in 2003. The closing of I Street between 23rd and 24th Streets provides for a pleasant plaza area at this juncture. Twenty-third Street also represents the boundary between the highlands to the east and the lowlands to the west.

During the first half of the 20th century, the lowlands area was largely occupied by a poor black population who inhabited the modest row houses and interior alley dwellings. **St. Mary's Church,** located at 23rd Street, was designed by James Renwick for a black congregation. Renwick was also the architect of the Renwick Gallery at 17th Street and Pennsylvania Avenue and the original Smithsonian Castle building. St. Mary's Church has played a continuing role in the community, as shown by St. Mary's Court, a housing project for the elderly, behind the church on 24th Street.

■ 8 **Townhouses at 24th Street.** Here you can still see streets of modest townhouses that formerly housed workers associated with Foggy Bottom's industrial past. These townhouses have been fully rehabilitated and are in high demand, even at more than half a million dollars each.

800 block of New Hampshire Avenue

■ 9 **Washington Circle** is one of the many circles and squares that formed important elements of the L'Enfant Plan. It was designated a local landmark in 1964. The center of the circle contains an imposing granite statue of George Washington in a military uniform, mounted on a horse. The statue is oriented to the east, looking toward the White House and Capitol.

■ **10 K Street between 24th and 25th Streets** represents the post–World War II planners' vision for Foggy Bottom: tall apartment buildings astride major thoroughfares. The construction of the K Street underpass was intended to facilitate commuter traffic to and from the Virginia suburbs. However, the traffic density and speed also effectively cut off the area south of K Street from its natural commercial strip along Pennsylvania Avenue. The high-rises along K Street represent an interesting mix of styles: art deco, modern, and postmodern. Several of the modern buildings have been converted into apartments and hotels.

■ **11** Turning south on **25th Street,** you can see one of the most intact residential streets in Foggy Bottom. Small alley dwellings, once notorious for their substandard level of housing but now rehabilitated and considered desirable, can be glimpsed along this street.

■ **12** The **Watergate** at 25th Street and Virginia Avenue was developed by the Societa Generale Immobiliare of Rome and designed by Luigi Moretti. It is an example of "packaged living"—with residential units and offices, restaurants, and shops. The Watergate is one of Washington's premier addresses. The Watergate scandal in no way diminished the luster of the complex's reputation. As you continue along New Hampshire Avenue toward the Kennedy Center, a major office section of the Watergate complex comes into view, as do the entrances to Gucci shops and other haute couture establishments. Directly north of the retail area is the former Howard Johnson hotel that was associated with the Watergate scandal; it has been purchased by George Washington University and converted into a student dormitory.

■ **13** The **John F. Kennedy Center for the Performing Arts** now comes into view. Completed in 1971 after the designs of Edward Durrell Stone, it represents the culmination of nearly two decades of plans to locate a major auditorium in Washington. The center houses five auditoriums—the Concert Hall, Opera House, Eisenhower Theater, American Film Institute, and Terrace Theater—as well as recently acclaimed restaurants. The view of Rosslyn, Georgetown, and the Potomac River from the main-floor and rooftop terraces should not be missed. Expansion of the underground garage is under way. Plans to expand the center are being developed.

■ **14** On the way back to Virginia Avenue, you will pass a building that was built as a privately owned office building for the Peoples Life Insurance Company in the late 1950s. That company has since relocated to North Carolina, and the building is in use as the Chancery of Saudi Arabia. The building, together with **Potomac Plaza** across Virginia Avenue (completed in 1955 on the former site of the Washington Gas Light Company), was an early high-rise entrant into the lowlands of Foggy Bottom.

■ **15 Columbia Plaza** (1968—Keyes, Lethbridge and Condon) comes next into view at 23rd Street and Virginia Avenue. Another "packaged living" complex of

Columbia Plaza

apartments, offices, and shops, Columbia Plaza represents the only residential product of two much larger urban renewal projects envisioned for Foggy Bottom in the post–World War II era. By the time ground was broken on the site in the mid-1960s, few planners could justify the project as a means to rid the area of substandard slum housing. The apartments have always been much in demand, although the ground-level shopping arcade has encountered difficulty in attracting tenants. Across the street at 525 is the headquarters of the World Bank.

■ **16** Continuing south along 23rd Street, you come upon the entrance to the **Naval Center** on the right, on the hill formerly occupied by the Naval Observatory. The **State Department** on the left was located in Foggy Bottom in the 1940s and, together with the World Health Organization, the Organization of American States, and the World Bank; it provides a distinctly international flavor to the area.

■ **17** At the crossroads of 23rd Street and Constitution Avenue, the **Lincoln Memorial** is in view (see Tour 4, The Mall—West, no. 9). The memorial, with its sculpture of a seated Lincoln by Daniel Chester French and the nearby Reflecting Pool, was a favorite among the followers of the City Beautiful movement. The **Arlington Memorial Bridge,** just beyond, carries traffic into Arlington Cemetery and points beyond.

■ **18** Turning left on **Constitution Avenue,** you now face the ceremonial street, with its views and monumental buildings that are seen on countless picture postcards. This area was carved out of the reclaimed lowlands and filled-in City Canal in the first half of the 20th century. On the left, the pedestrian will see a series of institutional and federal buildings designed by a host of nationally famous architects.

At the northeast corner of 23rd Street and Constitution Avenue is the first of this series, the **American Pharmaceutical Association** (1933—John Russell Pope). The next building is the **National Academy of Sciences** (1924—Bertram Grosvenor Goodhue). Don't miss the academy's **sculpture of Albert Einstein** just to the left of its building. Dedicated in 1979 on the centennial of Einstein's birthday, this statue was based on a bust that Robert Berks sculpted from life in 1953. Einstein sat for Berks in his study, dressed in casual attire, in a pose that translated into this sculpture as the scientist gazing down into the stars, arrayed at his feet. It contrasts with the highly formal environment of Constitution Avenue. As you continue east, the following buildings come into view: the **Federal Reserve Board** (1937—Paul Cret); the **Department of the Interior—South** (1931—Jules Henri de Sibour); the **Organization of American States Annex** (1948—Harbeson, Hough, Livingston and Larson); and the **Organization of American States** (1910—Albert Kelsey and Paul Cret). On the right are the parklands of the Mall, including the site of the **Vietnam Veterans Memorial** and **Constitution Gardens.**

■ **19** As you walk north along 18th Street, the large **Interior Department Building** (1937—Waddy Butler Wood) comes into view on the left. On the right are the rears of **Constitution Hall** and the **American Red Cross Building.**

■ **20** On the left at E Street is **Rawlins Park,** a pocket of tranquility that reaches its zenith in the early spring when its magnolia trees are in full bloom.

■ **21** At the northeast corner of 18th Street and New York Avenue is the **Octagon House** (1800—William Thornton). The Octagon, originally the home of Gen. John Tayloe, served as the temporary site of the president's house during the burning of the capital city by the British in 1814 and as the place where the Treaty of Ghent was signed, ending the War of 1812. The Octagon House is now operated by the American Institute of Architects and serves as a historic house museum and exhibition gallery.

■ **22** Behind the Octagon is the headquarters building of the **American Institute of Architects,** completed in 1973 after the designs of the Architects Collaborative. Although criticized by some as a less-than-distinguished product of a major design profession, the AIA building does not try to compete with its historic frontispiece. The lobby area contains an exhibition gallery, and its conference facilities are used by many design-related organizations in the city.

■ **23** The **General Services Administration** building stands on the left, the symbolic, if not actual, center of the federal government's public building design operations. The GSA building was built for the Department of the Interior in 1917 after designs produced by the Office of the Supervising Architect of the Treasury but was vacated by that department when its building to the south on C Street was completed.

Octagon House / AIA Headquarters

24 The crossroads of 18th and F Streets contains two architectural oddities. To the west is the historic **Ringgold-Carroll House** (also called the John Marshall House). The house and its garden are protected from development by a preservation easement held by the National Trust for Historic Preservation. The last owner, Mrs. Robert Lowe Bacon, endowed the Bacon Foundation, the house's present occupant. To the east stand the remnants of **Michler Row,** cemented onto a modern office facade. Michler Row was constructed in the 1870s and named for Gen. Nathaniel Michler of the Department of Public Buildings and Grounds. The firm of Skidmore, Owings & Merrill provided for a virtual reconstruction of part of the Michler Row facade, while allowing the office structure to rise behind it.

White House

(White House, Renwick Gallery, Lafayette Square, Corcoran Gallery)

Fred H. Greenberg, updated by John J. Protopappas

Distance: 1 3/4 miles
Time: 1 1/2 hours
Bus: 32, 34, 35, 36, 42, and 80
Metro: Farragut West (Blue and Orange Lines)

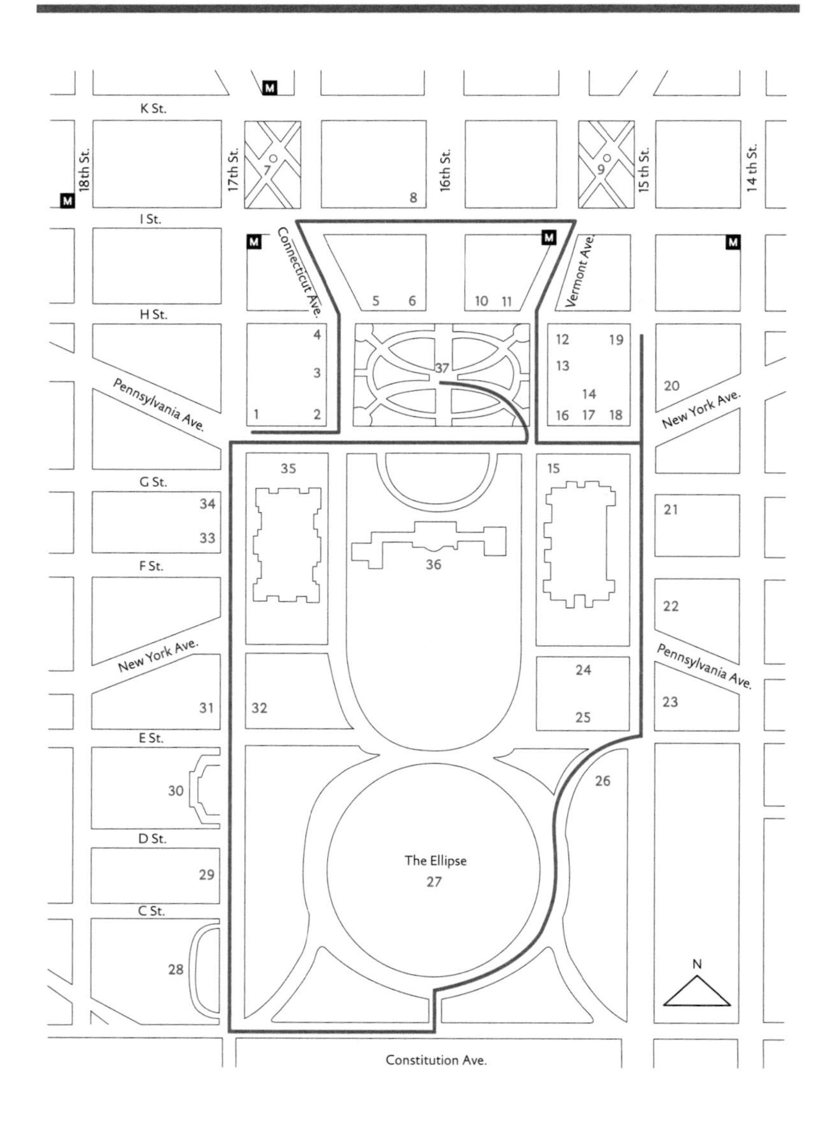

The White House precinct, the actual and symbolic center of the executive branch of government, is one of the most important and interesting areas in the city. Its core includes the White House grounds and the flanking Treasury and Executive Office Buildings, Lafayette Square, and the Ellipse. This area is almost entirely under federal ownership, deriving from the original "Reservation 1" purchased in 1791 as part of the original platting of the city. Beginning as a predominantly residential area around the White House, this precinct has evolved over time into an area that is now predominantly devoted to federal and private office buildings with related shops and services.

As a result of the initiatives of the Kennedy administration in the 1960s, a plan to build massive federal office buildings flanking Lafayette Square was discarded. Instead, a plan to restore and enhance the area was adopted. This included restoration of the townhouses facing the square and placement of the higher federal office buildings behind them. The old Corcoran Gallery building, threatened with demolition, was transferred to the Smithsonian Institution to be restored as a museum. Its opening in 1972, as the Renwick Gallery, represented an important step in bringing increased activity to the area.

Assets to the area are Pershing Park, with a cafe and a winter ice-skating rink; south of Metropolitan Square and the Willard InterContinental, The Metropolitan Square with offices, restaurants, and shops contained behind the restored facade of the old Keith-Albee Theater Building; and East Executive Park, between the White House and the Treasury. The White House precinct has undergone numerous changes in security since 9/11. Note the closing of Pennsylvania Avenue to vehicle traffic and the additional security barriers that has been extended to include the streets around the Lafayette Square.

■ 1 **Renwick Gallery of the Smithsonian American Art Museum** (Old Corcoran Gallery and US Court of Claims), 17th Street and Pennsylvania Avenue (1859—James Renwick; 1972 restoration—John Carl Warnecke and Hugh Newell Jacobsen). Originally designed as an art gallery for W. W. Corcoran, this building was used by the government during the Civil War. When he was able to occupy his own building, Corcoran found that it was too small for his collection, so he built a larger gallery at 17th Street and New York Avenue. The US Court of Claims took possession of the building in 1899 and used it for the next 65 years. The Smithsonian undertook the meticulous exterior and interior restoration beginning in 1965, and in 1972 the building was returned to its original function as an art gallery. The Renwick exhibits various aspects of US design and craftsmanship. Two rooms in the gallery are furnished in the styles of the 1860s and 1870s. Hours: daily 10:00 a.m.–5:30 p.m.

■ 2 **Blair-Lee Houses,** 1651 Pennsylvania Avenue NW (1824; 1931 restoration—W. Faulkner). Government officials entertain distinguished visitors from foreign countries in these fine houses. Blair House was completely restored and new entrance gardens were developed in 1988.

Renwick Gallery

■ 3 **Lafayette Square Restoration.** Architect John Carl Warnecke was engaged by the Kennedy administration to study the problem of development for Lafayette Square. The result was the integration of new buildings with the restored and infilling row houses. The "bookends" not only saved but also enhanced the scale, fabric, and marvelous sense of space of Lafayette Square. The townhouses are used as offices for the various commissions created during presidential terms of office. The two office buildings referred to as "bookends" flank the square on the west and east and contain secluded courtyards with fountains. They are the **New Executive Office Building** (west)**,** at 17th and H Streets (closed to the public), and the **US Court of Claims** (east).

■ 4 **Decatur House,** 748 Jackson Place NW (1818—Benjamin Latrobe). The house of Commodore Stephen Decatur, the suppressor of the Barbary pirates, was the first private house to be built on Lafayette Square. The upper two floors now serve as offices for the National Trust for Historic Preservation, and the rest of the house displays period furnishings. Be sure to visit the preservation bookstore around the corner on H Street. (The National Trust Regional Offices and Conference Center are also located on H Street.) Hours: weekdays 10:00 a.m.–5:00 p.m.; Thursday 10:00 a.m.–8:00 p.m.; weekends noon–4:00 p.m.; closed Monday. Admission charge. Tours are conducted 15 minutes after the hour.

■ 5 **US Chamber of Commerce,** 1615 H Street NW (1925—Cass Gilbert). The Chamber of Commerce and Treasury Annex (see this tour, no. 16) Buildings are the only completed portions of a plan to unify the architecture of Lafayette Square in the neoclassical style of the older Treasury Building.

■ 6 **Hay-Adams Hotel,** northwest corner of 16th and H Streets (1927—H. H. Richardson). This elegant hotel was built on the site of H. H. Richardson's houses for Henry Adams and John Hay. The hotel has reopened in 2002 following a complete renovation.

■ 7 "Damn the torpedoes! Full speed ahead!" said David G. Farragut during a Civil War battle in 1864 in Mobile Bay. A statue to the admiral is the centerpiece of lovely Farragut Square—and a roosting place for scores of pigeons. With good reason, **Farragut Square** is one of the most heavily used urban parks in Washington. At noon, the "lunch bunch" congregates to eat brown-bag lunches and be entertained by events ranging from concerts by the National Symphony to karate exhibitions.

Farragut Square

■ 8 The striking hexagonal **Third Church of Christ, Scientist** and the **Christian Science Monitor Building** (northwest corner of 16th and I Streets) were designed by I. M. Pei & Associates in 1972.

■ 9 **McPherson Square,** the eastern counterpart to Farragut Square, is one of the many public spaces provided in the L'Enfant Plan. A statue to Brig. Gen. James B. McPherson, who commanded the Tennessee Army in the Civil War, was erected in 1876. During the summer months, many local workers and tourists relax in the park while eating lunches and listening to free outdoor concerts.

■ 10 **St. John's Church,** 16th and H streets (1816—Benjamin Latrobe; 1883—James Renwick). St. John's is among the oldest Episcopal churches in the city. It is commonly referred to as the "Church of the Presidents" because a pew has been set aside for the president of the United States and the First Family. Since its first services in 1816, every president has worshiped here, some quite regularly.

■ 11 **St. John's Parrish House** (Old British Embassy), 1525 H Street NW (1822–24—St. Clair Clarke). This house was designed by its owner, St. Clair Clarke, and in the 1840s served as the British prime minister's residence. St.

John's Church acquired the building in 1954 for use as a parish house. On Wednesdays, between noon and 1:00, a French lunch is served, and there is an organ recital at 12:10. (www.stjohns-dc.org for tour information).

■ 12 **Cutts Madison House** (Dolley Madison House), at the corner of H Street and Madison Place, was built in 1820. This house was originally owned by James Madison and upon his death his widow, Dolley, took up residence here. The house was restored as part of the Federal Judicial Center in 1968.

■ 13 The **Benjamin Ogle Tayloe House,** at 21 Madison Place NW, was built in 1828. It served as a social center during the Tayloe Period and was later referred to by President McKinley as the "Little White House."

■ 14 **Howard T. Markey Building, National Courts and Appeals Court,** 717 Madison Place NW. An arcaded passageway leads pedestrians from H Street through a pleasant courtyard to Madison Place and Lafayette Square. The entrance to a "colonial-style" cafeteria faces the courtyard.

■ 15 **Treasury Building,** 1500 Pennsylvania Avenue NW (1836-69—Robert Mills, Thomas U. Walter). The Treasury Building is the third oldest federal building in Washington. The site, selected by Andrew Jackson, disrupts L'Enfant's grand concourse uniting the Capitol and the White House. The view down Pennsylvania Avenue as you walk past the Treasury on 15th Street is very dramatic. Free tours of the building's interior are available on Saturdays by appointment; call (202) 343-9136. The "cash room," added in 1868, was constructed with eight types of marble and is one of the tour's highlights. The Treasury building is undergoing renovation as a result of a serious fire.

Treasury Building

The following five buildings (nos. 16–20) anchor the old financial district of the city, clustering in front of the Treasury Building and along 15th Street. The united facade treatment of buildings 16–19, and their massive columns, gives the district a stately appearance.

■ **16 Treasury Annex,** Pennsylvania Avenues and Madison Place (1919—Cass Gilbert).

■ **17 Riggs National Bank,** 1503 Pennsylvania Avenue NW (1891—James G. Hill).

■ **18 Bank of America,** corner of 15th Street and Pennsylvania Avenue (1899—York and Sawyer).

■ **19 American Bar Association,** southwest corner of 15th and H Streets (1906—Wood, Donnard and Deming).

■ **20 SunTrust Bank,** northeast corner of 15th Street and New York Avenue (1880—James Windrim). The red brick Victorian-style structure provides a delightful relief from its more classic neighbors in the old financial district.

■ **21 Metropolitan Square (Keith's Theater and Albee Building),** southeast corner of 15th and G Streets (1911–12—Jules Henri de Sibour, 1982—facade retained and restored with offices, a restaurant and a major bookstore (Koubek and Skidmore, Owings & Merrill). The historic facade restoration highlights this private office and retail complex.

■ **22 Hotel Washington,** at the corner of 15th and F Streets (1917–18—Carrere and Hastings). The corner location of this fine hotel is one of the best in the city. During spring, summer, and fall, an outdoor rooftop terrace is open for dining and offers wonderful views of the Mall, the Potomac River, and parts of Rosslyn, Virginia (see Tour 10, Downtown—West, no. 39).

Willard InterContinental, at 14th Street and Pennsylvania Avenue, opened in 1901 and was one of Washington's top hotels for many years. In an earlier Willard Hotel on this site, Julia Ward Howe composed "The Battle Hymn of the Republic." The hotel building closed in 1968. Early plans for Pennsylvania Avenue called for tearing it down and building a huge national square at the west end of the avenue. The plans were changed in 1974, when the Pennsylvania Avenue Plan was revised to place more emphasis on historic preservation. The restoration of the hotel and an office building addition were completed in 1986 (see Tour 10, Downtown—West, no. 38).

■ **23 Pershing Park,** between 15th and 14th Streets on Pennsylvania Avenue (1981—Lindsey and Friedberg). The park is a memorial to Gen. John J. Pershing. The large pool at the center of the park, fed by a waterfall, converts into a public ice-skating rink in winter.

■ **24 Sherman Monument,** 15th Street and Hamilton Place. In addition to the statue of Gen. William T. Sherman, this monument includes the names of all of his battles and a chronology of his military assignments. The statues at the four corners represent branches of the army: infantry, artillery, cavalry, and engineers.

■ **25** **East Executive Park,** south of the Treasury Building, bordered by the White House, Hamilton Place, 15th Street, and E Street (1989—National Park Service). Tourist information kiosks and nearby restrooms are provided.

■ **26** In the areas surrounding the Ellipse are a number of notable monuments and points of interest: the **Boy Scout Memorial** and the Monument to the **Original Potentees** along 15th Street, and the **Haupt Fountains** and the **2nd Division World War II Monument** along Constitution Avenue.

■ **27** **The Ellipse.** Like Lafayette Square, the Ellipse (bordered by 15th and 17th Streets and Constitution Avenue) was part of the presidential grounds included in the L'Enfant plan. Note the visual relationship between the White House and the Jefferson Memorial and the strong axial relationship along 16th Street, through the White House to the Jefferson Memorial, enhanced by the Haupt Fountains. L'Enfant intended the monument to George Washington to be located along this north–south axis, but soil conditions prevented its construction there.

As you progress north along 17th Street to Pennsylvania Avenue, note the imposing variety of styles of the upcoming buildings.

■ **28** **Pan American Union** (Organization of American States), 17th Street and Constitution Avenue (1910—Albert Kelsey and Paul Cret). This building is the headquarters for the General Secretariat of the Organization of American States (27 member states are represented). The architectural styles of North and South America are blended into the building. The interior court, filled with many tropical plants, creates a wonderful space. Hours: Main Building—weekdays 9:00 a.m.–5:00 p.m. Museum of Modern Art of Latin America—Tuesday through Saturday 10:00 a.m.–5:00 p.m.; entrance on 18th Street NW.

■ **29** **Daughters of the American Revolution (Constitution Hall),** 1778 D Street NW (about 1930—John Russell Pope). The DAR complex consists of Memorial Continental Hall, a library, a museum, an administration building, and Constitution Hall, which was the home of the National Symphony Orchestra prior to the opening of the Kennedy Center. The hall's program now consists of various concerts and lectures. Revolutionary period museum tour: weekdays 9:00 a.m.–4:00 p.m.; Sunday 1:00–5:00 p.m.

■ **30** **American Red Cross,** 17th, D, and E Streets (1917—Trowbridge and Livingston). The building is a monument to the women of the Civil War and serves as national headquarters for the National Red Cross. Hours: 9:00 a.m.–4:00 p.m.

■ **31** **Corcoran Gallery of Art,** 17th Street and New York Avenue (1897—Ernest Flagg). This is one of Washington's finest art galleries, specializing in American art, fine art photography, modern art, and the education of artists. (The latter is accomplished through the Corcoran School of Art, located on the premises.) A

Corcoran Gallery of Art

fine example of beaux-arts style, the Corcoran has a magnificent atrium gallery. Hours: Tuesday through Sunday 10:00 a.m.–4:30 p.m.; Thursday until 9:00 p.m.; closed Christmas and New Year's Day. Free admission. The gallery is planning a major renovation and expansion, including a new wing designed by Frank Gehry.

■ 32 The **First Infantry Division Memorial** is the US Army's testimonial to those of the First Infantry Division who died in World Wars I and II and Vietnam. A bed of flowers in the shape of a "one" is at the base of the memorial.

■ 33 **Winder Building,** 604 17th Street NW (1847–48). Although the building pioneered the use of central heating and steel beams and was a veritable high-rise in its time, its significance is more historical than architectural. It was the first, among many more to come, of the inexpensive, speculative office buildings designed for use by the federal government—its use today.

■ 34 Headquarters building, **Federal Home Loan Bank Board,** 17th and G Streets NW (1977—Max Urbahn and Associates). An innovative and attractive design, the headquarters blends well with the renovated Winder building, harmonizing new with old. The project is significant in that it represents an effort by the General Services Administration to upgrade the quality of federal architecture and to incorporate lively commercial uses that bring much-needed nighttime activity into the area. The building features a lively urban park with an ice-skating rink in winter that converts into a fountain in summer, an outdoor restaurant, and retail stores at the street level.

■ 35 The **Executive Office Building** (Old State, War, and Navy Building), Pennsylvania Avenue and 17th Street NW (1871–88—Alfred N. Mullett).

Behind the 900 Doric columns was the world's largest office building at the time it was built. With its wealth of detail, it is probably the most eloquent government building in Washington. To beautify the nation's capital, President Kennedy saved the Old Executive Office Building from demolition. The Office of Management and Budget moved into the building in 1945. It is closed to the public.

■ **36** The **White House,** 1600 Pennsylvania Avenue NW (begun 1792—James Hoban, Benjamin Latrobe, and others). The simple, yet dignified, home of the US president has more than 132 rooms, including the 54 rooms and 16 baths in the living quarters. The John Adamses were the first presidential family to occupy the White House, and soon after, in 1814, the British burned it. It is speculated that the building was first painted white at the time to cover the charring from the fire. Hours: Tuesday through Saturday, 10:00 a.m.–noon, except holidays. Tour entrance is on East Executive Avenue.

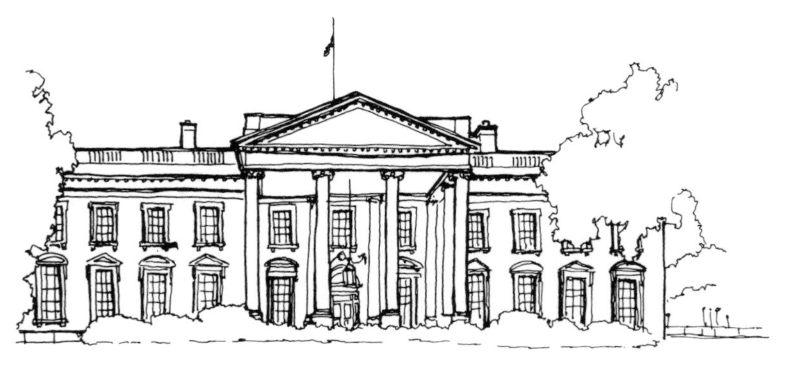

White House

■ **37** **Lafayette Square** was included in the President's Park in the L'Enfant plan of 1791. Jefferson authorized its separation into a park for public use. In 1824 the park was named in honor of the Marquis de Lafayette, a hero of the American Revolution. The central statue of Andrew Jackson, cast from the cannons captured by Jackson during the War of 1812, was the first equestrian statue in Washington, the second in the United States. The four other statues are of other American Revolutionary heroes: General Lafayette (southeast corner, 1890); Comte de Rochambeau (southwest corner, 1902); Gen. Thaddeus Kosciusko (northeast corner, 1910); and Baron von Steuben (northwest corner, 1910). Lafayette Square is one of the nicest urban spaces in any American city and is actively used during most of the year.

Federal Triangle

(Government office buildings, Old Post Office)

Sally Kress Tompkins, updated by Christopher J. Alleva

Distance: 1 1/4 miles

Time: 1 hour

Bus: 313A, 13B, 52; on Pennsylvania Avenue: 32, 34, 35, and 36

Metro: Federal Triangle (Blue and Orange Lines)

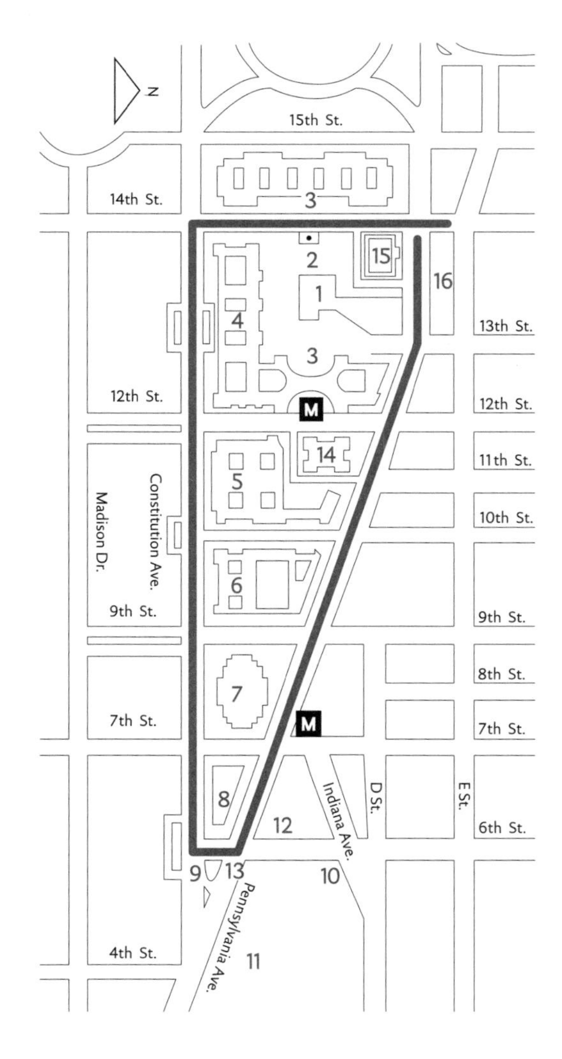

The Federal Triangle is formed by the intersection of Constitution Avenue with the diagonal Pennsylvania Avenue and is bounded on the west by 15th Street and on the east by 6th Street.

When Pierre L'Enfant created one of the most innovative land plans in the history of urban design that was to become the nation's capital, the Triangle was a swamp, subject to frequent flooding from the nearby Tiber Creek. L'Enfant transformed this barren wetland into the future sites of the buildings that now house much of the nation's government. Its exceptional location, south of Pennsylvania Avenue and north of the Mall between the White House and the Capitol, made it a natural place to locate the ministries and departments that run the day-to-day affairs of government.

After construction of the Tiber Canal in 1816 alleviated the flooding, the Triangle area developed rapidly, but as a commercial rather than a governmental center. The Center Market, between 7th and 9th Streets, lasted here from 1801 until 1870. Hotels, taverns, rooming houses, and printing and newspaper offices also filled the area. The Market Square Development across the avenue from the Archives Building recalls the historic markets in name only. It contains mostly offices with commercial space at the street.

The Triangle began to deteriorate after the Civil War. In 1899 the Old Post Office was erected at 12th Street and Pennsylvania Avenue, and it was hoped that this would be the beginning of a renaissance for the area. The McMillan Commission plan of 1902 pictured the Triangle as a park dotted with various government buildings of a municipal nature, and in 1908 the District Building was erected at 14th and E Streets, but no further action was taken. Conditions became increasingly scandalous: tattoo parlors, gas stations, and cheap hotels became prevalent, and Ohio Avenue (subsequently eliminated by Triangle construction) was lined with brothels. At the same time, the government's need for more office space was growing acute. The Public Buildings Bill, allocating $50 million for buildings in the District of Columbia, was finally passed by Congress and signed by President Calvin Coolidge on May 5, 1926. Two years later, Congress appropriated the money to buy the entire Triangle.

Secretary of the Treasury Andrew Mellon was responsible for the construction and design of the buildings, and in 1927 he appointed the Board of Architectural Consultants to draw up a plan for the entire Triangle area.

The architects and the members of the Commission of Fine Arts, who participated in formulating the plan, accepted the prevailing premise that the neoclassical style was the proper one for public buildings. They saw in the Triangle development a rare opportunity to plan a group of related monumental buildings designed to constitute a single great composition. Public enthusiasm was high for the project, and the Capital was caught up in a quest for grandeur. Everyone looked forward to Washington becoming the "Paris of America" and talked of a capital "worthy of a great nation."

In 1929 a model of the composition designed by the Board of Architectural

Consultants went on display. The Triangle had been given a treatment somewhat similar to that of the Louvre, with buildings reflecting a revival classical style. A series of courtyards surrounded a central circular court. Vistas from this court extended into the other plazas, one of which—the Great Plaza—was to be as large as Lafayette Square. The main entrances of the buildings were planned to open onto these courts, so that a sense of quiet would pervade the scheme. The buildings had a uniform cornice line drawn from the Natural History Museum and following the diagonal of Pennsylvania Avenue. Pylons at the entrances and specially designed sidewalks served to unify the composition.

Unfortunately, the Triangle never achieved the perfection for which its designers strove. The Great Depression—and the automobile—would sadly alter the final composition. The Great Plaza became a parking lot. The sweeping drives turned into major traffic arteries, and the pylons that were to flank them were declared a traffic hazard and were never constructed. The circular court was never completed because the Old Post Office, anathema to the Triangle's designers, was never demolished. Depression economies put the future of the final structure, at the apex, in doubt. When the Federal Trade Commission Building was finally constructed in 1937, it was a simplified version of the original design. By that time the neoclassical style was out of favor and there was little interest in the buildings or in completing the design. The Triangle's imperial facade was deemed inappropriate for a democratic country.

For over 60 years, the finished facade along Constitution Avenue has been somewhat forbidding, and the Pennsylvania Avenue street line, broken at 13th Street, exposed to view the huge unfinished parking lot that was to have been the Great Plaza. In 1981 GSA commissioned Harry Weese and Associates to design a master plan for the Triangle including the completion of this area. The intent was to create an urban design that would be more inviting to the public, exposing the historic courtyards and handsome architecture and providing new office, public use, and commercial space, thus creating a link between the Mall and Downtown. This idea evolved into the International Trade Center and DC Visitors Center, now the Ronald Reagan Building. Start your walking tour at the Federal Triangle Metro Station on the13th Street side of the Ronald Reagan Building.

■ 1 **Ronald Reagan Building.** In 1987, the Federal Triangle Development Act authorized the construction of a federal building complex and International Cultural and Trade Center on the 11-acre Federal Triangle property in the District of Columbia.

The complex was designed by Pei, Cobb, Freed & Partners of New York City, in association with Ellerbe Beckett, Architects and Engineers, of Washington, DC. Lead architect James Ingo Freed and his design team had a truly unique challenge. They would define the last vacant piece of land on Pennsylvania Avenue between the Capitol and the White House. They would complete the great complex of buildings whose construction was halted by the Depression. And, almost at the dawn of the 21st century, they would leave a statement about the relationship between traditional and contemporary architecture for future generations.

The building was originally designed to house operations for the International Cultural and Trade Center (ICTC) and offices for the Department of Justice. Some of the ICTC program components included an international club and reception center, two performing arts theaters, an IMAX theater, exhibition space, and retail and food services.

In 1992, the program for the project was revised to abandon the ICTC and retain approximately 500,000 square feet of space for the International Trade Center (ITC). Plans for the ITC included an auditorium and conference center, reception spaces, exhibit space, retail and food service, and office space for private sector trade-related firms. Parking for approximately 2,000 cars remained unchanged, as did the tunnels connecting the building to the Commerce building, the Customs building, and the Federal Triangle Metro station at the Ariel Rios building. The building opened in 1999, and its restaurants—particularly Jordan, named for Michael Jordan—have become popular with young people. Expect a large crowd if you visit at night.

■ 2 The **Oscar Straus Memorial Fountain** was designed by John Russell Pope, but a simplified version of his design was actually built. The figures were sculpted by Adolph A. Weinman.

■ 3 The **Department of Commerce Building** (14th Street between E Street and Constitution Avenue) was designed by Louis Ayres of the firm of York and Sawyer and housed all the bureaus of the department under one roof, except for the National Bureau of Standards. At the time of its construction in 1931 it was the largest government office building in the world—1,050 feet long, exceeding the Capitol by 300 feet. Arched gateways two stories high give direct access through the building at what used to be C and D Streets. The central section of the 14th Street facade is patterned after the Perrault facade at the Louvre. The relief panels, designed by James Earl Fraser, represent the various agencies of the department. The building encloses six courtyards providing light and ventilation, a design that was necessary before air conditioning. Enter the lobby to view the coffered ceiling with gilded accents and richly colored marble floors and columns. Look out the windows into the landscaped courtyards and you will begin to sense the feeling the planners and architects had in mind when the building was laid out.

Located in the basement of the Commerce Department Building is the **National Aquarium.** Enter from the 14th Street side. Hours: 9:00 a.m.–5:00 p.m.

Walk south on 14th Street and cross Constitution Avenue. The elaborate neoclassical facade of the Triangle buildings along Constitution Avenue can here be viewed from a distance. It is particularly impressive at night, when the facade is illuminated. GSA's master plan called for the projecting portico of the Andrew Mellon Auditorium to be flanked by major pedestrian paths through the monumental archways. The ICTC plan was designed to encourage public appreciation of the handsome architecture of the Triangle's interior.

■ 4 Arthur Brown Jr. of San Francisco, designer of the City Hall and War Memorial Opera House in that city, was the architect of the complex (between 12th and 14th Streets on Constitution Avenue) originally built for the Department of Labor, the **Andrew Mellon Auditorium,** and the Interstate Commerce Commission and now occupied by the **Enviromental Protection Agency (EPA).** Of particular interest is the second-story relief panel of the Departmental Auditorium, which diverges from the neoclassical allegorical sculpture typical of the building's exteriors. Designed by Edmond Romulus Amateis, it depicts Gen. George Washington with Major Generals Nathanael Greene and John Sullivan. Greene's face is that of architect Brown and Sullivan's is that of sculptor Edgar Waiter. The doors to the auditorium are often open, and this beautiful restored monumental space is worth seeing, as are the rotunda and hearing rooms of the ICC Building and the landscaped courtyard of the Customs Building.

Continue walking east along Constitution Avenue. As you cross 12th Street, note the new construction in the distance along Pennsylvania Avenue as well as glimpses of the Old Post Office Building.

■ 5 After crossing 12th Street, you will be looking across Constitution Avenue at the headquarters of the **Internal Revenue Service** and the comforting words of Oliver Wendell Holmes inscribed on it: "Taxes are what we pay for a civilized society." The building was designed by the Office of the Supervising Architect of the Treasury Department under the direction of Louis Simon. It was completed in 1930, the first of the group to be finished. It is constructed of Indiana limestone and granite with columns of Tennessee marble. The building has four handsomely landscaped inner courtyards, like the Commerce Department Building. The final wing, meant to form the eastern side of the circular court, was never completed.

Justice Department

■ **6** When you have crossed 10th Street you are opposite the **Justice Department Building.** It was designed by the Philadelphia firm of Zantzinger, Borie, and Medary and completed in 1934. Its architecture is notably simplified, reflecting the influence of the art deco or modern styles of the period. This is reflected in the extensive use of aluminum in decorative lighting fixtures and monumental doors as well as in the polychrome details at the cornice and the soffits at the entries.

■ **7** As you proceed across 9th Street you should stop to admire John Russell Pope's **National Archives Building.** This was to be the most important and tallest building in the complex, designed as a shrine for the nation's most treasured documents. The structure is purely classical with completely plain walls, except for windows to accommodate the offices on the Pennsylvania Avenue side. It is adorned by 72 Corinthian pillars, 52 feet high, grouped in colonnades about the building. The great pediment on the Constitution Avenue facade displays a figure representing the Recorder of the Archives and two eagles standing guard at the sides. The sculptor was James Earle Fraser, who also designed the large seated figures that flank the monumental steps leading into a public hall housing the **Declaration of Independence,** the **Constitution,** and the **Bill of Rights.** The Archives Building has reopened after several years of renovation. Please call 1-(866)-325-7208 for hours (note: Archives II is in College Park, Maryland; public tours are available).

National Archives

■ **8** Proceed along Constitution Avenue to the last of the Triangle group, the **Federal Trade Commission Building.** This building, designed by Bennett, Parsons, and Frost, was considerably altered from the original model to be acceptable to a nation in the throes of a depression. It is still a very satisfying building, however. This rounded colonnade of Doric columns, reminiscent of a blunted ship's bow, makes an excellent terminus to the Triangle composition.

■ **9** The **Canadian Chancery,** designed by Arthur Erickson, across Pennsylvania Avenue toward the Capitol, has an element of rounded columns designed to recall the FTC building.

■ **10** The H. Carl Moultrie I Court House of the **District of Columbia Courthouse** at 300 Indiana Avenue opened in 1977. It has one appellate and 44 trial courtrooms, plus ancillary space.

■ **11** The **E. Barrett Prettyman US Court House** on the east side of John Marshall Park has been the scene of many famous trials, including those held in connection with the Watergate and Iran-Contra affairs, and the trial of former mayor Marion Barry. A bold new courthouse addition on the Constitution Avenue frontage at 3rd Street, designed by Michael Graves, will open in 2004.

■ **12** The **Newseum,** the national museum of the news and journalism, is planning a new six-level, 215,000-square-foot interactive museum of news that will contain three times as much exhibition space as the original facility in Arlington, Virginia, which closed in 2002 to permit Newseum staff to focus exclusively on the Freedom Forum. The new museum on Pennsylvania Avenue is scheduled to open in late 2006 (see Tour 11, Downtown—East, no.45).

■ **13** The **Andrew Mellon Memorial Fountain,** across 6th Street from the Federal Trade Commission Building, is an exclamation point to the Triangle. The fountain, completed in 1952, could not be in a more appropriate position, filling the last sliver of the great Triangle that Mellon's influence brought to fruition and situated directly across from the National Gallery of Art, which he gave to the nation. The fountain was designed by Otto R. Eggers in bronze and granite. The signs of the zodiac, visible under the sheet of water formed by the overflow from the basins, are the work of Sidney Waugh. There are also benches to rest on before beginning the walk back along Pennsylvania Avenue.

The Pennsylvania Avenue side of the Triangle has been completely reconstructed. It is noticeable here that, in designing the Archives Building, John Russell Pope did not follow the diagonal of the avenue as did the other architects. The resulting triangular slice of land is a small park, a memorial to Franklin Delano Roosevelt, located there according to his wishes. The flanking statues at the building's entrance are the work of Robert Aiken.

The Justice Department Building returns to the concept of filling the entire block. Walk to the vehicular entrance in the center of its 9th Street facade for a glimpse of the largest and most elaborate of the Triangle's interior courtyards. Note the polychrome decorations of the soffits above the driveways.

At 11th Street, the short, truncated facade of the IRS Building testifies that the design here was never completed, awaiting the planned demolition of the Old Post Office. It is here that some of the most dramatic proposals of GSA's master plan will be realized.

A glassy pavilion is in the courtyard between the IRS Building and the Old Post Office. It provides additional retail space and thus complements the festival marketplace in the Old Post Office. The pavilion was designed by the architectural firm of Karn, Charuhas, Chapman and Twohy. Plans to renovate and alter this area are continuing.

■ **14** The **Old Post Office** was designed by Willoughby Edbrooke in the Richardsonian Romanesque style popular at the time of its construction in 1899. It was considered an "object of permanent regret" by the neoclassicist, and the Triangle designers drew up a plan that demanded its demolition. Its bulk cuts across the space that would have been the pivotal circular court designed after the "gay fashion of Paris." It is worth walking down 12th Street to see the great eastern facade of the Old Post Office that was to form half of that court. A small segment of the opposite side of the circular court is visible on the IRS Building behind the Old Post Office.

When completed in 1899, it was thought that the Post Office Building would stimulate revitalization of one of the worst neighborhoods in Washington. But the hoped-for results were not forthcoming. The early years of the building's history were marked with controversy and disappointment. The Old Post Office Building was less than ten years old when cries were heard that it should be torn down. One local man, Nathan Rubinton, carved by hand a model of the building so that when it was torn down people would remember how it looked. In 1914, the District of Columbia Mail Depot was moved to a larger building constructed next to Union Station. Although only 15 years old, the building at 12th Street and Pennsylvania Avenue was dubbed the "old" post office.

The Postmaster General moved to a newly constructed office building directly across 12th Street in 1934. The only reason that the Old Post Office was not then razed was the lack of money caused by the Great Depression. For the next 40 years the building served as overflow space for several government agencies. In the 1970s, when Congress finally appropriated the money to remove the Old Post Office, local citizens banded together for a desperate final struggle to save it. Nancy Hanks, the politically influential chairperson of the National Endowment for the Arts, joined the effort and prevailed in convincing Congress to reverse its decision. The Old Post Office was rescued. In 1983 the Old Post Office was officially renamed the Nancy Hanks Center in recognition of her devotion to the arts and the preservation of architecturally significant buildings.

After years of renovation, the Old Post Office reopened with several restaurants, bars, and specialty shops. Today, the government and privately owned businesses share its generous spaces. Many of the shops and restaurants have closed because of poor patronage; those that remain are very busy at lunch but not at dinner. Plans are under way to renovate and expand the retail space. The National Park Service provides tours of the Old Post Office Tower, which affords one of the most spectacular views of Washington from the 270-foot-high observation deck. An exhibit depicts the struggle for survival of the Old Post Office building and features the Rubinton model. While touring the tower, visitors can also view the Congress Bells, one of the largest sets of change-ringing bells in North America and the official bells of the US Congress.

■ **15** The **John A. Wilson Building** (1908, designed by Cope and Stewardson) is Washington's city hall, the site of the offices of the mayor and the Council of the

Old Post Office Building

District of Columbia and some other city offices. By the late 1980s the building was outdated and deteriorated, and the mayor and council moved out in the early 1990s. The beaux-arts building was renovated and enlarged by filling in a U-shaped space on the back frontage, creating a new atrium space. Shalom Baranes was the architect for the restoration and addition. The mayor, council, and related offices moved back into the building in 2001 (see Tour 10).

■ **16** In front of the District Building is the **Western Plaza,** designed by Robert Venturi for the Pennsylvania Avenue Development Corporation. The unique design incorporates a partial plan of the city into the paving of its raised platform. A water feature was added to the plaza at the western portion in the mid-1990s.

Downtown–West

(Central business district, Franklin Square, old Washington Convention Center Redevelopment Site, Ford's Theater, FBI Building, Old Post Office, Pennsylvania Avenue)

Robert N. Gray and Ellen Kotz, updated and expanded by John Fondersmith

Distance: 2 3/4 miles

Time: 2 1/2 hours

Bus: Major routes: 30, 32, 34, 35, 36, 42, 50, 52, 53, 54, 68, 80, 81, N7, P6, P17, P19, S2, S4, W13, and X2

Metro: Metro Center (Red, Blue, and Orange Lines); Gallery Place/Chinatown (Red, Green, and Yellow Lines); McPherson Square (Blue and Orange Lines); Archives/Navy Memorial (Yellow and Green Lines); Federal Triangle (Blue and Orange Lines)

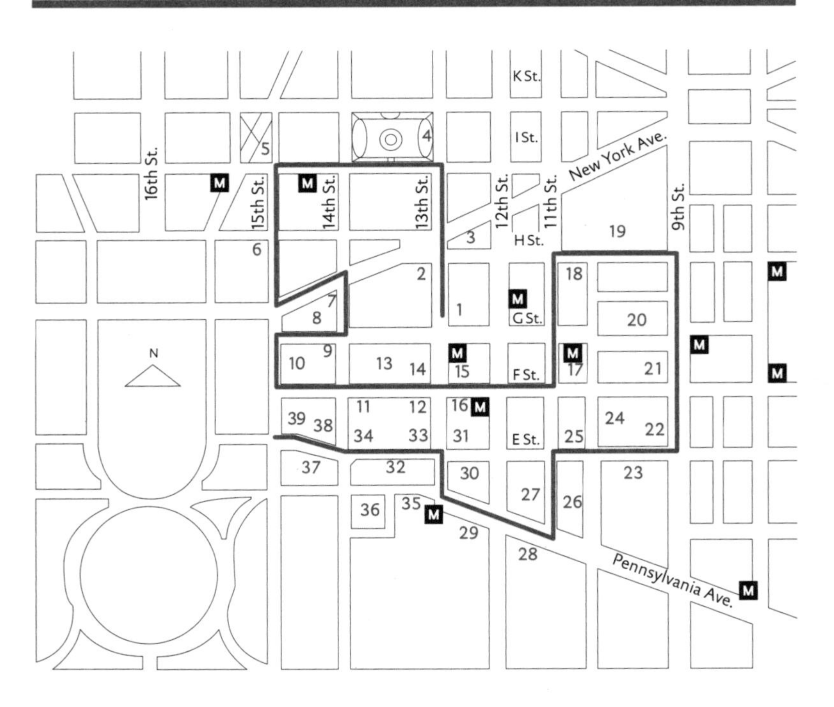

Beginning in the 1950s, Washington's original Downtown area north of Pennsylvania Avenue underwent the decline and change of functions that have affected other large American cities. In the early 1980s, the reversal of this trend began, stimulated by the still-expanding Metrorail system and a recognition of the area's economic potential by developers, the District of Columbia government, business leaders, and citizens. With guidance from the Downtown element of the comprehensive plan, extensive rebuilding continues, with aim of achieving a "Living Downtown." The work of the Pennsylvania Avenue Development Corporation (PADC), a federal development corporation, was important along Pennsylvania Avenue between 1972 and 1996, when the agency was closed. The Downtown Business Improvement District (BID) was formed and began work in 1997. The District government, through its Office of Planning and its development agencies, continues its work to transform Downtown. Revitalization—new development and the reuse of older buildings—has largely been completed in the area of this tour, west of 9th Street. However, some key projects remain unfinished, such as the 900 block of F Street and the rebuilding of the old convention center site. These developments, mingled among some of Washington's oldest and finest buildings, demonstrate the continuing potential of this area.

■ 1 **Metro Center** is at the core of the Metro system and has one of the most heavily used of the 83 Metro stations that serve the completed 103-mile regional rapid-rail system (three new stations are under construction in 2004, and other extensions are being planned). Metrorail service on a limited 4.5-mile segment through Downtown started in 1976. In the early 1970s, the District government acquired four renewal sites along G Street adjacent to the Metro Center station. The **Hecht's Department Store** on G Street between 12th and 13th Streets (opened in 1985) is the largest freestanding department store built in any American downtown since 1945. It has two direct connections to the Metro Center station. The original building was designed for additional development. **One Metro Center,** an additional six-story office building, was developed on top of the department store by Tishman Speyer Properties, Inc. (completed in 2003). On the west side of 13th Street is **700 13th Street NW.** The building lobby relates to a garden space adjacent to the historic **Church of the Epiphany** (1844, with later additions). Between 11th and 12th Streets is another office building, **700 11th Street NW.** This complex also includes the 450-room Marriott Metro Center Hotel at 775 12th Street NW, opened in 1989. These three buildings were designed by Skidmore, Owings & Merrill and developed by the Oliver Carr Company and the Theodore Hagans interests. Another new office building has been developed on the fourth renewal site, at 12th and G Streets.

■ 2 The **InterAmerican Development Bank Building** at 1300 New York Avenue NW, designed by Skidmore, Owings & Merrill, is one of the largest buildings in Downtown. It has a spectacular atrium space, which, unfortunately, is difficult for visitors to see because of security restrictions.

■ 3 The **National Museum of Women in the Arts** is housed in the landmark Masonic Building; Keyes Condon Florance were the architects of the renovation. The museum, which opened in 1987, is the only one in the United States exclusively devoted to art by women. An addition was completed in 1997.

■ 4 **Franklin Square** is both a park, bounded by K, I, 13th, and 14th Streets, and the name of a larger section that has developed as a prestigious office area since 1980. The park is surrounded by striking new buildings. On the southeast corner of the square, **1300 I Street NW** was developed by the Gerald Hines Interests and designed by John Burgee Architects with Phillip Johnson. On the east side of the square, the exterior of the landmark **Franklin School** (1869) was restored in the early 1990s as one of the amenities of the **Franklin Plaza** office project to the east. The large **One Franklin Square Building,** designed by Hartman Cox Architects, now frames the north side of the square. The two large towers add a new design feature. Use of towers on commercial buildings in Washington was popular in the 1980s as a way to give buildings a special design character even though the main building height is limited (generally to 130 feet in the central area of the city). Several other new and renovated buildings are located around the square. The office building at the southwest corner, designed by Arthur Cotton Moore, incorporates the western entrance to the McPherson Square Metro station (Orange and Blue lines). The square was improved in the early 1990s (plantings, new sidewalks, lighting, new fountain) through a cooperative effort of the District government, the National Park Service, and the Franklin Square Association. The Downtown BID and the National Park Service are working together to make additional improvements in 2004–2005.

Franklin Square

■ 5 **McPherson Square** is one of two squares centered on avenues radiating north from the White House (the other is Farragut Square, two blocks west). A mix of old and new buildings borders the square. At the southwest corner of the square is the former University Club (1911), later the headquarters of the United Mine Workers. The building, now known as the **Summit Grand Parc,** was renovated and a new building added to the west (in 2002) for housing (105 units) by Summit Properties/IBG Partners.

■ 6 **Fifteenth Street** between New York Avenue and K Street was once known as "Washington's Wall Street" because of the concentration of financial institutions. The area is now incorporated into the Fifteenth Street Financial Historic District. The Bowen Building at the southwest corner of 15th and I Streets NW began construction in 2003 (a major facadomy project), to be completed in 2005 (see no. 7 for discussion of "facadomies"). The Shoreham Building (formerly office) on the northwest corner of 15th and H Streets NW was converted to a 225-room Sofitel Hotel (opened 2002). Buildings of special interest are the **Southern Building** (1912) at 15th and H Streets, restored with two stories added on top, and the **National Savings and Trust Building** (1888), now a part of SunTrust Bank, also restored with a skillful addition. The **Wacovia Bank** and **Riggs National Bank** buildings, both with impressive banking halls and neoclassical facades, face the **Treasury Building** at the corner of 15th Street and Pennsylvania Avenue.

■ 7 **New York Avenue** extends northeast from the White House to Mount Vernon Square. Along the **south side of the 1400 block of New York Avenue,** notice the **Washington Building,** renovated in 1989 with two floors added on top, and the new section of the **National Commercial Bank** project (1420 New York Avenue NW). The **Bond Building,** at the southwest corner of New York Avenue and 14th Street, an example of a "facadomy," a preservation technique widely used in Washington. In a facadomy, the exterior facade of the building is retained and a new building built inside, sometimes rising above the facade and sometimes incorporating additions. The Bond Building complex, designed by Shalom

Riggs National Bank

Baranes and developed by the Sigal/Zuckerman Company, is a skillful demonstration of the facadomy technique.

■ **8** The landmark **Commercial National Bank Building** was renovated by the Oliver Carr Company in 1989 and joined to new construction to the west, which extends through to New York Avenue. Removal of an interim dropped ceiling revealed the full height of the impressive two-story banking hall, which now serves as the building's lobby off 14th Street. The **Colorado Building** (1921) across 14th Street was also renovated in 1989, by Greycoat Washington, Inc., and two stories were added on top. The renovation of these and other landmark buildings in the western portion of Downtown provides a link to an earlier era.

■ **9 Hamilton Square** (600 14th Street) at the northwest corner of 14th and F Streets is an office/retail building (renovation completed in 1998). The building formerly housed Garfinckel's, long Downtown's most fashionable department store. Garfinckel's closed in 1990. Retail now includes a major Borders book/music store and the Butterfield 9 restaurant.

■ **10** The **Metropolitan Square** complex (office/retail), developed by the Oliver Carr Company and designed by Skidmore, Owings & Merrill, was built in two stages between 1980 and 1986 and marked the movement of new development east of 15th Street. The landmark facades of the Keith-Albee and Metropolitan Bank Buildings along 15th Street facing the Treasury Building were retained as part of the project. The project occupies about three-quarters of Square 224. (City blocks in Washington are called squares no matter what their shape and are identified by numbers that date from 1792 in the original city). The complex has a large central atrium that includes the Old Ebbitt Grill, now in its third location. Some original furnishings were incorporated into the new space. The second phase of the project involved the controversial demolition of Rhodes Tavern.

■ **11** The **National Press Club Building,** at 14th and F Streets, has housed a concentration of media offices since it opened in 1924. The top floor is often the scene of talks by national and foreign leaders. The building underwent renovation in 1984, including a new facade, a central atrium, and a two-level shopping mall, which connects it to the adjacent National Place complex. Filene's Basement is the major retail anchor.

■ **12 National Place** is a retail/office/hotel project extending from F Street to E Street, developed by the Quadrangle Development Corporation, the Marriott Corporation, and the Rouse Company in the early 1980s. The Shops, a two-level mall, connects with the retail mall space in the National Press Building. The Shops offers stores, restaurants, and a food court.

■ **13** The **north side of the 1300 block of F Street** has a mix of old and new buildings. The new Westory at 14th and F Streets, designed by Shalom Baranes Associates and developed by the Steven A. Goldberg Company, incorporates the earlier Westory Building. The ground floor accommodates the colorful Red Sage restaurant. The new entrance canopy and lobby are noteworthy. The Romanesque 19th-century **Sun Building** at 1315–17 F Street NW, designed by Alfred N. Mullet in 1887, was Washington's first "skyscraper." Farney's Pens, in the Sun Building, is one of Washington's distinctive older businesses.

■ 14 **F and G Streets** in the retail core were once major shopping streets. The Downtown BID and the city are working to improve retail activity in this area.

■ 15 The **Homer Building** was built in the 1920s as a four-story structure with provision for additional stories. In view of that history, the District's Historic Preservation Review Board approved a design by Shalom Baranes Associates that retained the landmark facade and incorporated it into a large new building (developed by the John Akridge Company and completed in 1990). The structure has a dramatic atrium and an entrance to the Metro Center Metro station in an arcade in the corner at 13th and G Streets. Despite its success, this building (and others, such as Columbia Square, see no. 16) illustrates some of the conflicts between the design goals of office-building developers and the city's interest in obtaining more retail space. The SHOP overlay-zoning district, enacted in 1989 (incorporated into the Downtown Development District in 1991), requires more retail space in the retail core.

■ 16 **Columbia Square** was the first new building along F Street built by the Gerald Hines Interests. I. M. Pei and Associates designed it. It is another successful office complex with a spectacular atrium but limited retail space. An entrance to the Metro Center Metro station is in an arcade at the corner of 12th and F Streets.

■ 17 The **Woodward and Lothrop department store,** known to Washingtonians as "Woodie's," was once the area's leading department store. Woodward and Lothrop was the first retail establishment to move to F Street from Pennsylvania Avenue after the Civil War, beginning the present retail core. Its two buildings were built from 1901 to 1926, when they were joined to form one building. Woodward and Lothrop closed in 1995. The Douglas Development Corporation, with Shalom Baranes Associates as architect, is renovating the Woodie's Building for office use with retail space on three levels (opened 2004). H&M Clothiers opened in the Woodie's Building in August 2003. The Woodie's Building will again be an anchor in the retail area.

■ 18 **Washington Center** fills the entire block (Square 345) to the north. Designed by RTKL and developed by Quadrangle Development Corporation, it includes the 989-room Grand Hyatt Hotel on the north (built facing the old Convention Center), with a grand atrium, and an office building with a second atrium. The complex skillfully incorporates the landmark McLachlen Bank Building at the corner of 10th and G Streets. There is a direct link to the Metro Center station.

■ **19** The **"old" Washington Convention Center,** which opened in 1983, had 350,000 square feet of exhibit space and 40 meeting rooms. It was Washington's first "modern" convention center. Designed by Welton Becket Associates, Gray and West Architects, and H. D. Nottingham Associates, the building stretched for two blocks along the north side of H Street and spurred new development in adjacent blocks and elsewhere in the city. However, it proved too small for the expanding convention market. Planning for the new convention center began in the 1990s, groundbreaking took place in 1998, and the new facility (see Tour 11 Downtown—East, no.21) opened nearby, north of Mount Vernon Square, in March 2003. The old convention center closed at that time. The almost-10-acre site of the old convention center is one of the premier downtown development sites in the country. A development team has been selected, and the old convention center will be demolished. Tenth and I Streets will be reopened through the site, and the new mixed-use development will include open space and residential, retail, performing arts, and cultural anchors. Rebuilding of the entire new complex on the site is expected to be completed by 2010. During that period, visitors will have the opportunity to see a new urban complex taking shape. **1100 New York Avenue NW,** an office building west of the old convention center site, was designed by Keyes Condon Florance and developed by Manufacturers Realty, a Canadian firm active in Washington development in the 1980s. The complex is notable for retaining much of the 1930s art deco Greyhound Bus Terminal on New York Avenue. The old bus terminal lobby has been reconstructed as a focal point in the new building.

■ **20** The **900 block of G Street** was converted into a pedestrian mall in the early 1970s as part of the "Streets for People" program. That experiment proved to be a failure, and the street was reconstructed and reopened to traffic in 2001. The **Martin Luther King Jr. Memorial Library,** at 9th and G Streets, is the city's central library and the only work of the architect Mies van der Rohe in Washington. A mural in the library depicts the life of Dr. King. Across the street is the **Mather Building Studios**. Originally an office building, it was acquired by the District government for the University of the District of Columbia but later vacated. After a development competition in 2000, the building was sold to PN Hoffman and converted to a 40-unit residential condominium (completed 2003). Other buildings along this block include the YWCA, St. Patrick's Catholic Church, and the First Congregational Church.

■ **21** The **900 block of F Street** is interesting because of the eclectic mix of old buildings, because it is a transition area between the retail core and Gallery Place, and because it is the last block in Downtown west of 9th Street to undergo transformation. Two important landmark buildings anchor the eastern corners of the block. The **Convention Center Courtyard by Marriott Hotel** occupies the Richardsonian-style granite building at the southwest corner of 9th and F Streets (originally designed by James G. Hill for the Washington Loan and Trust Company in 1891 and for many years a branch of Riggs National Bank). Renovation was completed in 2000. The Gordon Biersch Brewery and Restaurant occupies the old banking hall on the first floor. On the northwest corner, the old Masonic Temple (1870) was renovated with a modern addition to house The Gallup Organization with McCormick & Schmick's Seafood Restaurant on the ground floor. These two buildings are part of a cluster of landmarks surrounding Gallery Place. On the west end of the north side of the block, the Akridge Company is developing Carroll Square, an office/retail project involving preservation of parts of some buildings as well as new construction. East of the Marriott Courtyard, the Douglas Development Corporation is undertaking **Jemal's Lofts,** a 66-unit residential project. Further east, Douglas Development/CarrAmerica is undertaking the **Atlantic Building** project, a new office/retail complex that retains historic facades.The landmark **National Union Building** (918 F Street) houses the American Immigration Lawyers Association and has a lobby museum about immigration. By 2006 the transformation of the 900 block of F Street should be complete, with retained landmark buildings and new activity.

■ **22** At **901 E Street NW,** an office building, designed by RTKL and developed by Quadrangle Development Corporation, has a lobby space designed to function as an art gallery. The gallery, **901 Arts,** hosts several changing art exhibitions a year and helps animate the Downtown Arts District.

The District government wants to enhance the **E Street Theater Row** as a key element of the Downtown Arts District. The idea is to fill in retail, restaurant, and entertainment uses along E Street, linking the National, Warner, Ford's, and Shakespeare Theaters as well as the **E Street Cinema** complex in Lincoln Square, which opened in 2004, and the new Woolly Mammoth Theater at 7th and E Streets.

■ **23** The huge **J. Edgar Hoover FBI Building** (between 9th and 10th Streets and Pennsylvania Avenue and E Street), completed in 1972, provides space for more than 8,000 employees. Its "brutalistic" architectural style reflects design ideas of the 1960s, and recent security restrictions have made its frontages even more unfriendly.

■ **24** **Ford's Theater,** where Abraham Lincoln was assassinated, was restored by the National Park Service and reopened as a museum and a theater in 1965. Across 10th Street, the **Petersen House** has also been restored to its appearance on April 14, 1865, when the dying president was carried there for treatment. The brick-paved portion of 10th Street between E and F Streets is known as "Lincoln Place." Just south of Ford's Theater is another cultural monument: Washington's **Hard Rock Cafe,** in the renovated 999 E Street Building.

■ **25** Two recent buildings to the west provide more office space for Washington law firms and add activity on E Street. **Lincoln Square** (555 11th Street), designed by Hartman Cox and developed by the Lawrence Ruben Company, combines office, retail, and cinema space. It integrates portions of older building elements with the new building and relates well to 1001 Pennsylvania Avenue across E Street, also designed by Hartman Cox (see no. 26). The more recent **E Street Cinema** (opened 2003), an eight-screen art cinema complex operated by Landmark Theaters, has an E Street lobby in Lincoln Square. The **Thurman Arnold Building** (555 12th Street) occupies the entire block to the west and is home to Arnold and Porter, one of the city's largest law firms. The E Street frontage is occupied by multilevel retail, an ESPN Zone (restaurant, bar, games, retail) at 11th Street, and a large Barnes and Noble books and records store at 12th Street.

■ 26 **1001 Pennsylvania Avenue,** designed by Hartman Cox Architects, is considered one of the most successful of the new buildings along Pennsylvania Avenue. Completed in 1985, it has a strong but subdued Pennsylvania Avenue facade. Facades of several older buildings on 10th and 11th Streets were retained and skillfully integrated into the overall design. Intersecting interior arcades meet in the center of the building in an impressive domed space.

■ 27 The old **Evening Star Building** (1898, Marsh and Peter), on Pennsylvania Avenue at 11th Street, has a beautiful neoclassical facade. The facade along 11th Street is especially prominent because of the setback of the FBI Building. The Ian Woodner Company, with Skidmore, Owings & Merrill as architects, completed renovation of the building in 1989. The project included the skillful integration of a slim new building element on Pennsylvania between the original building and a larger addition on 11th Street. In a sign of the times, Stacks Delicatessen replaced the previous Planet Hollywood restaurant on the ground floor in 2002.

■ 28 The **Old Post Office** (see Federal Triangle Tour 9, no. 14).

■ 29 One of the design triumphs of the PADC program has been the redesign of the **Pennsylvania Avenue streetscapes** between the Capitol and 15th Street with new trees (willow oaks) and special paving, lighting, and street furniture. The sections between 10th and 13th Streets are especially attractive and well used.

■ 30 **1201 Pennsylvania Avenue NW,** designed by Skidmore, Owings & Merrill and developed by Cabot, Cabot and Forbes, opened in 1981. It has an unusual atrium and office and retail space. **1275 Pennsylvania Avenue NW** is a successor to a 1950 building that was stripped to the bare structural system and rebuilt with a modern neoclassical-style facade, completed in 1988. Smith Segretti and Tepper were the architects for the renovations.

■ 31 The **Warner Theater,** at 13th and E Streets, has a long history as an entertainment center in Downtown Washington. The theater was renovated as part of the Warner, an office/retail/theater complex at 1299 Pennsylvania Avenue developed by the Kaempfer Company. Shalom Baranes was the architect of the Warner Building and theater renovation, which includes improvements to the "back of the house" theater facilities. Pei Cobb Freed and Partners were the architects for the related new office/retail building, with an interesting atrium, extending east along E Street to 12th Street. The District government plans to enhance the **E Street Theater Spine** to connect the National, Warner, and Ford's Theaters and other arts and arts-related activities along and near E Street to the Lansburgh Theater on 7th Street, as a feature of the Downtown Arts District.

■ **32 Freedom Plaza** (Venturi, Rauch and Scott Brown) is another of the five new open spaces developed by the PADC along Pennsylvania Avenue. It was formed by bending Pennsylvania Avenue into the line of E Street at 13th Street. The resulting rectangular plaza, used for national and local events, occupies a key site between the retail core and the monumental Federal Triangle complex to the south. The central part of the L'Enfant Plan is outlined in stone and grass in the center of the plaza, and there are interesting inscriptions about Washington, DC. The overall design of the plaza is not fully satisfactory (hot in summer, not user friendly, and too hard edged), but attempts to humanize the space are being made.

■ **33** The **American City Building,** designed by Frank Slessinger and developed by Quadrangle Development Corporation at 1301 Pennsylvania Avenue NW, completed in 1980, was the first new private office building on Pennsylvania Avenue in over a decade.

■ **34** The Pennsylvania Avenue frontage of the **National Place** complex (a joint design venture of Mitchell-Giurgola and Frank Slessinger Associates) includes offices, the 774-room **J. W. Marriott Hotel,** and the entrance to the retail mall. As part of the project, the adjacent **National Theater** was renovated in 1983.

■ **35** The **Ronald Reagan Building and International Trade Center** (see Tour 9, Federal Triangle, no.1).

■ **36** The **John A. Wilson Building** (see Tour 9, Federal Triangle, no.15).

■ **37 Pershing Park** is a delightful open space at the west end of Pennsylvania Avenue (designed as a joint venture of Jerome Lindsey/M. Paul Friedberg Associates). The central space is a pool in summer and a skating rink in winter. Nearby is a memorial to General Pershing. This park is generally considered the most successful design of the five new PADC open spaces.

■ **38** The landmark **Willard InterContinental Hotel,** at 14th Street and Pennsylvania Avenue, opened in 1901 and was one of Washington's top hotels for many years. In an earlier Willard Hotel on this site, Julia Ward Howe composed "The Battle Hymn of the Republic." The hotel building closed in 1968. Early plans for Pennsylvania Avenue called for tearing it down and building a huge national square at the west end of the avenue. The plans were changed in 1974 when the Pennsylvania Avenue Plan was revised to emphasize historic preservation.

Restoration of the hotel and an office building addition were completed in 1986. The Willard InterContinental reopened to great acclaim and is again one of the city's top hotels. The Oliver Carr Company and the Stuart Golding

Company were developers. Hardy Holzman Pfeiffer was the original architect and developed the concept of designing the new office wing to the west in the same style as the Willard. The firm of Vlastimil Koubek completed the construction documents. Walk into the Pennsylvania Avenue entrance to see the restored lobby and then proceed along "Peacock Alley," the grand hallway extending north to F Street. The Willard Room offers a special dining experience. On F Street, turn left and walk about 100 feet, then turn south again through the outdoor pedestrian passageway between the hotel and new office building. The Willard Collection, a group of small shops, lines the walkway. To the right is the Occidental Restaurant and Grill, a historic restaurant once adjacent to the Willard, now housed in a new setting. The collection of photos of Washington notables, mostly politicians and military leaders, which lines the walls, is especially interesting.

Willard InterContinental Hotel

■ **39** The renovated **Washington Hotel** (1917) anchors the west end of Pennsylvania Avenue. Notice the sgraffito (etching in stucco) frieze around the top of the hotel, restored in 1989 by the hotel with assistance from PADC. Inside are an interesting restored lobby and the Two Continents Restaurant. If you take this tour in late spring or summer, you would do well to end the walk with a visit to the rooftop cafe overlooking 15th Street (open May through September), which provides a splendid view over the White House grounds and other parts of monumental Washington.

Downtown—East

(Pennsylvania Quarter, Navy Memorial, Gallery Place, National Portrait Gallery/Smithsonian Gallery of American Art, MCI Center, Chinatown, Mount Vernon Square, City Museum, Convention Center, Judiciary Square, National Building Museum, National Law Enforcement Officers Memorial, National Postal Museum, Union Station, Canadian Embassy, Newseum)

John Fondersmith

Distance: 3 miles
Time: 4 hours
Bus: Major routes: 32, 34, 35, 36, 54, 70, D6, P6, P2, S2, and S4
Metro: Archives/Navy Memorial (Yellow and Green Lines), Gallery Place-Chinatown (Yellow, Green, and Red Lines)

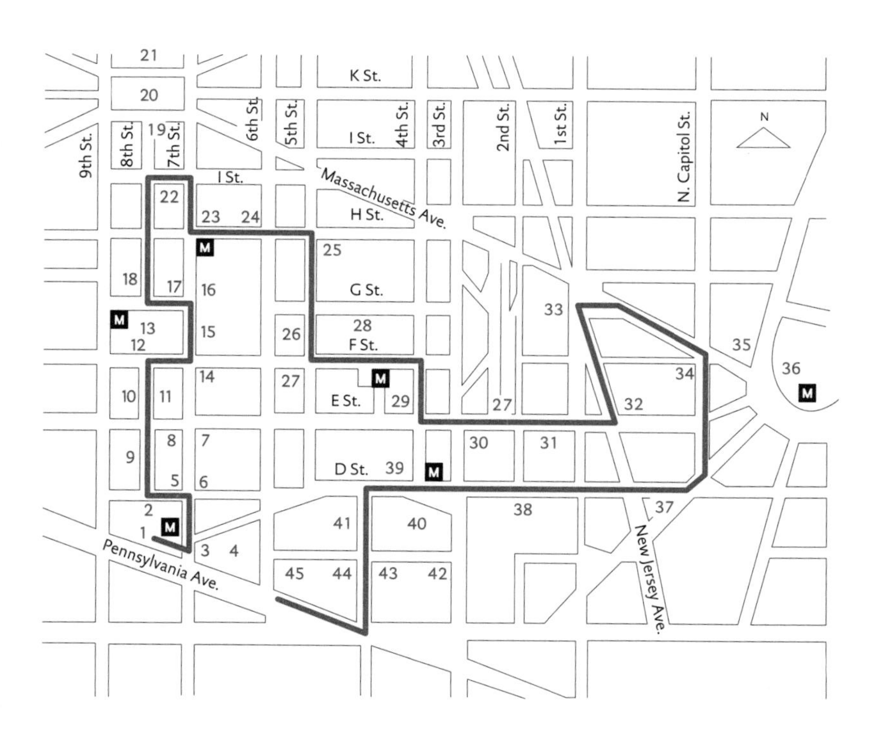

Seventh Street between Pennsylvania Avenue and Mount Vernon Square was once a primary retail street. Now it is emerging as an office/retail/residential/arts corridor, with a mix of old and new buildings. There are many restaurants of various cuisines in and near this corridor. This tour provides a view of the development that has been completed and is under way along 7th and 9th Streets between Pennsylvania Avenue and Mount Vernon Square. The tour extends east through Chinatown, Judiciary Square, and Downtown to North Capitol Street, providing an opportunity to visit Union Station before returning to the Municipal Center area and ending at the Canadian Embassy and Newseum site on Pennsylvania Avenue.

The PADC took the lead in the development of the southern portion of this area (Pennsylvania Quarter). The District government has worked to encourage development in the Gallery Place area and to preserve and enhance Chinatown. Attention is being focused on the Mount Vernon Square area.

The Downtown Business Improvement District (BID) has been important in providing security and maintenance services (see the SAMs personnel on the streets). The MCI Center (1997) and the new Convention Center (2003) have spurred revitalization. Most encouraging is the amount of new residential development in Downtown and adjacent areas. Since 2000, over 3,000 housing units have been completed, are under construction, or are planned, primarily in the area east of 9th Street.

■ 1 The **US Navy Memorial** is a circular plaza flanked by fountains, highlighting the oceans of the world in stone. The sculpture of the "lone sailor" by Stanley Blyfield symbolically represents all Americans who have served in the US Navy since the American Revolution. Bas-reliefs surround the base of the fountains, illustrating the various branches of the navy. A theater and information center in the adjacent Market Square East building provide orientation and sources for ex-navy personnel seeking information about their ships and former crewmates. The memorial, designed by Conklin Rossart, provides space for concerts. The Navy Memorial is part of Market Square Park, one of five open spaces along Pennsylvania Avenue developed by the PADC.

■ 2 **Market Square** is a mixed-use complex (retail and office space and 210 apartments) developed by the Trammell Crow Company. Hartman Cox Architects, a nationally recognized Washington architectural firm that has designed buildings in Downtown, designed the monumental complex. The two buildings frame the important **8th Street Vista** extending north from the National Archives Building to the National Portrait Gallery / Smithsonian Gallery of American Art at Gallery Place. There are several good places to eat before beginning the tour.

The area around Pennsylvania Avenue and 7th Street was Washington's first commercial center. A market was established in 1801 on the site where the Archives Building now stands south of Pennsylvania Avenue. The new residential / commercial / arts area adjacent to Pennsylvania Avenue (approximately 1,500 residential units when completed) is now called the **Pennsylvania Quarter.**

■ 3 **Indiana Plaza** is another new open space created by closing several streets and combining small park spaces into one plaza. Notice the **Temperance**

Market Square on Pennsylvania Avenue

Monument and the **Grand Army of the Republic** memorial. On the edge of the plaza is the Richardsonian-style **Argentine Naval Attaché Building** (1886), housing a branch of Riggs National Bank on the ground floor. To the south on Pennsylvania Avenue is the renovated former Apex Building, which was joined to several historic buildings in a complex designed by Hartman Cox Architects. This is now the **Dorothy I. Height Building,** the headquarters of the National Council of Negro Women. Walk around to the back of the National Bank of Washington to view the trompe l'oeil mural by Mame Cohalak.

■ 4 **Pennsylvania Plaza** is an office/residential/retail complex facing Indiana Avenue (technically it is joined to 601 Pennsylvania Avenue NW and thus has a Pennsylvania Avenue address). Notice the attractive entrances and the corner campanile structure at the corner of 6th Street and Indiana Avenue. The complex (completed 1990) was developed by the Sigal/Zuckerman Company and designed by Hartman Cox Architects.

■ 5 **Liberty Place** is an office building at 7th and D Streets, completed in 1990 by the Oliver Carr Company. The architect was Keyes Condon Florance. The project included the restoration of the Fireman's Insurance Company Building at 7th Street and Pennsylvania Avenue. As part of the restoration, the former gold dome on the building was replaced. The three smaller buildings to the east on Indiana Avenue, housing the Artifactory, the Dutch Mill Restaurant, and Litwin's Furniture, are some of the oldest commercial buildings in Washington, dating from the 1820s. **Litwin's** (637 Indiana Avenue) has one of the earliest elevators in the country.

■ 6 **Gallery Row** at 7th and D Streets was developed under the auspices of the PADC. The landmark facades were placed back onto a modern building, designed by Hartman Cox Architects, that includes the Zenith Gallery and the Andale Restaurant (contemporary Mexican), with office space above. Gallery

Row is one element in the program to create the **7th Street Arts Walk,** a concentration of public and private arts activities extending from the Smithsonian Institution's museums and galleries on the Mall to the National Portrait Gallery / Smithsonian Gallery of American Art at Gallery Place and on through Chinatown to the City Museum at Mount Vernon Square.

The **Jennifer Building** (400 7th Street) is a renovated building that includes office space and the Bead Museum. **406 7th Street** is a renovated building housing art galleries and Apartment Zero (home furnishings).

■ 7 The **Jefferson at Penn Quarter** (completed 2003) includes 428 residential units, retail space, and the Woolly Mammoth Theater (265-seat, courtyard-style theater, opened fall 2004). One building, which included a post–Civil War office of Clara Barton, has been retained and the space is being restored as a museum. This complex is being developed by JPI with Esocoff & Associates as architects. It is one of three major complexes completed along 7th Street in 2003–2004, essentially completing major development along 7th Street (see this tour, nos. 14 and 16).

■ 8 **The Lansburgh** is one of the most interesting building complexes along 7th Street. Developed under the auspices of the PADC, the complex was designed by Graham Gund Architects and developed by the Gunwyn Company. The project includes 385 apartments, the 500-seat Shakespeare Theater, and retail space. The design includes retention of a portion of the former Lansburgh's Department Store on 8th Street and two landmark facades, with a bold, colorful new building along 7th Street. Retail includes an Olsson's books and records store, the popular Jaleo restaurant (Spanish) and Austin Grill (Tex-Mex). Be sure to see the collection of old photographs of the area in the CVS windows at 8th and D Streets.

■ 9 Eighth Street from Pennsylvania Avenue to F Street is part of an important axis derived from the L'Enfant Plan. In this section, the Archives Building is to the south and portico of the National Portrait Gallery is to the north. The **Stables Art Center** (410 8th Street) is a renovated building leased by the District government to house local arts groups, the District of Columbia Commission on the Arts and Humanities, and the Marriott Hospitality High School. **Market Square North,** an office / residential / retail complex, occupies most of the remainder of Square 407. (See Tour 10, Downtown—West, no. 10, for an explanation of the square system in Washington.) Market Square North includes the major office building (401 9th Street) extending along the entire 9th Street frontage, developed by Gould Properties / Boston Properties, and two apartment buildings on 8th Street, the **Lexington** (86 units) at D Street and the **Lexington North** (49 units) at E Street, both developed by Gould Properties. Guy Martin at Studios Architecture was the architect for these three buildings. The Lexington houses Teaism, an unusual teashop and cafe.

■ **10** The **International Spy Museum** is housed in a renovated row of landmark buildings on the south side of the **800 block of F Street,** including the **LeDroit Building,** joined to new construction to the south. The LeDroit Building was an early Victorian office building (1875). The entire complex, which includes office space and 12 residential units, was developed by Douglas Development Corporation, with Shalom Baranes as architect. The intriguing International Spy Museum, opened in 2002, has proven to be very popular, as have the museum shop, Zola (restaurant and bar), and the Spy City Café.

■ **11** The **Hotel Monaco** (opened 2002) now occupies the landmark Greek Revival former **US General Post Office Building,** also known as the **Tariff Commission Building** (1829–1869, Robert Mills) at 700 F Street NW. This building first housed the Post Office Department and the city's post office and has provided space for other government agencies over the years, including the Tariff Commission. However, the building had deteriorated and was not suited for modern office use. In the late 1990s the General Services Administration decided to lease this historic building for private development. The resulting Hotel Monaco, developed by Kimpton Boutique Hotels, is one of the most interesting hotels in Washington. The renovation has made good use of the classical rooms and hallways. Turn through the archway from 8th Street into the courtyard to reach **Poste,** the hotel's restaurant, in the former mail handling room. An attached contemporary glass pavilion houses the bar.

■ **12** The **National Portrait Gallery/Smithsonian American Art Museum,** between F, G, 7th, and 9th Streets, was formerly the US Patent Office, a repository for the Declaration of Independence, and a Civil War hospital, among other uses, before its initial renovation and reuse by the Smithsonian Institution in 1968 for two important art museums. The building, erected in stages from 1836 to 1857 on a site that the L'Enfant Plan indicated for a national nondenominational church and pantheon, is an excellent example of Greek Revival architecture. Architects included Robert Mills and Thomas U. Walter. The building was closed in 2002 for renovation and will reopen in 2006. Office space and the Archives of American Art have been moved out to the nearby **Victor Building** at 9th and H Streets, so space for display of the art collections will be greatly increased.

■ **13** The wide expanse of F Street between 7th and 9th Streets, created by the slightly offset alignment of F Street for those two blocks, forms a space framed by surrounding buildings. This space, known as **Gallery Place,** has the largest grouping of landmark buildings in Downtown and will become even more interesting as nearby buildings are completed. In the 1970s this portion of F Street and the related section of 8th Street from E to F Streets were closed to traffic and converted to pedestrian areas as part of the "Streets for People" program. Over time, that program did not work. In 1997 the pedestrian areas were rebuilt to conventional street design and reopened to traffic.

■ 14 **Terrell Place** is a mixed-use complex (completed 2003) focused at 7th and F Streets that occupies much of Square 456. The Hecht Company department store, at 7th and F Streets, was a cornerstone of 7th Street retail activity, and the store eventually grew to encompass almost the entire block. In 1985, Hecht's moved to a new store at Metro Center (see Tour 10, Downtown—West, no. 1). The old Hecht Company main building at 7th and F streets (1924) and older buildings that had been joined together were closed. The new complex includes reuse of the completely renovated old Hecht Company building, a new building to the east on F Street, and new construction behind retained facades further south on 7th Street for office and related retail use. The building at 7th and E Streets has been increased in height (facade retained) for residential use (29 units). CarrAmerica is the developer. Terrell Place is named for Mary Church Terrell, a civil rights leader who led the fight in 1951 to integrate Hecht's lunch counter.

A new **Shakespeare Theater** (800 seats) will be built on F Street east of Terrell Place, near 6th Street (to open in 2007) with offices above. This theater and the reuse of the existing Shakespeare Theater on 7th Street will greatly increase Washington's role as a destination for classical theater in the United States. The first phase of rebuilding this square began in the late 1980s by the Oliver Carr Company with a dramatic neoclassical building at 6th and E Streets for the headquarters of the **American Association of Retired Persons,** designed by Kohn Peterson Fox.

■ 15 **MCI Center** is Washington's 20,000-seat state-of-the-art sports arena and special events center. It is home to the Washington Wizards, Washington Mystics, Washington Capitals, and Georgetown University's men's basketball team. The arena was developed by Washington businessman and team owner Abe Pollin, who decided in the early 1990s that the time was right to build a modern arena in Downtown to replace a 1970s arena located on the suburban beltway. The MCI Center was built on a site that included a previously cleared but undeveloped urban renewal site, the closing of the 600 block of G Street, and additional land to the north. The complex includes a sporting goods store, sports exhibit space, and a steakhouse other eateries. A large arcade entrance to the Gallery Place-Chinatown Metro station is built into the 7th and F Streets corner of the building, providing excellent Metrorail access from all parts of the Washington region. The MCI Center opened in December 1997 and has been a major catalyst for development in adjacent areas of Downtown, especially Pennsylvania Quarter, Gallery Place, and Chinatown.

■ 16 **Gallery Place** is a new mixed-use complex on 7th Street at H Street, in the center of Chinatown (opened 2004). It includes 250,000 square feet of retail space (including a 14-screen United Artists Cinema, Jillian's entertainment/dining, and other retailers), a new office building, 192 residential condominiums, and space for Chinatown community functions. A lively pedestrian walk, G Street Alley, provides a connection between 7th and 6th Streets along the north side of the

MCI Center. The Chinatown entrance to the Gallery Place/Chinatown Metro station is built in an arcade in the north end of Gallery Place at 7th and H Streets, adjacent to the Chinatown Archway. Gallery Place is a joint venture of Akridge and Western Development, designed by Architectonica and HTM Architects.

■ 17 The **buildings along the west side of the 700 block of 7th Street,** between G and H Streets, are the best remaining row of late-19th and early 20th century commercial buildings in Downtown. The Douglas Development Corporation has undertaken the historic restoration of these buildings, with ground-floor retail (mostly restaurants and food stores) and office space above. GTM architects have provided design services. This row of buildings adds a special character to this section of 7th Street.

■ 18 **Eighth Street** extends north from G Street to Mount Vernon Square, a continuation of the strong north–south axis derived from the L'Enfant Plan. Major development has taken place in this corridor. At 8th and G Streets, the Trammel Crow Company is constructing the **Portrait Building** (office with ground floor retail) with Leo A. Daly as architect. The project is being done in association with **Calvary Baptist Church.** The program includes the development of a new building behind the retained Greene Building facade for church use and restoration of significant historic elements on the church sanctuary, including reconstruction of the church's long-lost 150-foot-tall corner tower at 8th and H Streets. On the west side of 8th Street at G Street is the headquarters of the **Family Research Council** and, at 9th and G Streets, the new and striking **Edison Place** building, designed by Devrouax and Purnell. The building is headquarters for PEPCO, the local electric utility. The dramatic Zaytinya restaurant is a popular gathering place, one of several restaurants encircling the National Portrait Gallery/Smithsonian American Art Museum. Among the other new buildings between 8th and 9th Streets, notice the **Greater New Hope Baptist Church** north of H Street (originally built in 1897 as the Washington Hebrew Congregation).

■ 19 The **two city blocks bordering the south side of Mount Vernon Square** between 7th and 9th Streets, with 8th Street converted to a pedestrian plaza, constitute an interesting complex of four buildings, each with its own core and all built atop a common parking facility. The 8th Street pedestrian area passes below the four-story glass-faced bridge connecting two of the four buildings of the complex, creating a frame for the view between the north facade of the National Portrait Gallery/Smithsonian Gallery of American Art to the south and the City Museum and new Convention Center to the north. The original complex, known as "Techworld," consisted of two office buildings and the 800-room Renaissance Hotel. Developed by International Developers, Inc., the complex was intended to become Washington's high-tech center, but that concept was not realized. The complex has meeting and exhibit area space underground. There are also two Chinese gardens. In 2004, Akridge, a major local developer, completed 900 7th Street, a dramatic, glass-faced office building at

7th and I Streets. Designed by HOK Architects, the corner of the building will glow like a lantern at night, a fitting role for a building that will serve as the northern entrance to Chinatown. Future plans may include additional retail amenities that will complement the vibrancy and culture of the Mount Vernon Square area to the north and Chinatown to the south.

■ **20** In an open green space in Mount Vernon Square, the **City Museum of Washington, DC** (opened 2003), occupies the historic Carnegie Library building, which was constructed in 1902 to serve as the city's central library. After years of neglect, the building has been restored to house the museum, operated by the Historical Society of Washington. The City Museum is envisioned as a gateway to exploring the real Washington, the city beyond the monuments. In effect, the entire city becomes a larger museum. Visitors should see the multimedia show, *Washington Stories*, and the overview exhibit, *Washington Perspectives*, where you can walk across the city on a large aerial photograph map on the floor. Other exhibits provide information on aspects of Washington's history such as sports or the Civil War, and temporary exhibits highlight different neighborhoods. There is a state-of-the art research library, a cafe, and a museum store. This is the place for all residents or visitors to begin or continue their exploration of Washington.

Mount Vernon Square is also the name of a larger area extending from 12th Street on the west to New Jersey Avenue on the east and generally for several blocks to the north and south, overlapping part of Chinatown to the south. Mount Vernon Square will be Washington's next great urban neighborhood and will likely continue to develop over the first two decades of the 21st century. East of 9th Street the pattern will be mainly commercial with some residential. Just southwest of the square the new office building, **901 New York Avenue**, is under construction (completion 2004). A major **Marriott convention headquarters hotel** is planned at 9th Street and Massachusetts Avenue, just west of the convention center. The Mount Vernon Triangle east of 7th Street is proposed for residential development, approximately 5,000 units, with initial projects under construction along the south side of Massachusetts Avenue.

■ **21** The new **Washington Convention Center** at Mount Vernon Square opened in March 2003. With over 2.3 million square feet of space on almost six city blocks, it is the largest building in Washington. It has 725,000 square feet of column-free exhibit space, 70 meeting rooms, restaurant space, and a 52,000- square-foot ballroom. It also has a grand lobby facing Mount Vernon Square with magnificent stairways and views over the city from the upper ballroom floor. Although the building is huge, its size is less apparent because the building is borken into separate components and burrows into the slope of the land toward the north. The Mount Vernon Square/7th Street/Convention Center Metro station on 7th Street (Green Line) provides convenient Metro access. The Washington Convention Center Authority operates the convention center. The team of Thompson,

Ventulett, Stainback & Associates, Mariani Architects Engineers and Devrouax & Purnell designed this large and innovative complex. The Washington Convention Center will be important in promoting activity and spurring economic growth and new development. Most important, however, it will attract thousands of additional visitors to explore and appreciate Washington, DC.

■ 22 **820 7th Street,** an office / retail building developed in the early 1990s by DRI and designed by the Weihe Partnership, incorporates historic facades along 7th Street and includes Chinese design features. First floor tenants include the German Cultural Center (Goethe Institute Washington) and RFD (Regional Food and Drink), which advertises having 300 different bottled beers available and 30 beers on tap.

■ 23 The **Chinatown Archway** at 7th and H Streets marks the heart of Chinatown. With its seven colorful pagoda roofs, the archway is said to be the largest of its kind outside China. Erected in 1986, it was a joint project of the District of Columbia government and the Municipality of Beijing (Washington, DC, and Beijing are sister cities.) Alfred Liu was the architect for the District.

■ 24 The **600 block of H Street** forms the heart of Washington's Chinatown, with many Chinese restaurants and shops. It is an ideal place to stop for lunch or a snack. The **Wah Luck House,** at the northwest corner of 6th and H Streets, provides 153 apartments, a Chinatown community room, and a Chinese meditation garden. This modern building incorporates Chinese design features. The Office of Planning works with the Chinatown Steering Community to obtain Chinese design features and calligraphy on new and renovated buildings as part of the city's program to preserve and enhance Chinatown.

Chinatown Archway

■ 25 **St. Mary's Catholic Church,** at 5th and H Streets, was established in the mid-19th century to serve German Catholic immigrants. The design of the present church building (1891) was influenced by German gothic architecture. The large but not very inspiring **General Accounting Office** wraps around the St. Mary's Church complex on two sides. South on 5th Street, the **Avalon at Gallery Place** (203 units, opened 2003) is one of several new apartment buildings in and near Chinatown. It was developed by Avalon Bay Communities with Eric Colbert and Associates as architects.

■ 26 The **Jackson Graham Building,** designed by Keyes, Lethbridge and Condon, is the headquarters of the Washington Metropolitan Area Transit Authority, operators of Metrorail and Metrobus. It accommodates Metro's headquarters staff and houses the fare collection and central computer facilities for the entire Metrorail system.

■ 27 The **Keck Center of the National Academies** (Science, Engineering, and Medicine) at 500 5th Street is a striking new modern building, which also retains elements of previous historic buildings (designed by the Smith Group, opened 2002). The lobby has interesting and stimulating murals by Larry Kirkland. There is also a bookstore for scientific publications and the Marian E. Koshland Science Museum (entrance at 6th and E Streets).

■ 28 The **National Building Museum** is housed in the **Pension Building** (1882), 5th and G Streets, a Category I landmark in **Judiciary Square.** Montgomery C. Meigs, engineer of the Capitol dome and the Cabin John Bridge, designed the building. Its huge central hall, an innovation in lighting and ventilation at the time, was used for presidential inaugural balls in the late 19th century and is still used for balls and many special events today. The National Building Museum is a center for study and display of American building arts, including architecture, city planning, landscape architecture, and construction. The exhibit *Washington: Symbol and City* provides an overview of the planning and development of the city. The museum offers many programs and has an especially interesting museum shop.

■ 29 The **National Law Enforcement Officers Memorial,** designed by Davis Buckley, provides a landscaped setting in the center of Judiciary Square, just south of the National Building Museum. Names of law enforcement officers who have been killed in the line of duty are carved on two elliptical walls flanking the landscaped space. The northern entrance to the Judiciary Square Metro station is incorporated into the edge of the memorial. Dedicated in 1990, its meaning has increased with time. It was one of the first major national memorials to be built outside the monumental core.

■ 30 The **US Tax Court,** east of 3rd Street between D and E Streets, designed by Victor Lundy, uses innovative structural concepts of post-tensioning to sup-

Pension Building

port a cantilevered courthouse on six columns. A landscaped pedestrian plaza spans the adjacent Center Leg Freeway. Because the dramatic front of this building faces the freeway, most visitors do not see it. The original **Adas Israel Synagogue** is now located two blocks north of E Street at 701 3rd Street, on land next to the Center Leg Freeway. Dedicated a few blocks away in 1876, this was the first building constructed as a synagogue in the District of Columbia. It was moved to its present site in 1969 and restoration was completed in 1974. It has a small museum about Washington's Jewish community.

■ **31** The **Community for Creative Non-Violence Shelter** occupies the previous temporary federal office building on the east side of 2nd Street between D and E Streets. The shelter provides accommodations and facilities for homeless men and women.

■ **32** **New Jersey Avenue** is the spine of Downtown East. The **Capitol Place** complex, at New Jersey Avenue and F Street, includes the 265-room Washington Court Hotel and office space. The new national headquarters of the **National Association of Realtors** is being constructed on a challenging triangular site at New Jersey Avenue and E Street (completion 2004). This is the first new "green" office building in Washington.

■ **33** The **Georgetown University Law Center** now includes four buildings: the original semiclassical building (McDonough Hall, 1971) facing New Jersey Avenue at F Street, designed by Edward D. Stone; the neoclassical Edward Bennett Williams Law Library (1990) at the intersection of New Jersey and Massachusetts Avenues, designed by Hartman Cox Architects; the Bernard & Sarah M. Guars Student Center; and the Eric Hotung International Law Center and Georgetown Sports and Fitness Center (completed 2004), designed by Sheply Bullfinch Richardson and Abbott. F and G Streets between 1st and 2nd Streets have been closed to traffic to create a campus environment.

■ 34 **North Capitol Street** is the eastern edge of Downtown and the dividing line between the northwest and northeast quadrants of the city. Beyond North Capitol Street are the grounds of the Capitol complex. A cluster of hotels once extended along the west side of North Capitol Street, providing accommodations to rail travelers passing through nearby Union Station. Office buildings have replaced most of these hotels. The **Phoenix Park Hotel** at North Capitol and F Streets is the result of the renovation and expansion of an earlier hotel. **The Dubliner** is a popular Irish pub on the ground floor.

■ 35 **Postal Square** is a strong classical building originally constructed (1915, expanded 1935) as Washington's main post office. It was designed to relate to Union Station just to the east and to help form the northern edge of the Capitol grounds. The building was extensively restored and restructured in the early 1990s (completed 1993) by the Hines Interests (Shalom Baranes architect) working under the direction of the Office of the Architect of the Capitol. The classical facades were retained, as was the impressive former Post Office lobby that extends the length of the building along Massachusetts Avenue. The building is now used primarily for federal office space (the US Bureau of Labor Statistics), and there is a small post office accessible from North Capitol Street. Visitors will be most interested in the **National Postal Museum,** part of the Smithsonian Institution, which tells the story of the postal system in its intriguing exhibits. The large Capital Brewing Company provides food and drink.

■ 36 **Union Station** was designed by Daniel H. Burnham (1908) to provide a monumental entrance into Washington during the heyday of rail travel. The agreement to build this station and to remove railroad tracks from the future National Mall was a key element of the McMillan Commission Plan of 1902. By the 1970s, rail travel had declined. A program to use the station as a visitors center for the 1976 Bicentennial was less than successful, and deterioration of the main part of the building led to its closing in the late 1970s and early 1980s. A joint effort by federal, District, and private entities, under the direction of the Union Station Redevelopment Corporation, rescued the building. The renovated Union Station reopened in 1988 with a 200,000-square-foot retail mall, nine movie theaters, an improved Amtrak station, a huge parking garage, and office space. The former main waiting room is now the focal point of the complex. There are many specialized shops, the movie theaters, a large food court, and four major restaurants. The America and Thunder Grill restaurants offer views of the Capitol. B. Smith's, located in the former presidential reception room at the east end of the station, offers a special dining experience. The Union Station Metro station provides direct access to the Red Line. The **Columbus Monument** with fountain is located in front of the station.

Development continues around Union Station. East of the station is the **Thurgood Marshall Federal Judiciary Building** (1992, designed by Edward Larrabee Barnes Associates), a striking modern building with an interesting atrium. North of that building, the first phase of the large **Station Place** complex (developed by the Louis Dreyfus Property Group) is under construction, first phase to be completed in 2004. The Securities and Exchange Commission will occupy the first two phases of the complex. Future air rights development is planned north of Union Station (see Tour 1, Capitol Hill—West, no. 1).

■ 37 The **Japanese American Memorial to Patriotism during World War II** is a new memorial (opened 2001) on Louisiana Avenue at the edge of the Capitol Grounds. Designed by Davis Buckley, it is a reminder of the time during World War II when Japanese Americans were moved to detention camps. It also commemorates other Japanese Americans who served in the military during the war.

■ 38 The **Department of Labor Building,** between 2nd and 3rd Streets south of D Street, accommodates approximately 4,000 employees. Below this large federal building is the Center Leg Freeway, which tunnels under the Mall. The Department of Labor Building incorporates ventilation shafts for the freeway tunnel.

■ 39 The **Old City Hall** (1820–1881, George Hadfield architect) is a fine Greek Revival Building in Judiciary Square. The first public building constructed to house the District of Columbia government, it is now occupied by the Superior Court of the District of Columbia.

■ 40 The **District of Columbia Municipal Center (Henry J. Daly Building)** houses the headquarters of the Metropolitan Police Department and other District government agencies.

■ 41 The H. Carl Moultrie I Court House of the **District of Columbia Courthouse** at 300 Indiana Avenue opened in 1977. It has one appellate and 44 trial courtrooms, plus ancillary space.

■ 42 The **E. Barrett Prettyman US Court House** on the east side of John Marshall Park has been the scene of many famous trials, including those held in connection with the Watergate and Iran-Contra affairs and the trial of former mayor Marion Barry. A bold new courthouse addition on the Constitution Avenue frontage at 3rd Street, designed by Michael Graves, opened in 2004.

■ 43 **John Marshall Park,** created by closing John Marshall Place, is the fifth of five new open spaces along Pennsylvania Avenue created by the PADC. Designed by Carol R. Johnson & Associates, the park offers a quiet oasis for visitors and employees from the nearby court buildings.

■ **44** The striking **Canadian Embassy,** designed by Arthur Erikson and opened in 1989, frames John Marshall Place on the west and relates to the East Wing of the National Gallery of Art diagonally across Pennsylvania Avenue. The courtyard has a rotunda of 12 columns, representing Canada's 10 provinces and two territories, and an interesting sculpture, *The Spirit of Haida Gwaii,* by Bill Reid. The embassy includes a theater and an art gallery.

■ **45** The **Newseum,** formerly located in Rosslyn, Virginia, will occupy this key site on Pennsylvania Avenue next to the Canadian Embassy and across from the National Gallery of Art. The District government made the site available by moving the Department of Employment Services, demolishing the building, and selling the site to the Freedom Forum. The building has a dramatic design by Polshek Partners Architects and Ralph Appelbaum Associates. Completion is expected in 2006. The Newseum will be a six-level interactive museum demonstrating how news is made and reported, using the latest exhibit technology. The building also includes office space for the Newseum and Freedom Forum, a conference center, retail space, and approximately 100 residential condominiums.

From this point, the visitor can proceed west or east along Pennsylvania Avenue, south to the Mall, or back north into Downtown.

16th Street / Meridian Hill

(Elegant mansions, established churches, new and restored residential areas)

Perry G. Fisher, updated by Ryan Harris

Distance: 1 1/2 miles
Time: 2 hours
Bus: S2 and S4
Metro: Farragut North or Dupont Circle (Red Line)

Sixteenth Street is the most prominent of the numbered streets of Washington and is laid out along the north–south center line of the White House, just slightly east of the central meridian of the District of Columbia. The impressive boulevard mounts a series of gentle terraces shaped in the glacial period. One of the highest terraces encircling the original City of Washington is that stretching across Meridian Hill and Mount Pleasant at an average elevation of about 200 feet, a terrace bisected by 16th Street in its route from Lafayette Square to Silver Spring, Maryland.

The lower 16th Street corridor and the Meridian Hill district occupy land that at the time of the establishment of Washington was part of three large estates stemming from 17th-century patents from Lord Baltimore. When L'Enfant submitted his plan for the City of Washington in July 1791, development in this section of the Territory of Columbia was rather typical of the tidewater region of the time. Minor plantation houses occupied the higher elevations overlooking the Potomac River. There were some widely scattered clusters of shacklike frame houses near the stream banks, which developed with the active milling enterprises along the large, swifter tributaries of the Potomac. Settlement was sparse despite a good deal of speculation and subdivision of land in expectation of a real estate boom to accompany the move of the federal government to Washington. However, most of 16th Street above K Street remained vacant throughout the first three-quarters of the 19th century. Before the Civil War, small cottages near M and 16th Streets were built and occupied by semiskilled craftsmen and laborers. Many of these workers were black and were employed in the light industrial and commercial businesses that depended on the streams flowing through the area.

Under the territorial form of government imposed upon the District of Columbia in 1871 and the ambitious public works programs of Alexander Robey Shepherd, executive officer of the Board of Public Works, the fortunes of 16th Street and Meridian Hill took a different direction. The foundations were laid for the impressive later development that still sets the physical character of the street and district. Shepherd, as a successful local builder and real estate speculator, had a decided interest in the improvements of the West End of Washington. He began a pro-

N
Hobart St.
Mt. Pleasant St.
Irving St.
Harvard St.
Rd.
Harvard St.
Columbia
Girard St.
Fuller St.
Euclid St.
Kalorama Rd.
17th St.
16th St.
15th St.
Chapin St.
Crescent Pl.
Belmont St.
Florida Ave.
V St.
U St.
New Hampshire Ave.
T St.
Swann St.
S St.
Riggs Pl.
R St.
Corcoran St.
Q St.
Church St.
P St.
O St.
Rhode Island Ave.
N St.
Massachusetts Ave.
1
2
3
4
5
6
7
8
9
10
11
12
13
14
15
16
17
18
19
20
21
22
23
24
25
26
27
28
29
30
31
32
33
34
35
36
37
38
39
40

gram in the mid-1800s of deliberate cultivation of that section of the city as the most important residential and diplomatic quarter of the booming post–Civil War capital.

■ 1 **Scott Circle** (Massachusetts Avenue, Rhode Island Avenue, and 16th Street) is one of the original federal reservations planned by L'Enfant, although Andrew Ellicott subsequently modified its configuration. It was not until the early 1870s that a park was laid out and an upper-class residential neighborhood developed. The automobile underpass along 16th Street was completed in 1942.

Scott Circle takes its name from the statue of Gen. Winfield Scott in the center of the space, sculpted by Henry Kirk Brown. The figure was cast from a cannon captured in the Mexican War, and the statue was first erected in 1874. (See Tour 8, White House, for more information on the area south of the circle.) Note that many multistoried former office and residential buildings have been converted to hotels abutting the circle.

■ 2 In the small triangular park just to the east is the interesting **Memorial to S. C. F. Hahnemann** (1775–1843), founder of the homeopathic school of medicine. The memorial was designed by Charles Henry Neihaus and erected in 1900 by the American Institute of Homeopathy.

■ 3 In the corresponding small triangular park just to the west of 16th Street is Gaetano Trentanove's **statue of Daniel Webster** cast in bronze. The founder of the *Washington Post,* Stilson Hutchins, presented the statue to the city in 1900.

■ 4 1500 Massachusetts Avenue NW apartment house. This was the original **site of the Louise Home,** which was replaced by the present apartment house in the early 1950s. The Louise Home was erected in 1871 through the generosity of William Wilson Corcoran, Washington banker, art patron, and philanthropist, as a refuge for "Protestant women of refinement and culture who have become reduced in circumstances in their old age." It subsequently moved to Kalorama (see Tour 14, Kalorama, no. 10).

■ 5 **National Paint and Coatings Association,** 1500 Rhode Island Avenue NW. The present 1912 exterior of this building is John Russell Pope's classical entombment for most of architect John Fraser's 1879 house for John T. Brodhead, a wealthy Marine Corps officer from Detroit. In 1882 Brodhead sold the house to Gardiner Greene Hubbard, founder of the National Geographic Society. Hubbard bought it for his daughter and son-in-law, Alexander Graham Bell, who lived there until 1889.

For an example of architect Fraser's great domestic commissions in Washington, you may still view the James G. Blaine mansion (1881) at 2000 Massachusetts Avenue NW, a building in all its essentials very much like the Brodhead-Bell mansion (see Tour 13, Dupont Circle, no. 8). In 1889 Levi P. Morton, newly elected vice president, purchased the Rhode Island Avenue house.

■ 6 **Embassy of Australia Chancery,** 1601 Massachusetts Avenue NW. Built in 1965, this chancery firmly anchors Embassy Row at Scott Circle, despite the continuing move of embassies to the upper Northwest section of Washington. The building was built by Australian architect Bates Smart McCutcheon. The Australian government doubled the size of the building to the rear, along 16th Street, after demolishing three row houses during the 1990s.

■ 7 The **Johns Hopkins University School of Advanced International Studies,** 1619 Massachusetts Avenue NW. This is a much-praised work of the local architectural firm of Keyes, Lethbridge and Condon. The order and polish, the dignified restraint in the use of materials, and the proportioning of the main blocks and elements of the facade have pleased both critics and laypeople. A real understanding of the character of Washington and the design constraints it imposes is evident here.

■ 8 The **Embassy of the Philippines** is located on the west side of Scott Circle, between Massachusetts Avenue and N Street, 17th Street, and Bataan Place. The distinctive turn-of-the-century row houses formerly on the site housed a long list of notable persons. But Scott Circle is an area that has been totally transformed in the years since World War II, with many hotels clustered around the circle.

A major factor in the changes that have taken place is the rezoning of the District of Columbia, which was prepared in 1954–56 by Harold M. Lewis of New York and which became effective May 12, 1958. Among the several zoning categories was the Special Purpose (S-P) category, a classification that has had particular importance for areas like Scott and Dupont Circles, 16th Street, and the major diagonal avenues. The intent of the S-P zoning district was to stabilize areas of special architectural, historical, or functional character adjacent to districts of high-intensity commercial or central business district supporting uses. The conversion of several buildings to chancery, nonprofit organization, or professional office use is a matter of right within an S-P zone, and this provision has resulted in the conversion of many former residences to handsome adaptive uses. However, within an S-P zone, a new hotel or apartment house of a height of 90 feet is also a matter of right. Construction of new 90-foot-high office buildings for chancery, nonprofit organization, or professional use requires the approval of the Board of Zoning Adjustment of the District of Columbia.

■ 9 **First Baptist Church,** southwest corner of 16th and O Streets NW. This church building was designed in a pseudo-Gothic style in 1955 by Philadelphia architect Harold Waggoner. However, a church of a different style once occupied the site. In 1890 architect W. Bruce Gray designed a red brick and sandstone church that combined Romanesque and Italian Renaissance styles. An impressive campanile, flanking the main church on the north, reached a height of 140 feet. A magnificent arched recess sheltered the main entrance to the building.

The First Baptist Church building of 1890 marks the period when many downtown congregations sought new sites in the developing 16th Street and Dupont Circle areas for their church buildings, in an attempt to escape the increasing commercialism of the older parts of downtown Washington.

■ **10 Embassy of the Republic of Kazakhstan** (former **Gurley House**), 1401 16th Street NW. This is a fortunate case of adaptive use in a Special Purpose zone. The house was built in 1888 by Samuel and Charles Edmonston as a residence and was designed by one of the builders. This firm had been responsible for the construction of two 16th Street houses designed by H. H. Richardson. The Edmonstons borrowed heavily from Richardson in their plans for the house, which had been renovated during the 1980s for use as law offices and the office of syndicated columnist Jack Anderson. Restoration costs proved cheaper than rental rates in newer speculative office buildings nearby.

■ **11** The **Carnegie Institution,** southeast corner of 16th and P Streets. The Carnegie Institution is an internationally respected philanthropy devoted to research in natural science. The home of the institution features a rather uninspired beaux-arts design by the New York architectural firm of Carrere and Hastings. It was built in 1908 of Indiana limestone, and the portico, at least, deserves some recognition for its impressive adaptation of the Ionic order and magnificent urns. It is an important structure, since it marks the spread of institutional uses to 16th Street in the early part of the 20th century, and the growth of the scientific community in Washington.

■ **12 Foundry United Methodist Church,** northwest corner of 16th and P Streets. Foundry Methodist belonged to the period of 16th Street development in which the boulevard began to be referred to as the "Street of Churches." Following the common pattern of wealthier congregations of the era, Foundry Methodist—founded by Georgetowner Henry Foxall, who operated the Foxall-Columbia Foundry on the Potomac—moved uptown from a downtown location. The present Foundry Methodist Church was built in 1903-4 on the plans of prolific and versatile Washington architect Appleton P. Clark Jr., who was largely responsible for an important revision of the District of Columbia building code at the turn of the century.

Foundry Methodist has always been a socially active congregation and has developed many programs to serve the "free community" that grew up in this area in the 1960s. It has worked well with the changing demographics of the surrounding neighborhood. The congregation remains one of Washington's largest, even though most members live in the suburbs.

■ **13 Jewish Community Center,** southeast corner of 16th and Q Streets. It was quite an achievement in 1910 for the Jewish community in Washington (then centered in the old Southwest section) to be able to build an imposing building on 16th Street. The limestone structure—a work of B. Stanley Simmons—is in the classical manner, and perhaps its style and mass were inspired by the Carnegie Institution, built two years earlier. The classical tradition was rarely employed in the design of the Jewish religious structures. The University of the District of Columbia owned this building until 1990, when it was repurchased by a local Jewish group to be returned to its original use. It has been renovated as a Jewish community center, offering theater, meeting rooms, and a health club to the public.

■ 14 **C. C. Huntley House,** 1601 16th Street NW. This bracketed, stuccoed house is notable as one of the earliest examples of brick row houses on 16th Street and because its important stable building survives. The house was built in 1878 for C. C. Huntley, one of the principal owners of land along 16th Street.

C.C. Huntley House

■ 15 **The Cairo,** 1615 Q Street NW. This building was designed and built in 1894 by Thomas Franklin Schneider, who eventually built more than 2,000 structures in Washington, most in a very idiosyncratic interpretation of the Richardsonian Romanesque. Schneider here combines neo-Moorish and art nouveau elements in the facade of what is still the city's tallest nonmonumental building. Note especially the wonderful carved elephants.

The Cairo's 165-foot height so shocked turn-of-the-century, row house Washington that Congress imposed severe height restrictions in 1910 that in large part continue to shape the skyline of city. The Cairo was opened as a first-class residential hotel, fell on hard times in the mid-20th century, and was restored as rental apartments in 1976. The sponsor of the restoration was the Georgetown Inland Corporation and the architect was Arthur Cotton Moore. Although the partial federal funding of the rehabilitation required a percentage of low- to moderate-income tenants, only high-rent apartments were offered in the remodeled Cairo, a building located close to the commercial core of Washington and in the center of an a restoration area. The structure was converted to residential condominiums in 1979.

■ 16 **Church of the Holy City,** southeast corner of 16th and Corcoran Streets. Built as the Church of the New Jerusalem and dedicated May 3, 1896, it is constructed of Bedford limestone, designed on the English perpendicular order, with a good deal of French Gothic influence. The gargoyles are worth a careful look. The tower is modeled after the one over the main entrance to

Magdalen College in Oxford, England. The architect of this fine church was H. Langford Warren, head of the Department of Architecture at Harvard University, and Paul Pelz of Washington was construction overseer.

The Cairo

■ **17** The **1500 block of Corcoran Street,** immediately adjacent to the Church of the Holy City, is an interesting composite of late-19th-century domestic architectural styles in Washington row houses. A speculatively built "minor" street (originally an alley), Corcoran Street was totally restored during the 1980s and '90s by young white professionals, reflecting the trend of black displacement from the row-house blocks near 16th Street. At the turn of the millennium, this pattern has continued east beyond 13th Street NW to the Logan Circle area.

■ **18** **Denman-Hinckley House,** 1623 16th Street NW. This is one of Washington's finer Romanesque revival houses and was built in 1886 for Judge H. P. Denman. The architects were Fuller and Wheeler of Albany, New York.

■ **19** The **Mulligan House,** 1601 R Street NW. The house was built in 1911 for Navy officer Richard T. Mulligan and was designed by Jules Henri de Sibour, Washington's most gifted beaux-arts eclectic architect. The Mulligan House reflects the importance of the Georgian revival in the large-scale domestic architecture of early-20th-century Washington. The building currently houses the National Association of Colored Women's Club.

■ **20** The **Chastleton Apartments,** 1781 16th Street NW. The Chastleton opened in 1919 as an apartment hotel. It was built by Harry L. Wardman, an Englishman who came to the United States almost penniless in the 1890s and eventually built a Washington real estate empire. Wardman specialized in lavish apartment houses and luxury hotels, noted for the quality of materials and workmanship. It was Wardman who did much to introduce Washingtonians to apartment-house living.

■ 21 **Scottish Rite Temple,** 1733 16th Street NW. This is the headquarters of the Supreme Council of the Southern Jurisdiction of the Thirty-Third Degree of the Ancient and Accepted Scottish Rite of Freemasonry. The Scottish Rite Temple is one of the most architecturally significant buildings on lower 16th Street. John Russell Pope's design borrows from the famed Mausoleum of Halicarnassus. The cornerstone was laid in 1911 and the temple was dedicated in 1915. Two sphinxes by A. A. Weimann flank the main entrance to the building and represent Divine Wisdom and Power. The main space is beneath the ziggurat surmounting the Greek-temple base. The symbolism of the Masonic order is displayed in many facets of the design. For example, the Ionic columns of the colonnade are 33 feet high, representing the 33rd degree of Masonry. Despite the relation of architectural elements to the symbolism and work of the order, the temple is but a version of Pope's design for the Lincoln Memorial site.

■ 22 **Justice Brown House,** 1720 16th Street NW. The 1880s German Renaissance–style mansion of Supreme Court Justice Henry B. Brown is a rare design in Washington. The wings and carriage house along adjoining Riggs Place are superb.

■ 23 **Riggs Place NW,** one of Washington's more charming side streets, is largely a product of the speculative building activities of the 1890s. The stained glass and copper work of these modest row houses are worth noting.

■ 24 Proceed north on 16th Street through an area that is a mixture of **late-19th-century row houses** and small **early-20th-century apartment buildings.** Some of the properties had deteriorated in this vicinity, but considerable restoration took place in the late 20th century.

The 16th Street corridor in this area is zoned for medium- to high-density residential use (90-foot height limitation, 75 percent lot occupancy). Thus, from the realtor's standpoint, most of the existing structures underutilize the land. The rapidly gentrifying **14th Street corridor** two blocks to the east, ravaged by the 1968 riots caused by the assassination of Martin Luther King Jr., is experiencing retail rebirth and intense apartment and condominium construction, especially near the P Street intersection.

As 16th Street crosses U Street, it enters the **Meridian Hill district.** The major east–west artery connects the neighborhoods of Adams-Morgan and Shaw-Cardozo, with much revitalization following the 1991 opening of a Metro station on U Street at 13th and 10th Streets.

■ 25/26 **2001 16th Street NW, apartment house,** and 2101 16th Street, **The Roosevelt.** These are two of Harry L. Wardman's mammoth residential buildings of about 1916. The Roosevelt was originally an apartment hotel for the well-to-do but served as the Roosevelt Hotel for Senior Citizens from the early

1960s to the early 1990s. In 2001, the Roosevelt was renovated by a private development firm and converted into high-priced rental apartments.

■ 27 **Florida Avenue NW** (the original city limit of Boundary Street) marks the location of the fall line, which divides the older and harder Piedmont plateau from the softer deposits of the coastal plain. Merchant and mayor of Georgetown Robert Peter had assembled by 1760 some parts of a patent for land in this vicinity to form Mount Pleasant. His country farmhouse stood in the square bounded by 13th, 14th, and W Streets and Florida Avenue until the 1890s. Meridian Hill was originally referred to as Peter's Hill. In 1821 Columbian College (which grew into the George Washington University) built its first building on Meridian Hill, where it remained until moving to the downtown financial district in the 1870s. Another educational institution on Meridian Hill was the Wayland Seminary for the Training of Negro Baptist Preachers, which was built in the northeast corner of the present Meridian Hill Park in 1873.

The Meridian Hill area remained a combination of woodlots, orchards, and fields until after the Civil War. In 1867 Isaac Messmore subdivided Meridian Hill into building lots selling at 10 cents per square foot, but in those years there were few purchasers. Real estate values in this section of Washington peaked (in relation to the rest of the city) in the mid-20th century. In 1925, for example, so prestigious had the area become that the large houses on 16th Street itself sold for $250,000 and more. It was the extension of 16th Street north of Columbia Road along the true north–south line, and the bridging of Piney Branch Valley at the turn of the century, that prompted intensive development.

■ 28 **Henderson Castle Tract,** northwest corner of 16th Street and Florida Avenue NW. It was Mary Henderson, wife of John B. Henderson (the senator from Missouri who authored the emancipation amendment and cast the deciding vote that saved Johnson from conviction in his impeachment trial) who began and maintained the cultivation of 16th Street as the premier residential and embassy boulevard of Washington from the late 1880s until her death in 1931. The Hendersons bought the tract in 1887 for about $31,000, the first purchase in what would be the eventual assembly by Mrs. Henderson of a real-estate holding of some 300 city lots in the Meridian Hill area. The wall is all that remains of the turreted, crenelated, red Seneca sandstone house built in 1888 and popularly known as Henderson Castle. J. E. Gardner was the architect of the pile and J. H. Lane the builder.

From her Meridian Hill tower Mary Henderson directed her architect, George Oakley Totten Jr., in the improvement of 16th Street. She fought buses on the Avenue of the Presidents (she succeeded in having her street's name changed for one year) and Harry Wardman's apartment houses, which obstructed her view of the White House and degraded the capital city of villas. She also preached the evils of alcohol and oversaw the planning and partial construction of the great Meridian Hill Park opposite her home.

After many other plans and false starts, including proposals for a colony of homes for the elderly, the Henderson Castle tract was developed into a suburban styled, gated "colonial-style" townhouse development during the 1980s.

■ 29 **Meridian Hill Park,** east side of 16th Street between Florida Avenue and Euclid Street NW. At the turn of the century, when the White House was in a bad state of repair, it was Meridian Hill that was seriously considered for a new presidential residence. Mrs. Henderson was one of the most vocal supporters of the movement. When it became clear that the presidential mansion would not be moved to Meridian Hill, Mrs. Henderson pressured Congress to buy the site for a public park. The purchase of the 12 acres that became Meridian Hill Park was authorized in 1910.

The park is one of the most important examples of formal garden design in the United States. Actual construction did not begin until 1917, and the lower part of the park was not opened until 1936. George Burnap was the original landscape architect, and Horace W. Peaslee was responsible for the final plan and architectural design. The magnificent concrete work—in which aggregates were selected for varying sizes and colors, and the concrete was quickly washed with muriatic acid after it began to set in order to expose the aggregates—was begun as an experiment at Meridian Hill Park.

The use of massive retaining walls heightens the drama of the natural topography. The upper two-thirds of the park are designed in the formal French manner, with a large tapis vert bordered by promenades. The lower part of the park is inspired by the great Italian formal gardens of the 18th century and was later named in honor of the civil rights activist Malcolm X. An artificial cascade of 13 waterfalls of graduated size, representing the location of the park on the fall line, is the principal feature of this section. The park had become a haven for drugs and prostitution, but an organized neighborhood coalition has been largely successful in restoring a sense of safety to the park and it is often busy with strollers and impromptu games of soccer played by residents.

■ 30 **Envoy Towers Apartments,** 2400 16th Street NW. The Envoy Towers opened in the early 20th century as Meridian Mansions, a very fashionable apartment hotel, and later acquired the name Hotel 2400. The enormous structure—some of the apartments have dining rooms that seat 24 people—changed hands repeatedly in the early 1960s. After the 1968 riots, the District of Columbia leased space in the building to house displaced victims of the 14th Street civil disturbances. The handsome structure's use as this kind of housing angered many of the nearby residents. Recently, it was totally renovated and turned into condominiums and rental units.

■ 31 **Crescent Place—White and Laughlin Houses.** On the high ridge between Belmont and Crescent Places, opposite Meridian Hill Park, stand two of John Russell Pope's loveliest domestic commissions. Both represent departures from the usual ascetic classicism of Pope's work. **1624 Crescent Place NW,** in something of a Georgian Revival mode, was built about 1912 for Henry White, ambassador to France, and was long the residence of Eugene Meyer, publisher of the *Washington Post*. The building, which takes such command of a fine site, has been listed on the National Register of Historic Places and restored to its former glory. It is now a rental apartment building.

32 **Meridian House,** 1630 Crescent Place NW, is a richly decorated limestone house in the manner of an 18th-century French pavilion. It was built for Irwin Laughlin, ambassador to Spain, in 1915. The manicured garden, with its beautiful canopy of pollarded trees, is a rare example of landscaping art. The house is now the Meridian International Center.

Meridian House

33 **Council for Early Childhood Recognition,** 2460 16th Street NW. This chancery was built through the joint efforts of Mrs. Henderson and her architect, George Oakley Totten Jr. It was the first of 13 mansions erected speculatively to attract embassies to Meridian Hill. Totten, adept beaux-arts architect though he was, never escapes the late Victorian exuberance, vitality, and curiosity that shaped his early career.

34 **Inter-American Defense Board: The Pink Palace,** 2600 16th Street NW. This fanciful Venetian palace, built by the Henderson-Totten team in 1906, was

first occupied by Oscar Straus, Theodore Roosevelt's Secretary of Commerce and Labor. Mrs. Marshall Field was another prominent occupant, and for a long time the pink stuccoed house was the headquarters of the District of Columbia Order of the Eastern Star.

■ 35 **Warder-Totten House,** 2633 16th Street NW. Originally constructed in the 1500 block of K Street for a prominent real estate developer, Benjamin Warder, the sandstone house is a product of H. H. Richardson's office. George Oakley Totten bought the shell of the house from the wrecker in 1902 and stored the parts of the building until he was able to reconstruct it as his own residence. The mansion makes a far better detached villa than part of the original row-house block. The building has been converted to apartments with a nine-story building on the back of the lot facing 15th Street.

■ 36 **Former Embassy of Italy,** 2700 16th Street NW. Designed by the architects of Grand Central Station, Warren and Wetmore of New York, 2700 16th Street is an especially fine adaptation of the Italian Renaissance palazzo. The interiors are rich in works of medieval Italian art and the walled garden to the rear is an elegant, formal outdoor space that creates the illusion of being in Italy.

■ 37 **Mexican Cultural Institute,** 2801 and 2829 16th Street NW. The former Mexican Embassy, and previously the Spanish Embassy at 2801 16th Street was built for Mrs. Henderson and designed by George Oakley Totten in 1923. Mrs. Henderson had the mansion built in the hope that the federal government would purchase it as the official residence of the vice president.

2829 16th Street was built in 1911 for Franklin MacVeagh, Taft's secretary of the treasury, by his wife as a Christmas present. The architect was Washington designer Nathan Wyeth. The Italianate house is one of the most elaborate in Washington and has perhaps the largest private dining room in the city; it seats 250. The music room has an exact copy of the pipe organ at Fontainebleau. Beginning in 1934, Roberto Cuerva del Rio began his great series of murals for the new owner, the Mexican government.

Together, these two great houses and the chancery buildings to the rear facing 15th Street form what had been one of Washington's largest diplomatic complexes before the Mexican Embassy was relocated to 1911 Pennsylvania Avenue; this is one of the poorest examples of adaptive reuse in the city.

■ 38 **Harvard Square**—at the intersection of 16th Street, Columbia Road, and Harvard Street—was originally planned as a circle in honor of Civil War hero Gen. George Meade. The pleasantly landscaped area that actually developed just west of 16th Street is known, to however few, as Harvard Square. It was landscaped about 1915. Around the busy intersection are three important church buildings, erected during the years when the neighborhood was one of Washington's best residential neighborhoods. Columbia Road was here long before any other construction; it was an Indian route and later a post road to Georgetown from Baltimore. From this intersection, you are a short walk via Columbia Road to Adams-Morgan, east on Columbia Road to the recovering neighborhood of Columbia Heights, and northwest on Mount Pleasant Street to the gentrifying neighborhood of Mount Pleasant.

39 All Souls Unitarian Church, southeast corner of 16th and Harvard Streets. The architects of this skillful copy of James Gibbs's Saint Martin's-in-the-Fields, in London, were Coolidge and Shattuck of Boston. The church was constructed in 1924 at a cost of almost a million dollars.

Before the completion of the 16th Street church, the congregation was located downtown at 14th and L Streets. Today the congregation is integrated and something of a status church among Washington residents.

40 Mormon Washington Chapel, southwest corner of 16th Street and Columbia Road. This is a very interesting architectural period piece designed by Ramm Hanson and Don Carlos Young of Salt Lake City, completed in 1933. Young was the grandson of Brigham Young. Until September 1975, Washington Mormons used the elegant Utah marble edifice for worship. A gleaming, gold-leaf-covered statue of the Angel Moroni, which rested atop the lovely spire until the Mormons vacated the building, was a landmark seen from all parts of Washington. The building is now a branch of the Unification Church.

Dupont Circle

(Mixed uses and historic preservation; an area with diverse lifestyles.)

John Fondersmith, updated by G. Dan Hassman, Sherry Mauck and Ryan Harris

Distance: 2 miles
Time: 2 hours
Bus: 42 and L4
Metro: Dupont Circle (Red Line)

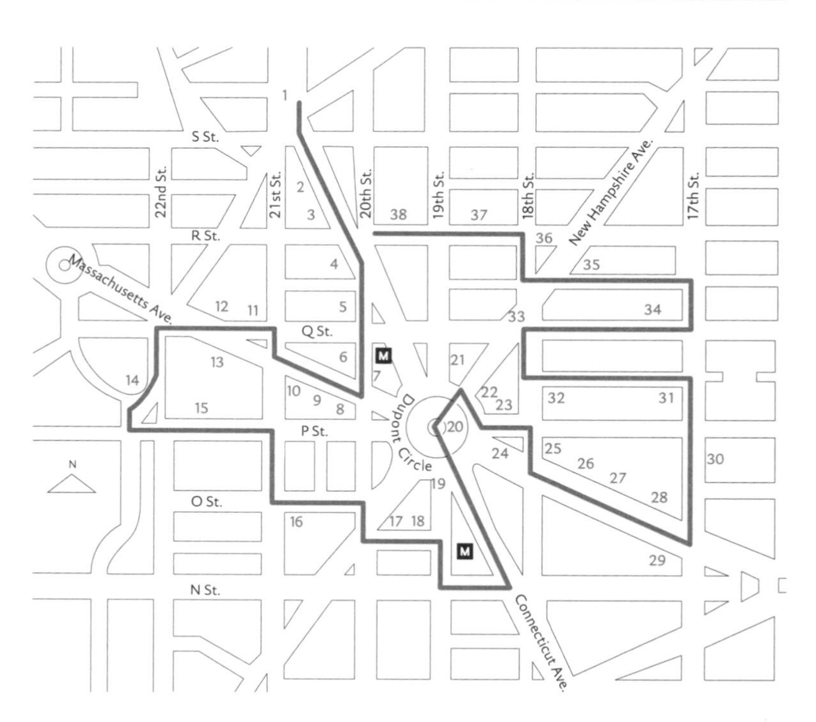

Dupont Circle is a fascinating area offering many points of interest. It was the prestige neighborhood in Washington at the beginning of the 20th century. The large mansions built by the newly wealthy from across the country reflected Washington's increasing importance on the national and world scene. The mansions also reflect the beaux-arts influence of the period and help give the neighborhood a distinguished character. In addition to these great houses are smaller townhouses and row houses along many streets, creating an intimate scale.

With the stock market crash of 1929, Dupont Circle's fortunes began to decline, and by World War II the elegance and prestige that had been slowly diminishing virtually disappeared as the mansions were converted into boarding houses for government workers. When the war was over, society had changed: commercial interests were expanding and families were moving to the suburbs. This too was reflected in the Dupont Circle area as many proud old structures were razed to make way for modern office and apartment buildings. Other large townhouses were put to use as rental apartments.

Today Dupont Circle is an area in transition. Many large row houses and apartment buildings have been renovated and converted into single-family homes or condominiums by people moving back into the city, again altering the demographic and economic balance of the community. The challenge facing Dupont Circle is to retain its historical quality, scale, vitality, and mix of residential and commercial activities while accommodating pressures for more intensive land uses and escalating housing costs.

■ 1 The tour begins at Connecticut and Florida Avenues. (Until 1902 Florida Avenue was known as Boundary Street, because it formed the original northern boundary of the city of Washington.) **Connecticut Avenue** between Florida Avenue and Dupont Circle (as well as the block south of the circle) has a bustling, cosmopolitan ambience; its array of bookstores, restaurants, cafes, antique stores, and other shops makes this one of the liveliest neighborhoods in the city. Although many of the buildings along this stretch of Connecticut Avenue date from the late 19th or early 20th century, the zoning has allowed construction of such glaring incongruities as the 90-foot-high office building housing the Benetton clothing store at 1666 Connecticut Avenue NW. Since the early 1990s, the trend toward massive, modern-style buildings has been modified. The District of Columbia Historic Preservation Office blocked the permit for an office building farther south on Connecticut Avenue, saying, "The primary standard must be that of the historic period."

■ 2 The building at **1718 Connecticut Avenue NW** demonstrates that it is possible to build attractive new buildings that do not clash with their surroundings. Designed by David Schwartz, it has been called the first really strong postmodernist building to go up in Washington. The facade features several interesting elements: the clock tower, gabled mansard roof, contrasting brick and limestone surfaces, and arched windows, all of which combine to create a modern structure that fits gracefully into its context.

■ 3 The block between Connecticut and Florida on R Street is lined with many small **art galleries** in renovated row houses. More continue to open and expand.

■ 4 The corner of Connecticut Avenue and Hillyer Place is the site of **a late-20th-century seven-story building** containing retail shops on the first floor and offices on the other six. Designed by GMR of Gaithersburg, Maryland, this structure features articulated stone entrances, window bays with keystones, and a cornice line with honed-down moldings; its style is thus architecturally consistent with its early-

1718 Connecticut Avenue

20th-century neighbors on the avenue. Its construction was the subject of much controversy and protest. The original design called for the structures on the site to be razed, including the building housing the historic Ben Bow (Ellen's Irish Pub), a popular neighborhood bar and gathering place. After months of petitioning and loud protesting, a compromise was reached; the facade of the Ben Bow was spared and is incorporated into the new structure. The bar itself, unfortunately, is gone.

Take time for a stroll down **Hillyer Place,** a short, quiet block lined with lovely trees and row houses.

■ **5** The **row of buildings** on 20th Street between Q Street and Hillyer Place represents a successful effort at preservation of old structures. These turn-of-the-century townhouses are now occupied by offices, restaurants, and shops and are an attractive feature of this part of the neighborhood.

■ **6** On the southwest corner of 20th and Q Streets, at 1520 20th Street NW, is the **Embassy of Colombia.** It was designed in 1920 by architect Jules Henri de Sibour, whose structures dot the Washington landscape. Built originally as a private residence, it was sold to the Colombian government in 1944. The house is designed in the style of a 16th- or 17th-century French country chateau. Its striking mixture of brick and limestone blocks on the facade and its wrought iron and glass marquee above the entryway are among the features that make it an interesting contrast to the buildings around it.

■ **7** Across from the embassy on Q Street is the northern entrance to the **Dupont Circle Metro station.** The precipitous descent through the circular entry into the station makes this a dramatic highlight of Washington's Metro system for tourists and commuters alike. This station is among the deepest in the system.

■ 8 At 2000 Massachusetts Avenue NW stands the **Blaine Mansion,** one of the oldest great houses to grace Dupont Circle. It was built in 1881 at a cost of $85,000 for James G. Blaine, one of the founders of the Republican Party and a three-time presidential candidate. Because it was originally designed for a different location, it seems somewhat misplaced on its present site. The dark-brick structure is an interesting combination of Victorian, Gothic, Romanesque, and Renaissance elements, with towers, seven chimneys, four skylights, and an elaborate covered carriage porch on Massachusetts Avenue.

Blaine Mansion

■ 9 Next to the Blaine Mansion at 2012 Massachusetts Avenue NW is the **Beale House,** a Renaissance Revival house constructed in 1898. The modern headquarters of the **American Home Economics Association,** it replaced a similar building to the east. If you happen to visit the area during the weekend, take time to view the produce available at the **Dupont Circle farmers market,** a well-established public amenity of the neighborhood.

■ **10** The **Indonesian Embassy,** the former **Walsh-McLean House** at 2020 Massachusetts Avenue NW, is one of Washington's truly great residences. It was designed in 1903 by architect Henry Anderson for Thomas F. Walsh, whose wealth came from his discovery and development of one of the world's richest gold mines;

it is rumored that a piece of gold from this mine is built into the foundation of the house. This ornate art nouveau mansion contains 60 rooms, some of which are among the largest, most elaborate in Washington. Throughout its history, the house has been the scene of many lavish parties, attended by such notables as Alice Roosevelt Longworth and Admiral Dewey, among many others. Thomas Walsh's daughter, Evalyn Walsh McLean, who lived in the house until 1916, was the last private owner of the Hope Diamond. In 1951 the Indonesian government bought the mansion for $355,000 for use as its embassy. A modern addition to the old building was built so that offices could be moved out of the mansion itself. Set back from Massachusetts Avenue, the curving facade of the addition was designed to respect the undulating art nouveau exterior of the original structure. The back of the new portion, situated on P Street, affords a much more jarring view, consisting of a glass-and-brick box with a cylinder attached to one side.

The **statue of Mohandas K. (Mahatma) Gandhi** (1869–1948) was dedicated in June 2000 in the pocket park at Massachusetts Avenue, 21st Street, and Q Street. The Indian American community and the Indian government created the statue and small park across from the Indian Embassy. Gandhi began a political movement aimed at creating an India free of British rule with the keynote of his political program centered on "nonviolent civil disobedience."

■ **11** Across Massachusetts Avenue, at 1600–12 21st Street NW, is the gallery housing the **Phillips Collection,** one of the most outstanding private art collections in the United States. The original brownstone structure, built in 1897, was the home of Duncan Phillips, an avid collector of the contemporary art that now fills the rooms. The collection was opened to the public in 1918. The extension, added in 1915, is stark and angular compared to the warmth of the old section.

■ **12** To the west, at 2121 Massachusetts Avenue NW, is the **Cosmos Club,** one of the most prestigious clubs in Washington. The structure was built in 1901 for railway magnate Richard M. Townsend and his wife, who superstitiously insisted that it be constructed around the shell of the home that formerly occupied this site.

■ **13** Across the street, at 2118 Massachusetts Avenue NW, is the **Lars Anderson House,** now the national headquarters of the **Society of the Cincinnati,** an organization of descendants of officers in the American Revolutionary Army. Constructed in 1900, the beautiful beaux-arts residence was one of the largest and costliest in the city and is distinguished by its early-18th-century English-style walled entrance court. The society's museum is open to the public on weekdays 1:00 p.m. —4:00 p.m.

■ **14** The **Church of the Pilgrims,** at 22nd and P Streets just south of Massachusetts Avenue, is a landmark on the western edge of the neighborhood. Across from the church in a triangular park is an incongruous memorial to 19th-century

Ukrainian national poet Taras Shevchenko. It consists of a modernistic frieze next to a traditional statue of Shevchenko. The monument was erected in 1964 amid controversy as to the suitability of a statue memorializing a Soviet national hero, but its defenders see it as a tribute to oppressed people everywhere.

■ 15 **P Street west of Dupont Circle** is a busy commercial strip, with many restaurants, stores, art galleries, and other establishments. Many of the older buildings have given way to modern high-rise apartments or hotels in which the lower floors consist of commercial space. P Street bustles day and night; some of the District's best-known night spots are here.

■ 16 **South of P Street,** between 22nd Street and New Hampshire Avenue, are several quiet, tree-lined blocks of older houses in varying stages of restoration and renovation. The residential character of this part of the neighborhood is a welcome respite from the high-rises and commercial activity of P Street and the large avenues.

■ 17 The 109-year old **Heurich House,** the home of the Historical Society of Washington, DC, for almost five decades, returned to the Heurich family in June 2003. The mansion, built in 1894 for German immigrant and brewing magnate Christian Heurich, is a splendid example of the Victorian architecture for which Washington is a treasure trove. It is the most intact late-Victorian home in the country, because only one family lived in the house and many of the original furnishings remain. The family foundation reopened the house in July 2003 as a historic house museum. The mansion's properties include the park and small carriage house along Sunderland Place. An earlier home designed by Christian Heurich in 1887 is located diagonally across the street in a building now occupied by the cultural and educational bureau of the Embassy of the Arab Republic of Egypt.

Heurich Mansion

■ **18** The **Sunderland Building** (1969—Keyes, Lethbridge and Condon) is an example of good design possible within the confines of the city's height limit.

■ **19** Walk north on New Hampshire Avenue to the **Euram Building** (21 Dupont Circle NW). It was designed by a local firm, Hartman Cox Architects, and opened in 1970. The inner courtyard is a pleasant addition urban landscape in this area.

Euram Building

■ **20** **Dupont Circle.** In 1882 an act of Congress changed the circle's name from Pacific Circle (so called because it formed the western edge of the city) to Dupont Circle, in honor of Civil War hero Rear Admiral Samuel Francis Dupont. In 1884 a statue depicting Dupont riding a horse was erected here. Public dissatisfaction with this memorial, combined with the erosion of its base, led to another congressional act in 1916 authorizing its removal and the erection of a marble memorial fountain in its place. Designed by Daniel Chester French (who also designed the statue of Lincoln in the Lincoln Memorial), the fountain consists of three figures representing sea, stars, and wind, traditional guardians of ships.

Over the years Dupont Circle has borne silent witness to the social and political changes taking place around it. It is frequently the starting point for political demonstrations and marches, and on warm days it is filled with people splashing in the fountain or relaxing on the benches around it. Permanent chess tables are located in the western part of the circle, and even on cold winter nights people congregate for spirited games.

Around the outside of the circle are entrances, now closed and filled with debris, to tunnels once used by trolleys. The two tunnels, built in 1949 to relieve congestion on the busy streetcar line have been closed since 1962, when the streetcars stopped operating. For a time they were used as fallout shelters. The tunnels are as wide as 26 feet in some sections, with 14-foot ceilings. The remnants of Dupont Down Under, an unsuccessful attempt to create an underground shopping venue in the tunnels, can be seen on either side of Massachusetts Avenue.

The windows of the CVS Pharmacy are decorated with interesting aerial photos and historical views of the streetcars in Dupont circle.

■ **21** The **Jurys Hotel** is typical of a type of design, especially for apartments, that was popular after World War II. The hotel replaced the famous Leiter mansion, one of the most fabulous houses of the time, and was considered a notable example of modern architecture when it was built in 1949. Note the bookstore to the east of the hotel, which is open 24/7 and adds to the nightlife of the area.

■ **22** The **Washington Club** now owns the **Patterson House** at 15 Dupont Circle NW. This is one of only two mansions remaining on the circle (the other is the former Wadsworth residence, now the Sulgrave Club—see this tour, no. 25) and it was possibly the most flamboyant of them all. The original owner, Elinor Patterson, was a well-known socialite, journalist, and owner of the *Washington Times-Herald*. She used this house mostly for entertaining, usually in the form of gala dinner parties. In 1927 Mrs. Patterson lent the house to President and Mrs. Coolidge while the White House was being refurbished, and they entertained the returning hero Charles Lindbergh there. Constructed in 1901–3, this building is an ornate example of neoclassical Italianate architecture. The face, of marble and glazed terra-cotta, is replete with winged figures, fruit clusters, and other elaborate ornamentation. This structure gives some idea of what Dupont Circle must have been like in its heyday, before the encroachment of "redevelopment."

■ **23** The **Embassy of Algeria,** formerly the **Boardman House,** at 1801 P Street NW, is considered one of the finest remaining Romanesque Revival houses in the city. Hornblower and Marshall built it in 1893.

■ **24** The **Sulgrave Club,** at 1801 Massachusetts Avenue NW, occupies an entire block. One corner of the triangular building points to Dupont Circle, the back is on P Street, and the front is on Massachusetts Avenue; the building's unusual site was clearly an important factor in its design. It was built about 1900 as the residence of Herbert Wadsworth and has been the home of the Sulgrave Club since 1933. This is one of the earliest beaux-arts mansions in the area and features interesting terra-cotta and cut-stone trim.

■ **25** The **National Trust for Historic Preservation** now occupies the **former McCormick Apartments** at 1785 Massachusetts Avenue NW. Constructed in 1917, this monumental beaux-arts luxury apartment building originally contained six apartments, one on each floor, along with living space for 40 servants. Considered the finest apartment building in the city, it was inhabited by such well-known personalities as Secretary of the Treasury Andrew Mellon, who lived there while planning the National Gallery of Art. The building was declared a national historic landmark in 1977 when the Brookings Institution sold it to the trust.

■ 26 The **1700 block of Massachusetts Avenue** is a study in change. It is zoned Special Purpose, a classification that allows for institutional buildings and apartments intended to serve as a buffer between the business district and residential areas.

■ 27 The **Brookings Institution,** 1775 Massachusetts Avenue NW, is a noted national research center. The original building has been expanded with additional space and uses. Across the street from Brookings is the Washington office of the American Planning Association, 1776 Massachusetts Avenue.

■ 28 The **Moore Residence,** at 1746 Massachusetts Avenue, is occupied by the **Embassy of Uzbekistan.** Constructed in 1906–9 under commission from Clarence Moore (an investor who would later go down with the *Titanic*), this residence is considered one of the finest examples of Louis XV architecture in the city. Its granite exterior, wrought-iron bar grilles, and casement windows present an orderly and symmetrical appearance.

■ 29 The section of **Massachusetts Avenue between 17th and 18th Streets** is part of the Dupont Circle historic district. The buildings between the Embassy of Uzbekistan and the corner of 17th Street and Massachusetts Avenue exhibit diverse architectural styles and periods that fit together harmoniously, unlike those across the street, which have little character and seem architecturally incongruous.

Located at 1724 Massachusetts Avenue NW, the headquarters of the **National Cable Television Association** is an example of a modern building that is nevertheless in keeping with its older neighbors. The southwest corner of 17th Street and Massachusetts Avenue is occupied by the **Chancery of Peru,** a classical Italian structure whose entrance faces the intersection.

■ 30 **Seventeenth Street** between Massachusetts Avenue and S Street is one of the most active retail and restaurant areas in the District of Columbia. Almost every block contains retail shops, bookstores, flower shops, and service establishments on the first and second floors, giving a real sense of community.

■ 31 **Church Street** is another attractive block of townhouses. At 1742 Church Street NW is the **Stanislavsky Theater Studio,** founded in 1997, which presents consistently fine productions of the work of young dramatists. Several of the houses on the west end of the block are used by small businesses and non-profit organizations, yet the street retains its residential quality.

■ 32 The **site of the original St. Thomas Episcopal Church** is now a park. The church, a splendid miniature Gothic cathedral, was destroyed by arson in 1970, but portions of the original altar and rear wall still stand at the back of the park.

The congregation now attends services in a renovated parish house behind the original church. The carefully landscaped park is a popular gathering place for lunchtime picnics, summer sunbathing, and quiet contemplation. In the shadow of the destroyed altar, the park retains a churchlike atmosphere of peace and solitude. A labyrinth has been constructed in the floor of the plaza facing 18th Street.

■ 33 The **Weeks House,** at 1526 New Hampshire Avenue NW, is now the home of the **Women's National Democratic Club.** Constructed in 1892, this turreted red brick house seems at the same time imposing and warmly inviting. An additional wing was added on the Q Street side. Tours are available by appointment.

■ 34 The **row houses** on the 1700 block of Q Street provide an indication of popular residential architecture of the late 19th century. Designed by Thomas Franklin Schneider and built in 1889–92, these stone houses are a lively mixture of Victorian architectural features, such as Richardsonian Romanesque arches, full turrets, and projecting bays. Each is different, yet taken together they form a coherent and unified whole.

Southwest corner of 17th and Q Streets

■ 35 The buildings on **Corcoran Street** were among the first in the neighborhood to be rehabilitated. This block has been almost totally restored. Notice the care and attention to detail reflected in the style and positioning of sculptures and reliefs in the houses on the south side of the street.

■ 36 Occupying a triangular site at the intersection of 18th Street and New Hampshire Avenue is the mammoth **Belmont House,** one of the largest on this tour. It was built in 1909 from the design of E. Sanson and Horace Trumbauer (the designer of the Philadelphia Art Museum) by Perry Belmont, who was a US congressman and minister to Spain at the time of the house's construction. Built in the Louis XVI style, it is massive and heavily ornamented, from the urns atop the eaves and the intricate wrought-iron balconies to the glass entrance doors. The Belmonts often held lavish parties in the exquisitely decorated rooms of this house. It was sold to the Order of the Eastern Star in 1935 and is the headquarters of that organization today.

■ **37** From the corner of New Hampshire Avenue and R Street walk past the **Thomas Nelson Page House** at 1759 R Street NW. Built in 1897, it was designed in the Federal Revival style by architect Stanford White. Farther west, between 18th and 19th Streets, are the headquarters of the **American Institute for Cancer Research** and the **World Cancer Research Fund.** The **National Museum of American Jewish Military History** is located at 1811 R Street; free admission. Both buildings feature additions that were thoughtfully designed to blend with the character and scale of the original buildings.

■ **38** The final stop on the tour is at the northeast corner of 20th and R Streets. The **Fraser Mansion,** a registered historic landmark that has housed a string of restaurants and clubs since the 1930s. It is sometimes referred to as the Scott-Thropp House because it was incorrectly thought to have been built by Thomas A. Scott, assistant secretary of war under Abraham Lincoln. The Italian Renaissance mansion was actually built in 1898 by Hornblower and Marshall for New York merchant George S. Fraser. In 1901 Fraser's widow sold it to Scott's daughter, Miriam Thropp—hence the misnomer. Marshall was probably the designer of the spectacularly ornate interior, which has recently been restored to its original grandeur, complete with beautiful carved-wood paneling in many of the rooms. The building is now the home to the **Founding Church of Scientology of Washington, DC.**

North of Downtown

Kalorama

(Historic area with embassies and beaux-arts mansions)

Perry G. Fisher, updated by John J. Protopappas

Distance: 1 1/2 miles
Time: 1 1/2 miles
Bus: N2, N4, and N6 or D2, and G2
Metro: Dupont Circle (Red Line); transfer to above bus routes or walk to Sheridan Circle

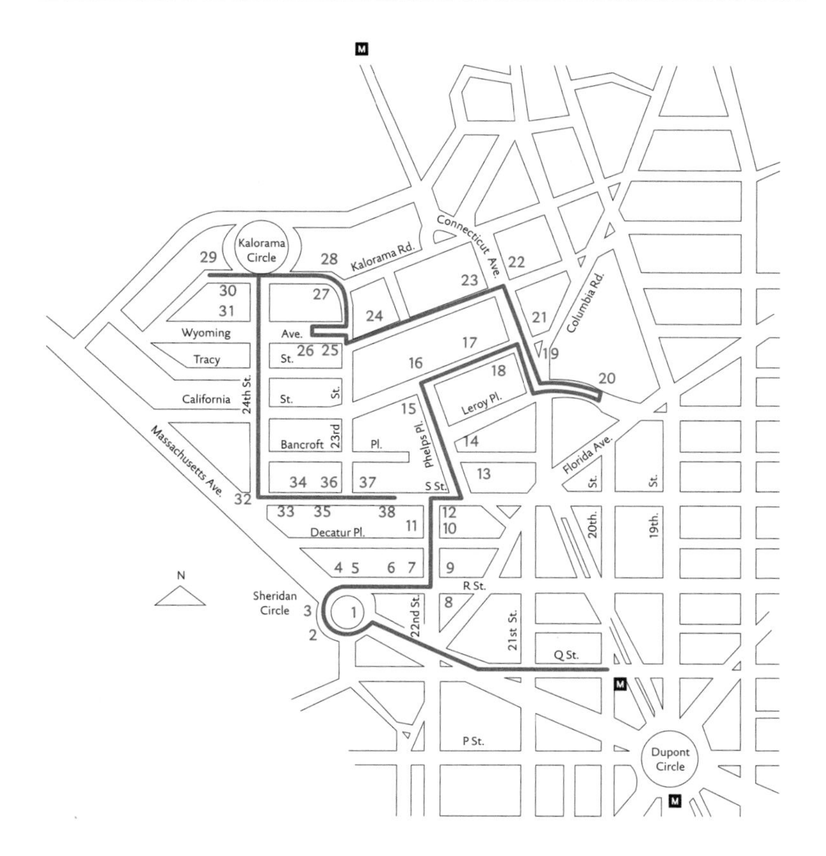

Kalorama is the center of the foreign diplomatic community and contains one of the finest collections of beaux-arts-inspired mansions in the United States. Handsomely developed, richly treed, and topographically varied, Kalorama is a pleasant island of quiet urbanity near central Washington.

For almost a century after the founding of Washington, DC, much of the elegant district was part of a large estate of great natural beauty. Superbly sited, the estate looked out over the Potomac, northern Virginia, and the infant capital city. The estate bore the same name as the modern neighborhood and was noted for its fine manor house, which stood until 1888. Kalorama was carved out of the Widow's Mite, a colonial patent of approximately 660 acres granted in 1664 to John Langworth by Lord Baltimore.

Kalorama, well known for the concentration of embassies and chanceries in its large mansions, is a phenomenon of the early-20th-century expansion of Washington. Its evolution into a beautiful and sophisticated neighborhood is closely related to several important developments: the termination in 1890 of the distinction between the City of Washington and the County of Washington (i.e., the area of the District of Columbia outside Florida Avenue); the extension of Massachusetts Avenue beyond Florida Avenue in the same period; the new bridges across Rock Creek; the commitment made in 1890 to preserve the Rock Creek Valley as a scenic and recreational resource; the proximity of Kalorama to established wealthy neighborhoods like Dupont Circle; and the filling up of older portions of the city in the dynamic post–Civil War years.

From the outset, Kalorama was intended to become a prime residential area. Intelligent and aggressive real estate promotion, very attractive building sites, and the astounding growth of the colony of wealthy people in Washington who wanted the most fashionable town residences made Kalorama. These developments provided an opportunity for architects working in the beaux-arts-influenced styles of the general classical revival period following the Chicago World's Columbian Exposition of 1893.

■ 1 **Sheridan Circle** (Massachusetts Avenue at 23rd Street). In November 1886 the Commissioners of the District of Columbia held public hearings to discuss plans for the extension of Massachusetts Avenue and a circle in honor of Stephen Decatur. The widow of George Lovett, last private owner of the Kalorama estate, protested the proposed improvements affecting her property. However, a New York real estate firm paid the Lovett heirs $354,000 for the remaining 60 acres of the estate. At an astonishing $5,900 an acre (in 1887), subsequent development by owners of the planned Kalorama Heights subdivision had to be either for a very wealthy population or for a very high-density population. It is clear to anyone standing in Sheridan Circle today that the new owners decided on the former type of development.

Decatur Circle became Sheridan Circle in 1890, when the officers of the Army of the Cumberland received authorization to commission a statue of Gen. Philip H. Sheridan, a Civil War hero who had died in 1888. Gutzon Borglum (sculptor of Mount Rushmore) was commissioned, and the model of his equestrian statue of Sheridan was accepted in January 1908. The statue was erected the following year. In the past, the statue has been compared to a traffic cop stuck in mud, but the harshness of critical opinion of the work has lessened over time. Mrs. Sheridan, of course, loved it instantly, and to be close to it she had built what is now the house at 2211 Massachusetts Avenue NW in 1905.

Sheridan Circle is perhaps the only one of Washington's circles that has maintained its grand residential character. It was the earliest part of the Kalorama neighborhood to develop, and the circle was a natural focus for neighborhood growth. Sheridan Circle is enclosed by a group of early-20th-century mansions whose mass, detailing, and styles are reflective of the wide, baroque boulevards of L'Enfant's original plan for the capital city. Embassies are now located in these buildings. Around the circle you can see the Greek, Korean, Rumanian, and Turkish Embassies, among others.

■ 2 The **Alice Pike Barney Studio House,** at 2306 Massachusetts Avenue NW next to the Korean Embassy (on the right), is now owned by the Smithsonian Institution. It was built in 1903 by Alice Pike Barney, a wealthy playwright and painter, for her many artistic pursuits and informal entertainments. The house, influenced by the mission style of architecture, was designed by Waddy Butler Wood of Washington. It includes studio and stage facilities and an interesting collection of 17th-century Spanish furniture. The Barrymores, Caruso, and James Whistler were among those Alice Barney entertained here.

■ 3 The **Edward H. Everett House,** now the **Embassy of the Republic of Turkey,** is located at 1606 23rd Street NW. It was built by Edward H. Everett, a multimillionaire capitalist-industrialist. Much of his fortune was the result of his patent on the modern fluted bottlecap. The architect of the Everett mansion was George Oakley Totten Jr. Begun in 1910, the house was not completed until 1915. As in so many of Totten's buildings, classical details are combined in a personal and idiosyncratic manner. Totten was too aware of architectural developments in America to remain uninfluenced by the pioneering work of Midwestern and California architects that was contemporary with the full-blown beaux arts. This native influence shows in features like the trellised roof garden on the Q Street side of the house. Similarly, the impact of Totten's time in Turkey shows in such features as the elaborate interior carving. It is hardly surprising that the Turkish government admired this house and has occupied it since late 1932.

■ 4 A **section of the Egyptian Embassy** is located at 2301 Massachusetts Avenue NW in the **Lieutenant Joseph Beale House.** The gently curved facade of this magnificent 18th-century Italian-inspired palazzo contributes a beautiful transition from R Street to Massachusetts Avenue. The architect of the detached house was Glenn Brown, who from 1899 to 1913 was secretary of the American Institute of Architects. The austerity of the exterior of the limestone and stucco mansion is not matched within. In 1928 Egypt acquired the Beale House for its ambassadorial residence.

■ 5 The **Embassy of the Philippines,** at 2253 R Street NW, is located in the **Gen. Charles Fitzhugh Residence** (1904). The scale of the building is somewhat

Turkish Embassy

smaller than that of most of the houses around Sheridan Circle, but the Fitzhugh residence holds its important position by clarity of form, plain surfaces, clearly articulated openings, and basic horizontality. Waddy Butler Wood, the architect, was subject to strong Mediterranean and even Wrightian influences; the unusual use of segmentally arched windows under the eaves is a typical Wood curiosity.

■ 6 Of the **row of three houses** at 2225, 2223, and 2221 R Street NW, the central building was the first constructed. It was built in 1904 for Alice Pike Barney, who just a year earlier had opened her studio house on Sheridan Circle. In 1931 Charles Evans Hughes, chief justice of the United States, purchased the house and lived there until his death in 1948. The government of Burma has been the owner since. George Oakley Totten Jr. was the architect of all three dwellings in the group. The smaller, stuccoed houses flanking the Barney residence were constructed in 1909. In general they harmonize well with the Fitzhugh residence just down the street. The repeating porte cocheres add great charm to the street.

■ 7 The **Gardner Frederick Williams House,** now the **Embassy of Pakistan's army, navy, and air attaché's office,** is located at 2201 R Street NW. This imposing, straightforward, clean-lined house was built in 1906–7 for Gardner Frederick Williams, a mining engineer who had been associated with Cecil Rhodes in Africa. George Oakley Totten Jr. was the architect.

■ 8 The **Palmer House,** at 2132 R Street NW, is a handsome Georgian row house and the home of A. Mitchell Palmer while he served as Woodrow Wilson's attorney general. Palmer was one of the chief figures in the "Red Scare" paranoia that swept the country after World War I; he saw communists everywhere. On June 2, 1919, an unidentified terrorist tossed a bomb into the Palmer home and in the process destroyed himself. Palmer was in the house at the time, but was uninjured.

■ 9 The **Franklin D. Roosevelt Residence,** now the **Embassy of Mali,** at 2131 R Street NW, is where Franklin Roosevelt lived from 1917 to 1920, while serving as assistant secretary of the navy. The house has 17 rooms and 6 1/2 baths and was well suited to the needs of the growing Roosevelt family. The house serves as the residence of the ambassador of Mali.

■ **10** In 1906 wealthy Boston spinster Martha Codman built her magnificent Washington home at 2145 Decatur Place NW. The designer was New York society architect Ogden Codman, one of her relatives. The **Codman House** is especially attractive because of its cherry-red brick and beautifully dressed stone. Although 18th-century England is the architectural inspiration, the approach to the house recalls a Parisian hotel. The superb garden terraces and the block of the mansion itself act as massive retaining walls for the Decatur Terrace slopes. The Codman House became the Louise Home in the early 1950s, when the original Louise Home for poor but genteel Southern Protestant ladies was demolished to make way for the apartment house at 1500 Massachusetts Avenue NW.

■ **11** Designed and constructed by the Office of Public Buildings and Grounds in 1911–12, the delightful **Decatur Terrace Steps and Fountain,** at 22nd Street between Decatur Place and S Street, solved the problem of linking Decatur Place with much higher S Street, in favor of the pedestrian. It is a rare occurrence in an American city when a street becomes a staircase, and Washington's example is unknown to many residents.

■ **12** The home located at 1743 22nd Street NW was built in 1904–5 for **Charles D. Walcott,** secretary of the Smithsonian Institution and a real estate promoter in northern Washington. The architect was George Oakley Totten Jr. in partnership with Laussat Rogers. The house has been modified and altered, but originally it was a beautiful Italianate mission–style home that took command of its fine site.

■ **13** Closer to Connecticut Avenue, the character of Kalorama changes. As early as 1873, streetcars ran along Connecticut Avenue from 17th Street to Florida Avenue. In the blocks of Kalorama adjacent to this major diagonal avenue of L'Enfant's plan is the speculative row-house development typical of a streetcar suburb; **1801–9 Phelps Place** is a good example of the pattern. The row was built in 1896 by William Alexander Kimmel, an active speculator and building contractor responsible for 17 Washington churches in addition to countless houses. Most of the Phelps Place buildings now serve foundation or educational purposes. The row houses of the nearby blocks of S Street near Connecticut Avenue, as well as Bancroft and Leroy Places, have long been popular with government officials. There was an especially heavy concentration of prominent New Deal personalities in this section of Kalorama. Most of the pleasant row houses in this favored district were built between 1900 and 1915.

■ **14** The **Conrad Miller Residence,** at 1823 Phelps Place NW, now has **offices of the Russian Federation.** It was designed by Washington architect Thomas Franklin Schneider for Conrad Miller, celebrated lecturer and publisher, and his wife, Anna Jenness Miller, author and lecturer. It was constructed in 1896–97 and displays all of Schneider's full-blown mannerisms.

■ **15** At the southwest corner of Phelps Place and California Street NW is the **St. Rose's Industrial School,** more recently used as the **Mackin Catholic High School for Boys,** which has been closed. Organized originally in a downtown location in 1872, St. Rose's Industrial School (for the training of orphan girls in home economics and "feminine" manual arts) was built about 1904 in what was then open country. Later the building became the St. Ann's Infant Asylum. In the 1960s it was the Cathedral Latin School and the Mackin Catholic High School. The impressive Roman brick and brownstone structure is one of the few buildings in Kalorama not intended as a residence. A structure of this size would not be permitted in the area if built today.

■ **16** The **2100 and 2200 blocks of California Street.** At California Street, Connecticut Avenue, and Columbia Road is the only concentration of large apartment houses in the Kalorama district. At the turn of the century the height above Florida Avenue attracted massive apartment house development, which aroused the ire of many residents who felt that such structures were alien to the character of the city.

■ **17** Typical of the grander apartment houses of about 1905, **California House,** located at 2205 California Street NW, has very large, handsomely appointed apartments. Justice Louis Brandeis resided here for many years.

■ **18** The **Westmoreland,** at 2122 California Street NW, was built in 1905. It is a fine example of Washington's "apartment-house baroque" architecture and now is a cooperative apartment development.

■ **19** **Equestrian statue of Maj. Gen. George B. McClellan,** Connecticut Avenue and Columbia Road. The bronze statue, completely lacking in personality, of the commander of the Army of the Potomac was designed by Frederick MacMonnies in 1907 and rests on a base designed by James Crocroft. MacMonnies had attracted worldwide attention and praise with his sculpture for the World's Columbian Exposition in 1893.

From the vantage point of the Lothrop House site (see this tour, no. 21), one can imagine the wonderful view that the early houses on Kalorama Heights must have had. The commanding view was possible until the development of the Washington Hilton Hotel site across Columbia Road from the Lothrop mansion.

■ **20** At Columbia Road and T Street is located the **Washington Hilton Hotel–Universal Office Building.** The large tract of land occupied by the Hilton and large office buildings directly south was long called Oak Lawn, after the huge and ancient oak tree that stood there. In the 1920s the site was proposed to accommodate a national Masonic memorial, which resulted in the submission of an interesting scheme by Frank Lloyd Wright. The erection of the hotel in the early 1960s totally changed the fabric of this neighborhood. The attempted assassination of President Ronald Reagan took place at the entrance to this hotel.

■ **21** At the northeast corner of Connecticut Avenue and California Street is the **Alvin Mason Lothrop House,** now part of the Russian Federation offices. This 40-room, Italianate limestone mansion was built in 1901 for Alvin Mason Lothrop, partner in the dry-goods firm of Woodward & Lothrop (once Washington's largest department store and now closed). The architects were Joseph Hornblower and James Rush Marshall.

Alvin Mason Lothrop House

■ **22** Of all the mammoth luxury apartment buildings erected on this stretch of Connecticut Avenue in the early 20th century, the **2101 Apartments** are perhaps the most impressive. Built in 1928 by the same firm that built the Shoreham Hotel, it has only 66 apartments. All have at least seven rooms with three baths and three exposures. Of special interest are the sculptured parrot gargoyles and lion's-head medallions above the entrance portals. Some of Washington's most prominent people have lived here. In its art deco decorative flair and in its excess of elegant spaciousness, the building might be considered the last of the truly lavish and significant phase in grand apartment house construction in Washington.

■ **23** The **Mortimer J. Lawrence House** (1907), at 2131 Wyoming Avenue NW, was built for Mortimer J. Lawrence, the publisher of *The Ohio Farmer, The Michigan Farmer,* and *The Pennsylvania Farmer.* He was a Cleveland bank president as well. The house was Lawrence's wedding gift to his bride, Carrie Snyder. Both were infatuated with Italy and had their architect, Waddy Butler Wood, model the house after a Tuscan villa. Throughout, there is fine marble and mosaic work; barely any surface, interior or exterior, is wood. Note the beautiful soffiting.

■ 24 The **William Howard Taft House** was the home of former President Taft from the time he returned to Washington as chief justice of the united States, in 1921, until his death in 1930. Mrs. Taft lived on in the house until her death in 1944. Taft purchased the large, Georgian Revival–style house from Massachusetts congressman Alvin Fuller. The building was constructed about 1904.

■ 25 The **Anthony Francis Lucas Residence,** now the **Embassy of Zambia,** is located at 2300 Wyoming Avenue NW. The cost of this delightfully pretentious house at the time of its construction in 1913 was an incredible $20,000. The architect was Clark Waggaman, a local resident, who during his short career specialized in large suburban homes for the wealthy. Undoubtedly, this house is one of the most unusual in the city, so closely is it tied to the products of Italian mannerism, particularly the work of an architect like Giulio Romano. The most important space in the building is the two-story room behind the loggia on 23rd Street. The roof groin is vaulted and splendidly articulated. The dining room is noteworthy for its richly carved oak paneling.

■ 26 The **Warren G. Harding Residence,** at 2314 Wyoming Avenue NW, is where Harding lived as senator from Ohio from 1917 until becoming president in 1921. The house is more important for its historical than for its architectural values. However, the use of a side entry is unusual in Washington, and the interesting use of classical elements and overall sculptural quality make the building more intriguing than a first glance might acknowledge.

■ 27 The former **Royal Thai Legation,** at 2300 Kalorama Road NW, is one of the few Kalorama buildings built for a foreign mission. The Royal Thai Legation dates from about 1915. Note the Eastern symbolism incorporated into the concrete works, for example, the garudas (a mythological bird that was the vehicle of Vishnu) atop the pilasters of the Kalorama Road facade.

■ 28 The **W. W. Lawrence House** is now the **Embassy of France.** Located at 2221 Kalorama Road NW, it occupies a dramatic and beautiful site high above Rock Creek and is the largest house in Kalorama. It was built in 1911 for W. W. Lawrence, whose fortune was made in mining. The government of France purchased the house in January 1936 for about $400,000, including furnishings and household equipment. The Kalorama Road mansion has served as the residence of the French ambassador ever since.

The architect of the splendid Tudor house was Jules Henri de Sibour, who was born in France in 1872 but grew up in the United States. De Sibour, who studied architecture at the Ecole des Beaux-Arts, had an extremely successful Washington career. He worked most often in eclectic borrowings from French classicism, and thus the house for W. W. Lawrence marks an unusual venture into the Tudor country manor house heritage. The mansion is actually perfectly symmetrical, but it creates the impression of a rambling asymmetry because it is impossible to approach head-on from any of the surrounding streets.

■ **29 The Lindens,** 2401 Kalorama Road NW. The section of Kalorama west of the French Embassy dates entirely from the period since 1925. Kalorama Circle is unusual among the circles of Washington in that it was planned for development, rather than as a public park. None of the houses on the circle is especially good architecture, but the overall quality of development, the superb views across **Rock Creek Park,** and the cut-off, quiet character of the neighborhood keep this one of the city's most expensive and prestigious sections. By way of comparison over time, the two charming Tudor, or Norman, stone houses at 33 and 29 Kalorama Circle were designed by Horace W. Peaslee and built in 1926 for Leslie F. R. Prince for a combined price of $45,000. And the decade of the 1920s was a period of extreme inflation!

In this neighborhood of re-created historical styles, the Lindens is an example of the real thing—almost. The Georgian house was actually built in 1754 in Danvers, Massachusetts, for Marblehead merchant Robert Hooper. The Lindens served as the summer home of Thomas Gage, the last royal governor of Massachusetts, and for this reason is sometimes known as the Gage House. The Robert Hooper mansion was moved to Washington by Mr. and Mrs. George Maurice Morris in 1936. At the time, they were searching for a suitable home for their antiques, and by acquiring the Lindens, the Morrises spared the house from planned destruction. Walter Macomber, resident architect of Williamsburg, directed the disassembly of the building, which was carried out by Williamsburg workmen.

■ **30/31** The **Devore and Stewart Residences,** 2030 and 2000 24th Street NW, were built for two sisters whose father, Canadian-born Wisconsin lumber magnate Alexander Stewart, had in 1909 built the family's first Washington home at 2200 Massachusetts Avenue NW on the site of the Kalorama estate cemetery. In 1931, 2000 24th Street NW was built. The architect was New Yorker William L. Bottomley, who has been described as the "master of the old new House," and the Devore residence justifies his reputation. It is a limestone demipalace in the style of a French hotel of the Louis XV period. In 1961 G. Howland Chase offered 2000 24th Street NW to the US government as a permanent home for the chief justice of the United States, along with an endowment to maintain it. The government refused the gift offer. A minor scandal erupted in 1982 when the public learned that the Roman Catholic Diocese of Washington planned to buy the home for its bishop. The building was subsequently purchased as a conference-reception center for a Christian businessmen's organization.

The Lindens

In 1938–39 the other sister built 2030 24th Street NW next door. The architect was Philadelphian Paul Cret. Again, France is the source of the design, although in the Stewart house there is a sort of Morman country house inspiration. The stonework and detailing are exquisite throughout.

■ 32 Proceed south on 24th Street and take note of the many embassies along the way. When you reach S Street, you will see to your right the **Robert Emmett statue,** located at the corner of 24th and S Streets near Massachusetts Avenue. Emmett was an Irish revolutionary who looked to America as a guide to his country's independence. The Hon. Victor J. Dowling, chairman of the Emmett Statue Committee, presented this statue to the Smithsonian Institution on June 28, 1917, in the presence of President Wilson. It was erected on this site on April 22, 1966, 50 years after the proclamation of Irish independence.

The quote on the back of the statue reads: "I wished to procure for my country the guarantee which Washington procured for America. I have parted from everything that was dear to me in this life for country's cause. When my country takes her place among the nations of the earth then and not until then let my epitaph be written."

■ 33/34 Next, proceed east on S Street and visit the **Woodrow Wilson House** (2340 S Street NW) and the **Textile Museum** (2310–30 S Street NW). Both are open to the public and well worth seeing.

Woodrow Wilson House

■ **35** The **William A. Mearns Residence,** at 2301 S Street NW, was built in 1906 for Mearns, a banker and president of the Washington Stock Exchange. The architects were Frost and Granger of Chicago.

■ **36** The **Gales-Hoover House,** 2300 S Street NW, now the **Embassy of Burma,** was one of the earliest houses built on Kalorama Heights. This house was originally the home of Maj. Thomas M. Gales, who was connected with the realty firm that developed the Kalorama section. The Gales House was built in 1901–2 and the architect was Washingtonian Appleton P. Clark Jr. It is unmistakably a late-19th-century house trying desperately to become Georgian. It is far more famous as the home of Herbert Hoover, who moved here in 1921, when he was appointed secretary of commerce by Harding and who returned here after serving as president. Precisely in front of the Hoover

House, in the middle of S Street, is the location of the original Kalorama mansion, which stood until 1888, when it was demolished to accommodate the building at S and 23rd Streets.

■ 37 **Mitchell Playground** and the site of the **Kalorama Square** development (north side of S Street between 23rd and 22nd Streets). The land for Mitchell Playground was donated to the city by Mrs. E. N. Mitchell in 1918. She and her husband had planned a large residence there, but his death terminated the project. The only proviso of Mrs. Mitchell's generous bequest was that the city care for the grave of her pet poodle, Bosque, perpetually. The dog's grave remains, surrounded by a white chain fence, in the middle of the play area.

The fortresslike Kalorama Square townhouse project represents an important chapter in the long development of Kalorama. The pseudo-Georgian dwellings are the enterprise of a Kalorama resident, architect Walter Marlow. A landscaped central mall covers the parking area between the rows of houses.

■ 38 The **Frederick A. Delano House,** now the **Embassy of Ireland,** is located at 2234 S Street NW. Georgian Revival architecture dominates the upper portions of Kalorama. It was the most popular style of domestic design in early-20th-century Washington. Waddy Butler Wood designed this house for Frederick A. Delano, an uncle of Franklin D. Roosevelt and president of the Wabash and several other midwestern railroads.

Adams-Morgan

(Grand apartment houses, lively commercial area, ethnically diverse neighborhood)

Anthony Hacsi and Susan Harlem, updated by Ryan Harris and Alvin R. McNeal

Distance: 1 3/4 miles
Time: 1 1/2 hours
Bus: L4
Metro: Woodley Park/Zoo/Adams Morgan (Red Line)

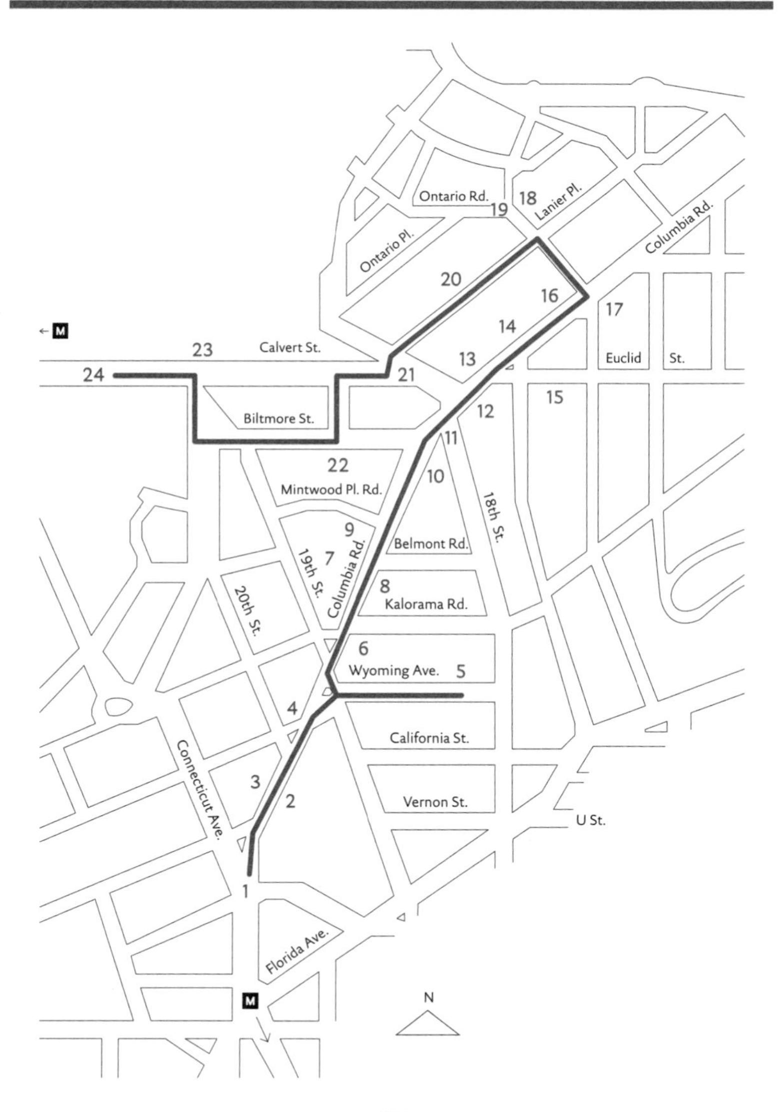

Adams-Morgan is now Washington's most ethnically and economically diverse neighborhood, but it started as a community for the wealthy. A hundred years ago the area was mostly rural. With cool breezes and good views of the city, its location on a hill made it attractive, but before the extension of streetcar service in the 1890s, it was not practical for many to live so far from the city. In about 1900 construction began on large apartment houses and roomy row houses, and most of the buildings now in the area were in place by 1920. What in the 1950s would come to be called Adams-Morgan then consisted of handsome subdivisions known as Washington Heights, Lanier Heights, Meridian Hill, and Cliffbourne. For the first half of the century the area was known for its elegance and its many politically or socially prominent residents.

With the Great Depression and later the World War II housing shortage, the area began to decline. Townhouses were converted to rooming houses, and large apartments were split into smaller units. In the postwar years, middle-class flight to the suburbs was coupled with an increase in lower-income residents. The new people found the area a good place to live but, along with longtime residents, they became concerned about further decline. Although local citizens' organizations had been active since before the turn of the century, cooperation between the racially segregated groups failed, and a new integrated organization was formed in 1955. Taking the names of two elementary schools in the area, the all-white Adams and all-black Morgan, it was called the Adams-Morgan Better Neighborhood Conference. It marked the beginning of an era of increased neighborhood activism, and it created a new name for the area. An urban-renewal plan that evolved from the citizens' concerns was debated through the early 1960s but was never adopted. It was rejected largely because of fear of the displacement that had resulted from other urban-renewal projects, particularly in Southwest Washington.

During the 1960s Adams-Morgan became known as the Hispanic center of Washington. Unlike Hispanic enclaves in other American cities, Washington's is heterogeneous, with representation from the Caribbean, Mexico, Central America, and South America. (At one time a plan was proposed to develop a highly commercial "Latin Quarter" here.)

Another group of "immigrants"— young middle-class whites—arrived in the 1970s. In a pattern repeated in inner cities across America, they found the close-in, low-cost housing very attractive. With higher demand, widespread renovation, and real estate speculation, prices soared. The displacement of the poor, feared in the 1960s as part of organized urban renewal, has become a reality as a consequence of the gentrification that began in the 1970s. Shoppers frightened away from Adams-Morgan by its proximity to the 1968 riots have returned. New stores and restaurants, often appealing to the middle class, open with increasing frequency. Merchants are advertising Adams-Morgan as Washington's "Village," and many Washingtonians are predicting, as often as not with regret, that it will become another Georgetown. The main question concerning Adams-Morgan's future is whether it will retain its "Unity in Diversity" (the area's motto) or return to the posh district it was in its early years.

■ 1 **Columbia Road** was an Indian footpath before the District of Columbia was established and then an early post road between Georgetown and Baltimore. In the early 19th century it was known as Tayloe's Lane, when it led to a popular race track near 14th Street, where Gen. John Tayloe (for whom the Octagon House was built—see Tour 7, Foggy Bottom, no. 21) and others ran their horses. It has always been Adams-Morgan's main thoroughfare, and has become a major commercial street for the area. Over the years, Columbia Road has evolved into one of the more colorful and diverse thoroughfares in Washington. Neighborhood and international restaurants are juxtaposed with nightclubs, bookstores, antique shops, and neighborhood grocery stores. As you walk up Columbia Road, to your left is Kalorama Triangle (its other two sides are Connecticut Avenue and Calvert Street—see Tour 14, Kalorama), Adams-Morgan's wealthiest section and one that has remained largely white.

■ 2 **The Wyoming,** 2022 Columbia Road NW (1905, 1909, 1911—B. Stanley Simmons). Dwight and Mamie Eisenhower and their son John lived here in apartment 210, and then in 302, from 1927 to 1935. This was their longest stay anywhere except the White House and their farm in Gettysburg. Twenty-four members of Congress and 70 high-ranking military officers have also lived at the Wyoming, and four countries have maintained their legations here. This large apartment house was constructed in three parts: the southern portion in 1905, the northern part and entrance pavilion in 1909 (you can see how the original entrance has been bricked up), and a rear addition in 1911. The monumental entrance pavilion has Corinthian columns and limestone ornamentation (note the lion's head). The original revolving doors were replaced long ago, but the pavilion retains its iron marquee. The lobby features white Italian marble walls and stairways, a tobacco leaf motif in the ceiling moldings, and mosaic tiled floors designed to simulate Oriental carpets. The largest of the 106 apartments includes five bedrooms, a parlor, a library, a reception hall, and a trunk room.

Until the Washington Hilton Hotel was constructed in the early 1960s, the Wyoming enjoyed an exceptional view of the city. In 1980 this building and two adjacent apartment houses were threatened by a proposed expansion of the Hilton, but neighborhood groups protested, and the plan was disapproved by the city zoning commission. The Wyoming was converted into condominiums in 1982.

■ 3 **Chao Phraya Gallery,** 2009 Columbia Road NW (1889—William L. Conley). The oldest building on this tour was designed as a single-family home and used as such until 1947. It was split into apartments and was once also used as a dance studio. An art gallery and home for the owners since 1979, it was extensively renovated. The eclectic design combines classical elements with a homey front porch and Victorian hooded windows. Notice how the first-floor columns and pediment are imitated on the third floor.

Chao Phraya Gallery

■ 4 **The Altamont,** 1901 Wyoming Avenue NW (1915–16—Arthur B. Heaton). Col. George Truesdell, a commissioner of the District of Columbia from 1894 to 1897, lived on this property for many years in his mansion, Managasset, before he had The Altamont built. It was designed in the Italian Renaissance style and has a tile roof with twin towers, a loggia, vaulted frescoed ceilings in the entrance halls, an Italian carved stone mantel and fireplace in the reception room, and patterned tile floors in the public hallways. The original tenants were offered an exceptional array of amenities: fireplaces, wallpapered bedrooms, copper cooking utensils, garbage incinerators, sitz baths, some oval and circular rooms, and sweepers in each apartment connected to the vacuum-cleaning plant in the basement. The upper floors contained only three apartments each: one with three rooms plus bath, and two with 12 to 13 rooms plus five baths and a sleeping porch. Many of the large apartments were divided into smaller and less expensive units during the Depression. The seventh floor originally had the Palm

Room, a cafe opening onto the loggia, and additional kitchens for entertaining. These spaces, along with the former billiard room in the basement, have been converted into apartments. The Altamont has been a cooperative since 1949.

The **Adams Elementary School,** the source of half of the name of this community, is located south on 19th Street at California Street. It was named for John Quincy Adams. The former **Morgan Elementary School,** now the Marie Reed School, is at 2200 Champlain Street NW. Thomas P. Morgan was a commissioner of the District of Columbia from 1879 to 1883.

■ 5 **Admiral Peary Residence,** 1831 Wyoming Avenue NW (1913—George N. Ray). Adm. Robert E. Peary, who led the first expedition to reach the North Pole in 1909, bought this house in 1914 and died here on February 20, 1920.

■ 6 The **Kalorama,** 1882 Columbia Road NW (1910—Merrill Vaughn; 1913—northern addition, Appleton P. Clark Jr.). To the casual observer it may not be apparent that the Alwyn was designed in two stages by two different architects. This is because Appleton Clark's addition has the same scale, wall surface, and roof style as the original. But while Merrill Vaughn's portion has squared corners and many oval and circular windows, Clark's has a rounded corner and only squared windows. Clark also added wrought-iron balconies, decorative carving, and a corner tower. The *K* on the tower refers to the 1913 owner, William Pitt Kellogg, a US representative, senator, and governor of Louisiana. A somewhat incompatible penthouse structure was added in the early 1990s.

■ 7 **Kalorama Park,** with its fine old oak trees, is all that remains of the woods and farms that once covered the entire area from Florida Avenue to Rock Creek. In 1828 Anna Maria Thornton, wife of architect of the Capitol William Thornton, sold two large farms to Christian Hines and his brother, Matthew. They planned to cultivate silkworms on the property and planted a grove of mulberry trees for this purpose. The venture was not successful, however, and the mulberry trees were eventually removed. Members of the Hines family were buried in a plot in an oak grove in the northern section of their land, now the rear of stores at 2440–44 18th Street. The Hines brothers sold their property to John Little in 1836. "Little's Woods," as the area was known, became smaller and smaller as parcels were sold during the next hundred years. This last remaining section was considered for development in the 1940s, but citizen pressure to make it a public park prevailed.

■ 8 **The Norwood,** 1868 Columbia Road NW (1917—Hunter & Bell), was known only by its address until 1974, when the residents voted to name it in honor of longtime resident manager Kathryn M. Norwood. Actress Tallulah Bankhead lived here from 1918 to 1921, when she was a teenager. Her father, William B. Bankhead, was a US representative at the time and later became Speaker of the House. Her grandfather was a US senator while he lived there, from 1918 to 1922. William Edmund Barrett, author of *Lilies of the Field,* lived here in the 1970s. The Norwood's facade is extremely elaborate, with extensive white terra-cotta decoration and an ornate classical portico with flanking entrance lanterns. Above the front columns are ram's heads. Note also the swan's-neck pediment above the third floor, and the brickwork above the fifth floor.

■ 9 **The Woodley,** 1851 Columbia Road NW (1903—Thomas Franklin Schneider). This was the first apartment house on Columbia Road. It was designed and built by Thomas Franklin Schneider, architect of The Cairo (see Tour 12, 16th Street/Meridian Hill, no. 15). Schneider used light brick extensively, to simulate stone. This gives the building a heavy, solid look, reinforced by the massive porte cochere. There is less stone simulation on the upper floors, where a lighter look is desired. Note the two-story gallery and the highly decorated frieze. On the roof is a cupola, although it is difficult to see from most vantage points. The original six apartments on each floor have been broken up into efficiencies and one-bedroom units and in 1976 were converted into condominiums.

The Woodley

■ 10 **Southwest corner, 18th Street and Columbia Road** (Perpetual American Federal Savings and Loan: 1979—Seymour Auerbach). This is the site of the worst disaster in Washington's history. On this corner stood the Knickerbocker, an elegant movie palace built by Harry M. Crandall in 1915 as part of his prestigious chain of theaters. The Knickerbocker had a full orchestra, which played during intermissions, and patrons often attended in formal dress. On the evening of January 18, 1922, during the city's heaviest recorded snowfall, the roof of the Knickerbocker collapsed onto a full house, under the weight of 50 tons of snow. Rescue operations involving the fire and police departments, the Marines, and the Walter Reed Hospital Corps continued through the night, greatly hampered by the snowstorm. The final toll was 97 dead and 127 injured. Although investigations determined that the building contractor had failed to follow the design specifications, architect Reginald Geare, his career ruined, committed suicide five years after the accident. Harry Crandall hired Thomas Lamb to redesign the ruined building, and the Ambassador, another fine movie theater, opened in 1923. It was demolished in 1969 after several years of diminishing business.

The site remained vacant for the next decade. During the 1970s, community groups were successful in preventing the construction of a gas station on this prominent corner. The Perpetual American Federal Savings and Loan was constructed after months of negotiations with citizen groups, who fought for and won the right to community involvement in the bank's loan policies. The building now houses a SunTrust Bank and the District of Columbia Office on Latino Affairs. An open-air market, which had blossomed on this corner before the bank's construction, continues on the plaza. On Saturdays, the busiest day for this community market, you can buy fresh fruits, vegetables, cheeses, breads, and flowers; shop at a flea market; and enjoy an occasional concert by local musicians.

■ 11 The **intersection of Columbia Road with 18th Street** is considered the "heart of Adams-Morgan." The community's commercial section began here in the early 20th century; the 18th and Columbia Road Business Association's businesses opened their first stores near here, including Ridgewell's Caterers, Dart Drug, Toys-R-Us, and the General Store. Eighteenth Street is now a colorful shopping strip, with restaurants, cafes, and shops representing many cultures—Salvadoran, French, Mexican, West African, Jamaican, Italian, Ethiopian. There are also galleries, picture-framing shops, and antiques and second-hand stores. Angle parking has replaced parallel parking here to make room for more cars and to create a more informal atmosphere.

■ 12 **Southeast corner, 18th Street and Columbia Road** (1899 [original structure]—Waddy Butler Wood). Architect of the Department of the Interior Building and many large homes in the Kalorama neighborhood, including the Woodrow Wilson house (see Tour 14, Kalorama, no. 33/34), Waddy Wood designed this building as a single-family residence. Within four years after it was constructed, the commercial potential of this site was exploited by conversion of the first floor into a pharmacy. It continued as a pharmacy until 1969 (from 1922 to 1969 it was a People's Drugstore), and since then it has been a McDonald's. Note the steeply pitched roof with shed dormers.

■ 13 **Northeast corner, Columbia and Adams Mill Roads** (1915—B. Stanley Simmons; 1920 addition—B. Stanley Simmons and Charles S. Holloway). You should have no difficulty here in differentiating between the original building and its addition. The older tapestry-brick section was built to house shops on the ground floor and apartments on the upper floors. The newer section, with its classical facade of limestone and granite, was added as the home of the Northwest Savings Bank. From 1949 to 1969 Gartenhaus Furs was located here. The original bank vault is still in the building and has been used as a tiny auditorium for theatrical productions.

■ 14 **Avignone Frères Building,** 1777 Columbia Road NW (1928—Frederic B. Pyle). When this neighborhood was a home for wealthy people who entertained, several catering and confectionery establishments in the area served their needs. The Avignone Frères Building is the sole survivor of that era, and the caterer and restaurant was probably the oldest continuously operated business in the community until renovated as a PayLess shoe store in 1993.

■ 15 **First Church of Christ, Scientist,** 1770 Euclid Street NW (1911—Marsh & Peter and E. D. Ryerson). This classical-style church with its colonnade entrance porch is constructed of brick and limestone. There are regularly scheduled services in Spanish.

■ 16 **1743–51 Columbia Road NW.** In 1906–7 Harry L. Wardman, the most prolific Washington developer of his time, built six small apartment buildings on this site. They were designed by his chief architect, Albert H. Beers. Wardman named them the Derbyshire, the Hampshire, the Cheshire, the Wilkshire, the Yorkshire, and the Devonshire. In the early 1950s they were replaced by a Safeway grocery store, which in turn was expanded eastward in 1981.

■ 17 The **Beverly Court,** 1736 Columbia Road NW (1914–15—Hunter & Bell). For many years artists have lived and worked in this building, with its large and unusual spaces well suited for studios. After the death of Beverly Court's owner in 1977, the tenants formed an association to purchase the building. They became the first tenant's group in Washington to finance the rental-to-cooperative conversion through private lending institutions. Also in Beverly Court is Ayuda, a nonprofit organization offering legal services to low-income residents.

■ 18 **2809 Ontario Road NW** (1909). Paul Pelz, architect with John L. Smithmeyer of the original Library of Congress building, designed this house for Henry Park Willis, a secretary of the Federal Reserve Board and a framer of the Federal Reserve Act of 1914. Note the unusual rounded end walls, the arched dormers and entrance, and the lion's-head rainspout.

■ 19 **The Ontario,** 2853 Ontario Road NW (1903–4 and 1905–6—James G. Hill). Archibald M. McLachlen, founder of Washington's McLachlen National Bank, gave up his home on this property to build The Ontario. Although designed as a whole, it was constructed in two stages: the western portion in 1903–4 and the eastern, larger portion, in 1905–6. (The smaller of the two entrance porticoes served as the original entrance.) Constructed in a part of Washington that was at the time quite rural, the building had an unobstructed view of nearby Rock Creek Park and the new National Zoological Park.

Some of The Ontario's special features are the decorative keystones above the windows, cast-iron entrance doors and balconies, and a turret crowned by a cupola. Inside, there are brass mailboxes, tile-bordered floors in the lobby and hallways, and rare cast-iron staircases with marble stairs. The 20 apartments on each floor range from two to nine rooms, with 10-foot ceilings, gas-burning fireplaces, and extensive wood trim.

Architect Hill, former supervising architect of the Treasury Department, lived here from the time the building opened until he died in 1913. Other notable residents have included Gen. Douglas MacArthur, Sen. Robert LaFollette, Adm. Chester Nimitz, and, more recently, author Nora Ephron and Watergate journalist Carl Bernstein.

■ **20 Engine Company No. 21,** 1763 Lanier Place NW (1908—Appleton P. Clark Jr.). When this site for the firehouse was announced in 1906, some in the neighborhood objected to it, not only because it was on a narrow street in a residential neighborhood, but also because it was not centrally located for its area of service. The justification given was that the only nonresidential street, 18th Street, on a hill (difficult for the horses), and the price of land there exceeded the appropriation. Another factor in favor of siting the facility here may have been that, from this northern high ground, the horses could run downhill to fires. This stuccoed-brick building looks more like a Spanish mission than a firehouse. The tower was needed for drying hoses, but in this context it looks as if it should house bells. Notice how the design incorporates the rainspouts.

In 1925 the *Washington Evening Star* began an annual competition among fire stations to see which could most quickly get its fire engine out of a station. Engine Company No. 21 set a "world record" of six seconds the following year. Architect Clark lived on this block at no. 1778 from 1905 until his death in 1955. His home has been replaced by condominiums. Al Jolson's parents also lived on Lanier Place, at no. 1787, and the Stafford (1911—Hunter & Bell), at no. 1789, was one of the first two cooperatives in the city.

■ **21 Calvert Street.** From Lanier Place you reach Calvert Street (called Cincinnati Street until 1905) where it intersects Adams Mill Road (so named because it once led to a flour mill owned by John Quincy Adams). The **Beacon,** on the northwest corner of Calvert Street and Adams Mill Road at 1801 Calvert Street NW (1911—J. J. Moebs), makes maximum use of its triangular lot. The **mirror-image duplex** at nos. 1847–49 was designed by Arthur Heaton. Notice how the right facade has been simply painted and the left has fallen into disrepair. At no. 1855, The **Cliffbourne** (1905—N. R. Grimm) has an unusual variety of window heads, while next door at no. 1915, The **Sterling** (1906—Appleton Clark Jr.) has Palladian windows and a loggia on the fourth floor. On the southwest corner of Calvert Street and Cliffbourne Place, **2516 Cliffbourne**

Engine Company No. 21

Place NW (1901—Waddy Butler Wood) is a charming house with tile roof, shed dormers, two open porches, and a second-floor balcony.

■ 22 **Biltmore Street** is one of Adams-Morgan's loveliest residential streets. Named Baltimore Street until 1905, it was once known informally as General's Row because of the many military officers who lived here. Coming from Cliffbourne Place, your first view is of four large row houses, nos. 1848–50–52–54, each with its own distinctive facade. Down to the left is the duplex, nos. 1822–24 (1906—Albert H. Beers). When its building permit application was filed, the question, "Will the roof be flat, pitch, or mansard?" was answered "All kinds." Toward the other end of Biltmore Street, at no. 1940, is the tapestry-brick **Biltmore** (1913—Claughton West) with its balustraded roof and overhanging Italian cornice. There are only four apartments to a floor, and each apartment has its own fireplace. The hearths are arranged so that when one pulls a slide the ashes drop through a metal chute to a bin in the cellar.

■ 23 **Trolley turnaround.** On this site was a trolley turnaround known for many years as the Rock Creek Loop. Streetcar service, which spurred the development of

Biltmore Street

what is now called Adams-Morgan, came to the area in September 1892. The first line ran north on 18th Street, then west on Calvert, across the bridge, and north on Connecticut Avenue to Chevy Chase Lake, Maryland. In 1935 the section of the run from here to Chevy Chase was replaced by bus service, and Rock Creek Loop became the end point of the streetcar line. Streetcar service continued here until Washington's last trolleys were replaced by buses on January 28, 1962. Buses now use this loop to turn around, and a small structure from the streetcar days remains.

Another streetcar line began to serve the area in 1897, coming up Columbia Road as far as 18th Street. In 1900 that line was extended east on Columbia, then north on what is now Mt. Pleasant Street to Park Road. It was replaced by bus service in December 1961.

■ 24 **Duke Ellington Memorial Bridge** (1934–35—Paul Cret). As a requirement of its streetcar charter, the Rock Creek Railway built a 125-foot-high steel trestle bridge on this site in 1891. In 1911 it became shaky and had to be reinforced and narrowed. Finally, in 1934, construction of a replacement bridge was begun. Traffic here was too important to interrupt, so the old bridge was moved 80 feet downstream to be used as a detour until the new one was completed. To do this, the bridge's footings were put on rollers on top of parallel rails. The bridge was then moved by machinery powered by horses. Auto traffic resumed the same day, and streetcar traffic was interrupted for less than 48 hours. The new Calvert Street Bridge, as it was called for many years, was constructed of concrete faced with Indiana limestone. It was renamed in the 1970s for Washington native Edward Kennedy ("Duke") Ellington. The abutments are embellished by Leon Hermant's relief panels representing four modes of travel: ship, train, automobile, and airplane. This bridge has a reputation as the favorite Washington bridge for people seeking to leap to their death. It underwent extensive renovation in the 1980s with the addition of a security fence and railings to discourage suicides.

A pleasant way to end this tour is to stop in at the nearby Mama Ayesha's Restaurant for some Middle Eastern food, or retrace your steps to the many interesting cafes to be found on both 18th Street and Columbia Road.

Woodley Park and The National Zoological Park

(Early-20th-century apartments, National Zoo, prestige residential areas, and convention hotel area)

Floy Brown, updated by Christopher J. Alleva

Distance: 1/2 mile
Time: 3/4 hour
Bus: On Connecticut Avenue: L2 and L4; on Calvert Street: 90 and 92
Metro: Woodley Park/Zoo/Adams Morgan (Red Line)

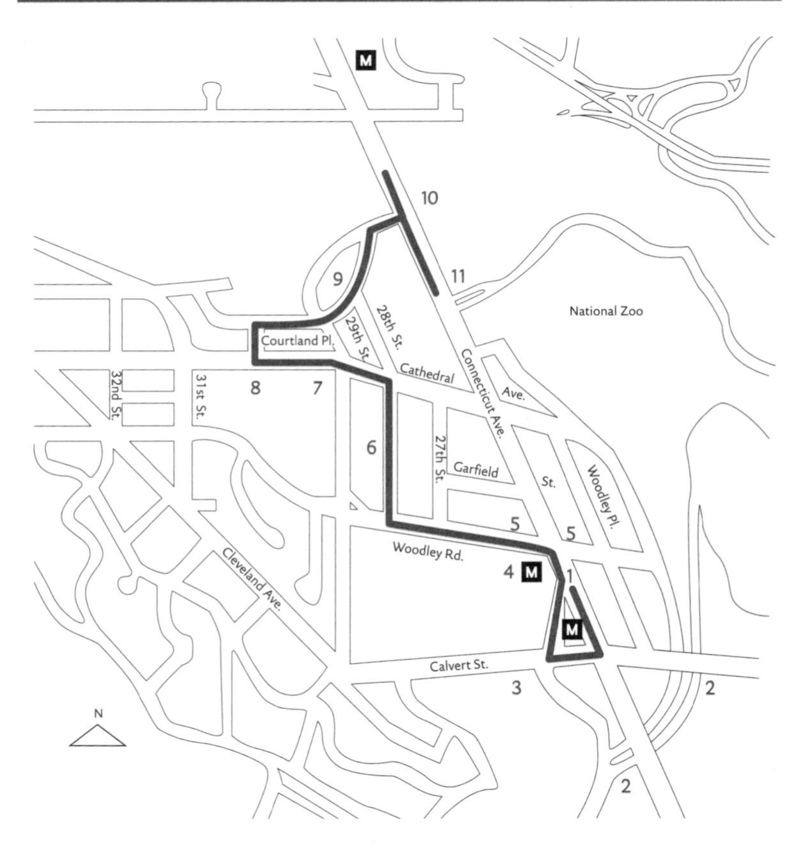

Woodley Park was originally part of a 1,000-acre tract of hilly, wooded land purchased by Gen. Uriah Forrest shortly after the American Revolution. Around 1800 the general transferred 250 acres to a wealthy Georgetown lawyer named Philip Barton Key, uncle of Francis Scott Key. The house that Key built was known as Woodley House, named after the old bachelor hall in Elizabeth Gaskell's novel, *Cranford.*

Natural topographical borders locate Woodley Park on the peak of land that rises from the valley of Rock Creek, extends northward for a mile, and then slopes downward to a spring branch of the creek. The altitude and cooler summer temperatures made the area a desirable summer retreat from the city during the 19th century.

In the 1890s Sen. Francis G. Newlands of Nevada, owner of the Chevy Chase Land Company, purchased Woodley Park. Newlands was also principal owner of the newly chartered Rock Creek Railway of the District of Columbia, a line that would connect Chevy Chase with downtown Washington. Put into operation in 1892, the streetcar route opened the area to suburban development.

This area has two of the largest convention hotels (the Shoreham and the Marriott) in the District of Columbia.

■ 1 As you exit the Woodley Park/Zoo/Adams Morgan Metro station, proceed south along Connecticut Avenue. Reflective of the eclectic residential character of Woodley Park, the shops and restaurants along Connecticut Avenue include everything from the neighborhood drugstore to international haute cuisine. Numerous **sidewalk cafes** provide congenial resting places.

■ 2 The original steel-deck truss bridge crossing Rock Creek Valley at Calvert Street has long since been replaced by the existing concrete structure, now known as the **Duke Ellington Memorial Bridge** (see Tour 15, Adams-Morgan, no. 24). The "million-dollar" **Connecticut Avenue Bridge** opened in 1907. At that time it was the largest concrete bridge in the world, and its name and presence highlighted the appeal of Woodley Park.

■ 3 Proceed west along Calvert Street. The **Shoreham Hotel,** constructed in 1930 by Harry Bralove, proved a worthy rival to the Wardman Park. It has been said that the Shoreham attracted so many prominent Washingtonians that you could ring a bell there anytime and summon a quorum of senators. Jimi Hendrix stayed at the Shoreham, where he wrote some of the lyrics to his songs on Shoreham stationary during a tour stop in 1968 at the Washington Hilton Ballroom just south on Connecticut Avenue. The hotel has recently reopened after renovation.

West of the hotel is a good example of the reuse of a public school site. The complex includes a new public elementary school for the District of Columbia school system and upscale rental apartments, developed by the LCOR, a national mixed-use developer.

■ 4 Proceed north along 24th Street back to Connecticut Avenue. At the corner of Connecticut Avenue and Woodley Road stands the **Wardman Tower,** now part of the Marriot Hotels. Harry L. Wardman, the master builder of Woodley Park, constructed the 1,500-room luxury hotel in 1918. Washingtonians called it "Wardman's Folly," little realizing that a hotel in the suburbs could prove so popular. Now primarily a residential wing of the larger complex, the tower has served as home to many of the nation's vice presidents and other VIPs. Doskned Mesrobian built the tower portion of the hotel in 1928, now a category 1 historic landmark. (The original crescent-shaped main building was demolished in the late 1970s and replaced with the present structure.)

Wardman Tower

Turn left at Woodley Road. Adjoining the original Wardman Tower at the corner of Connecticut Avenue, the complex now includes 16 acres of landscaped grounds and large convention facilities.

■ 5 The **apartment buildings** at 2700 and 2701 Connecticut Avenue NW and the extensive Cathedral Mansions at 3000 Connecticut Avenue NW are also Wardman's work. By constructing reasonably priced houses and apartments along the streetcar line, Wardman converted rural property into comfortable town living.

■ 6 Turn right onto 28th Street. The **neo-Georgian brick townhouses,** many of which have been modernized to contemporary standards, are characteristic of the Wardman subdivision south of Cathedral Avenue, known as Woodley Park. No longer a suburb, the area is desirable now to old and young alike, offering a variety of lifestyles.

■ 7 Turn left on Cathedral Avenue. Proceeding down Cathedral Avenue away from Connecticut Avenue, you pass **Single Oak,** built in the mid-1920s by Senator Newlands as a residence for a married daughter and now the home of the Swiss ambassador.

■ 8 High on a hill behind a row of stately oaks stands elegant **Woodley Mansion.** The white stucco Georgian house served as the summer home of four 19th-century presidents, including Van Buren, Tyler, Buchanan, and Cleveland. Henry L. Stimson lived there while serving as secretary of state for President Herbert Hoover and secretary of war for Franklin D. Roosevelt. The building is now owned and operated by the private Maret School.

■ 9 Turn right at the alley and cut through to Courtland Place. Take another right on Courtland Place and proceed past the playground that joins Klingle Creek Valley to Devonshire Place. Many of the homes in this mixed residential neighborhood were part of the exclusive Wardman subdivision north of Cathedral Avenue known as **English Village.** The crescent-shaped streets give a picturesque effect.

At the intersection of Connecticut Avenue and Devonshire Place, decide whether you want to see the National Zoo (see this tour, no. 11), to the south. To the north is Cleveland Park (and the nearest Metro station). Or take the Cleveland Park and Washington Cathedral Tour (Tour 17) in reverse.

■ **10** Notice the **Kennedy-Warren** apartment building, 3133 Connecticut Avenue NW, at the east side of Connecticut Avenue where it intersects Devonshire Place. It was built in the early 1930s in art deco style. Notice also the bridge of the same era and style, including eight **bridge lights** that were illuminated until a reconstruction in the late 1970s. A long-planned addition to this apartment complex, which will double its size, is scheduled to be completed in 2005. Prior to the construction of the convention hotels in the area, this complex hosted many events in its glorious ballroom.

Kennedy-Warren

■ **11** At the crest of the hill is the entrance to the **National Zoological Park,** a Smithsonian facility. Designed by the famous landscape architect Frederick Law Olmsted, the world-renowned, 175-acre zoo exhibits over 3,000 animals of more than 800 species and subspecies, many of them rare and not exhibited elsewhere in the country. The zoo's most famous residents are the giant pandas Tian Tian and Mei Xiang, in their new home since December 6, 2000. On loan for 10 years from China, the pair are the result of a negotiation with China since the passing of Hsing-Hsing on November 28, 1999. Hsing-Hsing and his mate Ling-Ling were a gift from the People's Republic of China following Richard Nixon's visit there in 1972. The zoo contains many well-marked paths that are not included in this guide. You can obtain a guidebook at the zoo shop.

Cleveland Park and Washington Cathedral

(Turn-of-the-century residences; Gothic cathedral)

Charity Vanderbilt Davidson, updated by John J. Protopappas

Distance: 2 miles
Time: 2 1/4 hours
Bus: L2, L4, H2, and H4
Metro: Cleveland Park (Red Line)

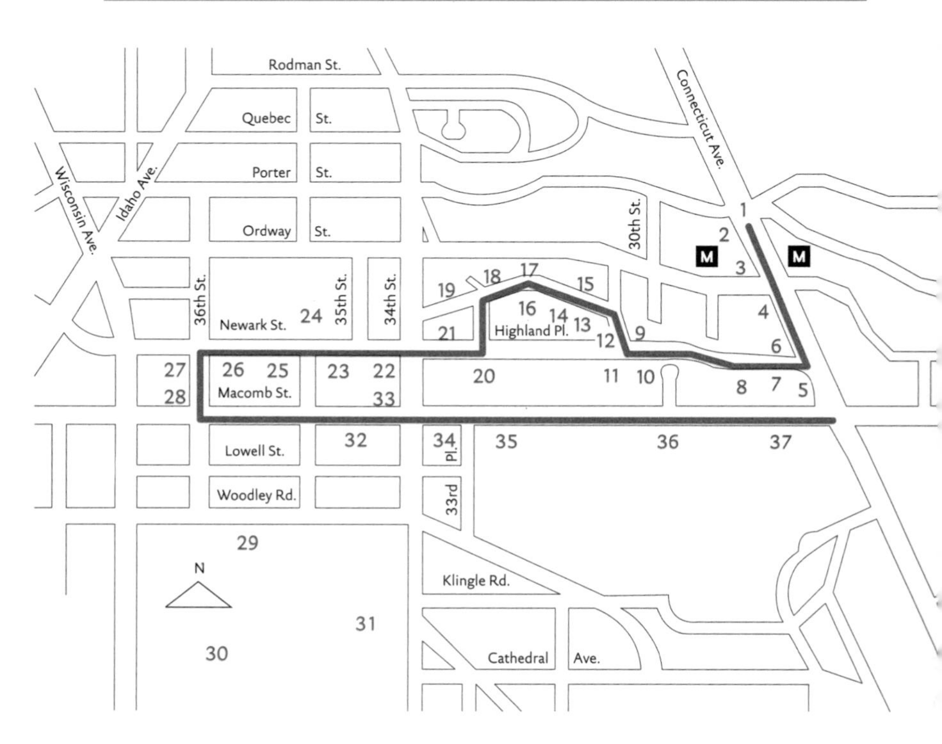

Cleveland Park is significant as a neighborhood with a strong sense of community and distinctive architecture. With its tree-lined streets, brick sidewalks, and large frame houses, it has successfully retained much of its late-19th- and early-20th-century atmosphere. Many of the architectural styles that gained popularity in the late 19th century are represented in Cleveland Park's houses.

Cleveland Park and the Close of the Washington Cathedral (officially known as the Cathedral Church of St. Peter and St. Paul) were originally part of about

12,000 acres purchased about 1790 by Georgetown merchants Benjamin Stoddert (who was also the first secretary of the navy) and Gen. Uriah Forrest (former mayor of Georgetown, friend of George Washington, and representative from Maryland to the US Congress). Forrest bought Stoddert's share in the property and in 1794 moved with his family to the house he built and named Rosedale after his ancestral home in England. The area remained rural until the late 1880s, when it became a fashionable retreat from Washington's hot, humid summers. Wealthy Washingtonians, including President Grover Cleveland (from whom the area derived its name after he established his summer White House at Oak View in 1886), built large, rambling summer "cottages," of which Twin Oaks is the sole surviving example.

In 1892 streetcar service began on Connecticut Avenue, connecting Chevy Chase to the city center. Cleveland Park was one of the chief beneficiaries and quickly became a desirable area for year-round residence. Housing starts mushroomed in the years between 1894 and 1920. The Cleveland Park Company, formed in the early 1890s with John Sherman as its president, was responsible for the most varied and interesting houses in this "streetcar suburb." Sherman was an enlightened developer who hired local architects to design his houses and provided certain amenities (a streetcar waiting lodge, stables, and a fire station), to make Cleveland Park life more attractive to his prospective residents. The residential development of Cleveland Park was virtually complete by 1920. At that time, residential and commercial development along Connecticut and Wisconsin Avenues intensified to provide services for the residents, who previously had ridden the streetcar into the city to purchase all of their provisions.

Cleveland Park has remained a popular in-town residential area with a touch of rural atmosphere because of the preserved open space. Its residents consistently have been professionals (especially lawyers), high-level government officials, academicians, and journalists.

■ 1 **Cleveland Park Metro station** opened in December 1981. Accessible from both sides of Connecticut Avenue NW, it is among the deepest stations in the Metrorail system. After ascending the long escalator, walk north to Porter Street NW.

■ 2 **Firehouse No. 28** is on the west side of Connecticut Avenue. It opened December 1, 1916, making it the second building on this strip of Connecticut Avenue. Snowden Ashford, who was appointed the first municipal architect in 1909, designed it. This was a progressive fire station when it opened, with motorized equipment replacing the less efficient horse-drawn engines. Notice the handsome stone arches and angle quoins as well as the red brick with white trim, especially the central swan's-neck pediment with a pineapple as a centerpiece. All are details of the Georgian Revival style, recalling the early plantation houses along the James River. Next to the fire station is the Yenching Palace resturant, site of several historic events. During the Cuban missile crisis of 1962, the Yenching Palace was one of the meeting places of President Kennedy's personal intermediary, ABC News correspondent John Scali, and the emissary of Soviet premier Nikita Khrushchev. It was during the last of these meetings at the Yenching Palace that the final terms were agreed upon that ended the crisis and avoided war. In addition, the ABC documentary, "The Cuban Crisis," narrated by John Scali, was filmed at the Yenching Palace. Lastly, in 1971, when President Nixon initiated rapprochement discussions between the United States and the People's Republic of China, the Yenching Palace was the chosen site for diplomatic exchanges between then-national security adviser Henry Kissinger and high-ranking representatives of the Chinese delegation to Washington in their efforts to normalize relations between the two countries. After viewing the fire station, walk south on Connecticut Avenue. The renovated shopping center on the east side of Connecticut Avenue was one of the first shopping centers in Washington built to accommodate the automobile.

■ 3 **3520 Connecticut Avenue NW** (apartment building, 1919); **3500–18 Connecticut Avenue NW** (unified series of townhouses, 1920). These were the first residences to be built along this stretch of Connecticut Avenue. Harry L. Wardman built them before he built the Wardman Tower in Woodley Park. The first and second floors of many of the townhouses along this street have been converted to restaurants and retail shops.

■ 4 The **Uptown Theater** joined the commercial strip in the early 1930s, providing a new kind of entertainment. Notice the art deco details: decorative features in stone and brick, etched glass, and the marquee with its decorative use of lights and color. The movie theater has one of the largest viewing screens in the Washington metropolitan area.

■ 5 Cross Newark Street and notice the **public library** built in 1952. This site was designated in 1898 by John Sherman to be the location of an architect-designed stone-and-stucco lodge in which early residents could wait for the streetcar in warmth and comfort; it was also used for community meetings and activities. The lodge was largely destroyed by fire about 1910 and was not rebuilt. Today the library serves a similar function as a focal point for the community. It is slated to be replaced by a larger library over the next five years. Turn right and walk up Newark Street.

■ 6 **2941 Newark Street NW** (1898—Robert Head). A local architect, Robert Head designed at least 17 houses that were built in Cleveland Park from 1897 to 1901 in styles ranging from the informal Queen Anne, which this house represents, to the more formal Georgian Revival. Notice the turret, the tall, ribbed chimney that joins the two distinct parts of the house, the variety of roof forms and window shapes, and the first use by Head of the rope-dipped-in-plaster motif on a gable on the west side of the house.

■ 7 **2940 Newark Street NW** (1903—John Sherman, architect-developer). This was one of the first houses built by the Cleveland Park Company after John

Sherman had ceased employing architects. The change probably was the result of the imminent bankruptcy of Thomas Waggaman, who appears to have been the primary landholder and financial backer. This house was at one time home to the famous Arctic explorer Adm. Robert E. Peary.

■ 8 **2960 Newark Street NW** (1899—Robert Head). This Georgian Revival house was the residence of O. T. Crosby, who founded PEPCO, the local electrical power company in the District of Columbia and Maryland, in 1896. Notice that the house serves as a visual focal point as you ascend the hill. Also note the classical details.

■ 9 **3035 Newark Street NW** (1898—Robert Head). This magnificent Queen Anne–style house has a commanding view of the city. Notice the twisted columns and sunray motif on the porch, the swags in the frieze area, the varied roof forms (including a central, bell-shaped turret), and the window forms (including leaded and stained-glass windows).

■ 10 **3038 and 3042 Newark Street** (1903—John Sherman). Notice the use of rope dipped in plaster and applied over the entrance of no. 3042 as a decorative motif.

■ 11 **3100 Newark Street NW** (1897—Waddy Butler Wood). Notice the varied windows, including an eyebrow window in the roof, and the decorative effects achieved by the cut shingles and the rope dipped in plaster in the arched shape above one window.

■ 12 **3121 Newark Street NW** (1903—Ella Bennett Sherman). Notice the two oriel windows on the east side of the house, the rope-dipped-in-plaster motif, and the handsome brackets supporting the central third-story balcony. The architect was the wife of John Sherman, the developer of Cleveland Park.

Turn around and retrace your steps to Highland Place, where you turn left.

House on Highland Place

■ 13 **3100 Highland Place NW** (1896—Frederick Bennett Pyle). Notice the Palladian window in the dormer, the elliptical oculus window by the front door, and the varied shape of the porch, including a porte cochere.

■ 14 **3138 and 3140 Highland Place NW** (1901—Robert Head). These are two of the last houses designed by Head. They exhibit a Japanese influence in the sticklike brackets under the overhanging eaves and in the gentle upward flare of the roof on the central dormer of no. 3140.

■ 15 **3141 and 3155 Highland Place NW** (1895-96—Robert I. Fleming). These "twin houses" were the first to appear on Highland Place. They were built on the unsubdivided portion of Cleveland Park, which was still considered to be agricultural land. The irregular course of Highland Place seems to derive from a property line.

No. 3155 is significant as the home and first office for the brothers W. C. and A. N. Miller, who formed their real estate company as very young men just after their father died. W. C. & A. N. Miller is still an active real estate development firm in Washington today.

■ 16 **3154 Highland Place NW** (remodeled 1905—William Dyer). This early house has received its distinctive appearance through successive renovations. Early photographs show it as a simple frame house until the shingled pagoda-style porch was added in 1906, and then it was further modified in 1916, when the red tiles you see today replaced the shingles.

■ 17 **3209 Highland Place NW** (1906—Hunter & Bell). This was the first brick house built in Cleveland Park. Notice the formality and symmetry of this Georgian Revival house and the use of darkly glazed bricks similar to those found in Williamsburg.

■ 18 **3225 Highland Place NW** (1898—Robert Head). This represents Head's first attempt at a Georgian Revival house, with the Ionic columns on the porch and the Palladian window motif on the side. Once again, the house has a commanding presence on the street.

■ 19 **3301 Highland Place NW** (1912—B. F. Meyers for W. C. & A. N. Miller). This is one of the earliest houses constructed by W. C. and A. N. Miller. They employed B. F. Meyers to design many of their early Cleveland Park houses. They are representative of the second wave of developers active in Cleveland Park after the demise of the Cleveland Park Company in 1909.

Turn left at 33rd Place and walk to Newark Street.

■ 20 **3300 Newark Street NW.** This house was built in 1920 on the site originally occupied by a frame building that housed the chemical fire engine and the police office. The Cleveland Park Company provided these in 1901 for the comfort and safety of the early residents.

■ 21 **3301 Newark Street NW** (1895—Pelz and Carlyle). This modified Italian villa–style residence was the first house built on the east side of 34th Street. Pelz (one of the architects of the Library of Congress) and his partner, Carlyle, were the first architects hired by John Sherman. The site of this house marks the beginning of the subdivided area of Cleveland Park, which was laid out in 1894 in a regular grid pattern from Wisconsin Avenue to 33rd Place on Newark Street. The area you have just walked through was unsubdivided agricultural land; consequently, the developer or prospective owners determined the large, irregularly shaped lots, and the curvilinear streets owe their charming character to property lines and the natural contours of the land. You will notice the increased regularity of lot sizes during the remainder of your tour.

Cross 34th Street with extreme caution and continue on Newark Street.

■ 22 **3410 Newark Street NW** (1895—Pelz and Carlyle). Notice the tower rising out of the west side of the house as you walk by. Look back to catch a glimpse of the Palladian window beside the tower, which lights the landing on the stairs.

■ 23 **3418 Newark Street NW** (1982—Sam Dunn). This house is sensitively designed of wood to match the traditional building materials of the neighborhood. Architect Sam Dunn said he wanted to create a "1982 Cleveland Park house" with a creative flair of its own.

■ 24 **Rosedale, 3501 Newark Street NW** (1794). This 8-acre tract is all that remains of the large acreage Gen. Uriah Forrest originally owned in the 1790s. It can be entered from the drive near the corner of Newark and 36th Streets. A stone building on the property (referred to as the "old kitchen") is believed to have been built in 1740; Forrest built the weatherboard farmhouse, typical of the 18th century, about 1794. The Forrests made this their permanent residence, and George Washington is believed to have been a guest at Rosedale while the new capital city was being built. Pierre L'Enfant, also a personal friend, is rumored to have helped design the original gardens.

In 1796–97 Forrest mortgaged Rosedale (420 acres and the house) to obtain a loan from Maryland so that the new government could complete construction of the Capitol. Forrest then lost most of his money when the Greenleaf real estate syndicate collapsed in 1797. His brother-in-law, Philip Barton Key, who built the Woodley Mansion (now the Maret School), bailed him out by buying all of this land at auction, paying off the mortgage, and then dividing the land into generous parcels, which he sold. He conveyed the farmhouse and 126 acres to Mrs. Uriah Forrest, who was the sister of Key's wife.

Rosedale remained in the family until 1920, when Avery Coonley, a Chicago philanthropist, and his wife purchased it. Frank Lloyd Wright visited his former clients at Rosedale and is reported to have proclaimed it "honest architecture."

In 1959 the Coonleys' daughter and her husband, Waldron Faulkner, sold the house and 8 acres to the National Cathedral School for Girls. The brick buildings that now surround the farmhouse (1968—Waldron Faulkner) were intended as dormitories and faculty housing for the school. The Rosedale Conservancy uses the modern buildings for its offices and classrooms while preserving and restoring the 18th-century farmhouse. Architect Winthrop Faulkner designed the three white brick townhouses on 36th Street at the entrance to Rosedale.

■ 25 **3512 Newark Street NW** (1895—Pelz and Carlyle). Notice the Palladian window on the side of the house as you approach it, and then look back as you walk by to see the oriel on the west side of the house, which rises and has its own terminating roof form.

■ 26 The **stone wall** that you encounter just after passing 3518 Newark Street NW, with its distinctive Hugh Newell Jacobsen renovation, is all that remains of Grover Cleveland's summer home, Oak View. In 1886 President Cleveland purchased an 1868 stone farmhouse and hired architect William M. Poindexter to wrap fanciful wooden Victorian porches around it, giving it a totally new appearance. This was to become the summer White House for the president and his new bride, the handsome young Frances Folsom, who was the daughter of his former law partner. This set a precedent for the area; prominent Washingtonians followed his example and established summer homes nearby. Cleveland's home deteriorated and was razed in 1927 to make way for the present brick house, built the same year for a descendant of Robert E. Lee. The stones from Cleveland's house were used to build this wall.

■ 27 **3320 36th Street NW,** stable for 3601 Macomb Street (1900—Sherman & Sonneman). You will pass on your right a most interesting Palladian window motif, which replaced the large opening in the upper story of the stable that had provided easy access for the storage of hay for the horses. The former stable, built out of Rock Creek granite, makes a very attractive little house.

■ 28 At this point you can continue on 36th Street to reach the Washington Cathedral (see no. 29), or you can turn right on Macomb Street to reach Wisconsin Avenue, where you will find restaurants and public transportation. To continue the walking tour of Cleveland Park, turn left on Macomb Street and begin to descend the hill. Most of the **houses in the next two blocks** were not built until the second decade of the 20th century, when developer Charles Taylor was at work with architect R. G. Moore.

■ 29 The **Cathedral Church of St. Peter and St. Paul** (also known as the **National Cathedral** and the **Washington Cathedral**). Late in 1891, a group of Washingtonians interested in planning a cathedral in the city met at the home of Charles Carroll Grover, a prominent local banker and the prime mover in an effort to establish Rock Creek Park. Two years later, in 1893, Congress chartered the Protestant Episcopal Cathedral Foundation to oversee the construction and operation of such a cathedral and to carry out an educational program. Mount St. Alban, rising above the flatlands of the city, was selected as the site, and in 1906 Bishop Henry Yates Satterlee and the Cathedral Chapter decided on the Gothic design submitted by George Frederick Bodley, England's leading Anglican church architect. Henry Vaughn, a prominent American proponent of the neo-Gothic style, was selected as the supervising architect. More than 20,000 people attended the laying of the foundation stone in 1907. The Bethlehem Chapel, opened in 1912, was the first section completed. Construction was halted during World War I and was resumed in 1922, under the supervision of Philip Hubert Frohman, of Frohman, Robb & Little. Frohman, the cathedral architect for more than 50 years, modified the original design of the nave and the central tower. The choir, apse, and north transept were opened in 1932, the south transept in 1962, and the 301-foot Gloria in Excelsis tower (with its magnificent carillon and ring of bells) in 1964. The west front (Frederick Hart, sculptor) was dedicated in 1982. The west tower was completed in 1990. It is the sixth largest cathedral in the world, offering worship, concerts, tours, gardens, views from the towers, magnificent stained glass, carvings, dramatic architecture, three shops, and more.

The Pilgrim Observation Gallery, high above the west facade, is open from 10:00 a.m. to 3:15 p.m. (admission charged) and offers a panoramic view of the city and suburbs.

The cathedral itself can be entered from the north or south transepts or from the west end. The Cathedral Foundation conducts guided tours of the interior. Call (202) 537-6200 or go to www.cathedral.org/cathedral for information.

Leave the cathedral by the south transept or the west front and follow the stone wall to the entrance to the Bishop's Garden.

■ **30** The **Bishop's Garden** (1928–32—landscape design, Mrs. G. C. F. Bratenahl). Turn right through the Norman arch. The Bishop's Garden actually consists of several gardens, including a rose garden and a medieval herb garden, connected by boxwood-lined, stone-paved walkways. With its pools and ivy-covered gazebo, it is among the city's most pleasant and peaceful places.

Return to the main roadway and continue east to the Pilgrim Steps and the equestrian statue of George Washington (Herbert Haseltine, sculptor). Those wishing to explore the woodland path should descend the 40-foot-wide steps and cross Pilgrim Road.

■ **31 Woodland Path.** This curvilinear walk, maintained by local garden clubs, leads to St. Alban's School or to a lower section of Pilgrim Road. The branch to Pilgrim Road includes a large wooden footbridge (1961—Walter Dodd Ramberg); the bridge is noteworthy for its composition, the size of its members, and its overall character. Cross the footbridge to Pilgrim Road and then walk south on Pilgrim Road to Garfield Street, to the St. Alban's Tennis Club (1970—Hartman Cox Architects). This small, well-ordered building is notable for its varied but dignified facade.

Return to the main road. Beyond the Pilgrim Steps and the deanery (1953—Walter G. Peter) is the greenhouse, which offers a great variety of herb plants for sale (catalogs are available upon request).

The low, modern building (1964—Falkner, Kingsbury & Stenhouse) to the right of the greenhouse is Beauvoir, the cathedral elementary school (founded in 1933). Other structures on the western end of the Close include buildings for administration, the College of Preachers, the Cathedral Library, and canons' housing (all 1924–29—Frohman, Robb & Little).

Washington Cathedral

Retrace your steps past the south transept entrance and Pilgrim Steps and walk west toward Wisconsin Avenue. The Herb Cottage on your left, one of the earliest buildings on the Close, was originally built to house the cathedral's baptistery but now serves as a gift shop. Continue around to the left and notice the panorama of Washington stretching before you from the Peace Cross (dedicated in 1898). The buildings in this section of the Close house the St. Alban's School for Boys (founded in 1903) and St. Alban's Parish (consecrated in 1855; substantially altered in the early 1920s).

You can leave the Close via Wisconsin Avenue and/or Massachusetts Avenue, both of which are served by major bus routes, or return to the Cleveland Park tour, using the entrance at 36th Street.

■ **32 3426 Macomb Street NW** (1897—S. A. Swindell). This little house set so far back from the street is the oldest house on Macomb Street and represents the cottage style popularized by Andrew Jackson Downing. Notice the change in the sidewalk at this point as you leave the early subdivision of Oak View and enter Cleveland Heights (Macomb and Lowell Streets from this point to 33rd Place). This house stood alone for almost 20 years before W. C. and A. N. Miller and George Small built some neighboring houses in Cleveland Heights.

■ **33 Macomb Playground** appeared on the real estate maps as early as 1937. In 1954 the neighborhood mothers raised $1,000 in one week to pay for trees and sod to beautify the playground.

■ **34 John Eaton School** (1911—west wing, Appleton P. Clark Jr.; 1923—east wing, Arthur B. Heaton; 1931—auditorium; 1981–82—renovation, Kent Cooper Associates). As you cross 34th Street, you are looking at the rear of the school, which opened in 1911. From here you can see the oldest wing, with the entry from the playground marked for boys and the tall chimney designed by Heaton. The school and the community particularly appreciate the newly enlarged and landscaped playground.

■ **35 Twin Oaks** (1888—Francis Richmond Allen). 3200 Macomb Street NW (rear entrance); 3225 Woodley Road NW (main entrance). This is the only remaining example of a house designed to be a summer home located in the Cleveland Park area. Twin Oaks is an extremely early example of a Colonial (Georgian) Revival house—perhaps the earliest one surviving in the United States. It bears a close resemblance to McKim, Mead and White's H. A. C. Taylor House of Newport, Rhode Island, of 1886 (demolished in 1952). Gardiner Greene Hubbard, a Bostonian, hired architect Francis Richmond Allen from his native city to design his summer home, which resembles the large, rambling New England frame seaside summer houses. Hubbard was the founder of the National Geographic Society and also was the chief financial backer for Alexander Graham Bell, a partnership that made possible the establishment of worldwide telephone service.

Twin Oaks remained in the possession of this family until it was sold in 1947 to the Republic of China. It then became the residence of the Chinese ambassador. In 1978, with the US recognition of the People's Republic of China, Twin Oaks became the property of the Friends of Free China. It is private property and therefore not open to the public, but the house, its wooded site, and the rolling lawns are visible from the lower ends of both driveways.

■ **36 Tregaron (formerly The Causeway),** 3100 Macomb Street NW (original rear entrance); 3029 Klingle Road NW (original main entrance). The entire estate, including buildings and grounds, is a Category 3 landmark. This 20-acre portion of Gardiner Greene Hubbard's 50-acre estate was sold in 1911 by Alexander Graham Bell to James Parmelee, an Ohio financier. Charles Adams Platt, who was then the nation's foremost country house architect, designed the estate in 1912. Landscape architect Ellen Shipman assisted him. Platt's brick neo-Georgian mansion sits on the crest of the hill surrounded by sloping meadows and landscaped rustic woodland areas, including the bridle paths. The property was acquired by Joseph E. Davies (ambassador to the Soviet Union from 1934 to 1938) and his wife, Marjorie Merriweather Post. It was renamed Tregaron after the ancestral home of Davies's mother in Wales. Davies, who occupied the house until his death in 1958, added the Russian dacha (cottage).

In 1980 the property was sold and divided into two parcels. The 6 acres at the top of the hill, which include all of the present buildings, belong to the Washington International School, which has established its middle and upper schools on the site. The remaining 14 acres are owned by the Tregaron

Development Corporation, which applied for permission to construct 120 townhouses that would have wrapped around the existing mansion on three sides. This proposed development was soundly rejected by the students, their parents, and residents who raised funds to buy the property. Tregaron is also a privately owned site to which public access is limited. Both the Tregaron and Twin Oaks sites are visible from the surrounding streets.

■ **37** As you complete your tour of Cleveland Park by walking down Macomb Street to Connecticut Avenue, you will be passing through the final phase of development completed by the Cleveland Park Company between the years 1905 and 1909. Notice **3031 Macomb Street NW,** at the corner of Ross Place, with its Palladian window decorated with a fan shape in the arch and motif of rope dipped in plaster. This house, with its large arch set in the main gable of the house, is repeated at **2929 Macomb Street NW.** You may also enter it from Newark Street. As you approach Connecticut Avenue you can probably pick out the other Sherman frame houses with their expansive porches, flaring roof eaves, and commanding positions above the street. You will also walk past the location of the **Cleveland Park Stable** (2932 Macomb Street NW). If you turn left, you can return to the Cleveland Park Metro station.

LeDroit Park

(Historic African American residential area, Howard University, Howard Theater)

Suzanne Ganschinietz, updated by Maybelle Taylor Bennett

Distance: 1 1/2 miles
Time: 1 1/2 hours
Bus: 90, 92, 96, G2, and G8
Metro: Shaw/Howard University (Green Line)

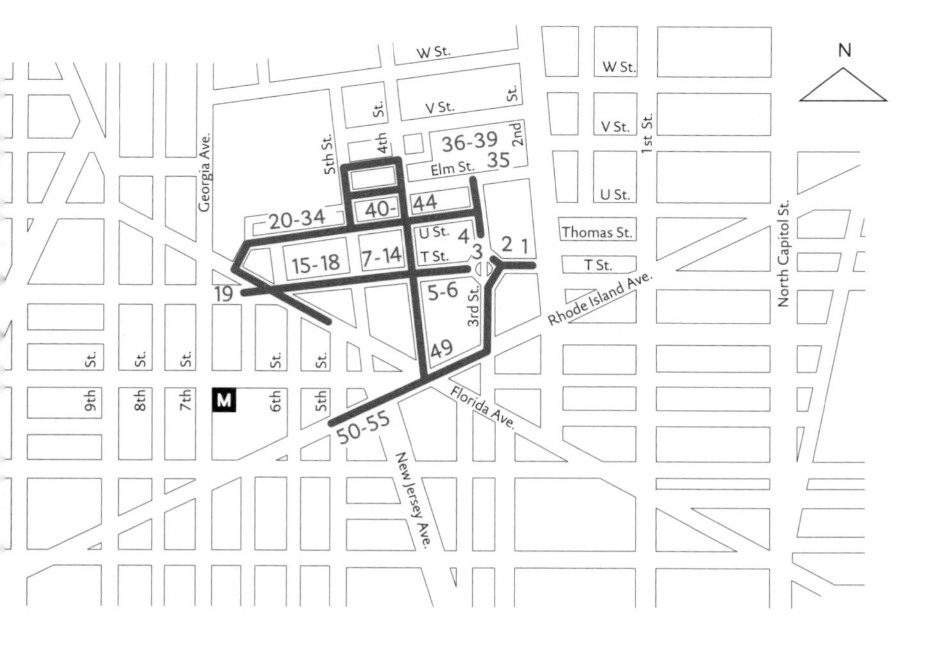

LeDroit Park is a Category 2 landmark of the National Capital and is listed on the National Register of Historic Places. It is a small, unified subdivision built during the 1870s that has been, since its inception, inextricably linked with Howard University. Upon the resignation of his trusteeship at Howard University, Amzi L. Barber purchased 40 acres of land owned by the university (that was later to become known as LeDroit Park, named for Barber's father-in-law and realtor LeDroit Langdon) on a $115,000 promissory note without a down payment between 1872 and 1873. The new subdivision first appeared on the map in 1873, and in 1874 the university accepted $95,000 in full payment of the note. By 1877, 41 new houses had been erected, all of them designed by well-known architect

James McGill. In time, more than 60 detached and semi-detached homes were designed by McGill in the Calvert Vaux cottage tradition. The area, which was adjacent to the boundaries of Washington when built, was advertised as offering the advantages of city living with the open space of the country. No fences were erected between the homes, although the entire area changed in the 1880s and 1890s as developers sold the remaining land within the district for the erection of row houses. An additional change occurred near the turn of the century as the area became a predominantly African American community, upon the removal of racially restrictive covenants.

For many years the area has been the home of prominent black citizens. Located adjacent to Howard University and the Howard Theater, two nationally significant black educational and cultural centers, the neighborhood has served as an important cultural and political center for the entire District of Columbia. Indeed, it was once considered the area's hub for the black intelligentsia and boasted renowned black poets, statesmen, attorneys, jurists, educators, artists, politicians, clergy, scientists, and medical professionals.

Today, LeDroit Park retains much of the same scale and character and most of the architecture that it had at the turn of the century. Many of the original detached houses scattered among the slightly later brick-and-frame row houses are still standing. The row houses, constructed in the late 1880s and 1890s, are primarily low-rise brick structures with fine terra-cotta and decorative brickwork. They have roof lines frequently accented with turrets, towers, pedimented gables, and iron cresting that combine to provide a varied and rhythmic pattern to the streets. Many of the detached and row houses retain decorative ironwork fences and balustrades. Unique in the District of Columbia are the twisted porch columns found in the row houses on 3rd Street near the Anna J. Cooper Circle.

More important, the area is undergoing a renaissance catalyzed largely by substantial investments by Howard University, Fannie Mae, and the Fannie Mae Foundation in the rehabilitation of existing row houses, the in-fill new construction of single-family row homes, and the upgraded infrastructure. This revitalization effort is part of a larger redevelopment scheme called the "LeDroit Park Initiative," which involves extensive housing, infrastructure, commercial and cultural district improvements as well.

Together with other nonprofit housing developers and private property owners, the area is experiencing an increase in units being upgraded and occupied after decades of decline that began in the 1960s and continued through the 1970s and 1980s. New households include families of Howard University employees, community members who are returning to the city from the Washington suburbs, and first-time homebuyers in the area. New residents represent the income diversity of the existing neighborhood through the purposeful efforts of Howard University, Fannie Mae, and the District of Columbia, whose partnership resulted in moderated prices for new and rehabilitated housing, below-market mortgage interest financing, down payment and closing cost assistance, and substantial housing counseling efforts. To complement the new housing development and rehabilitation activities, the District of Columbia Department of Public Works and the US Department of Transportation provided support for ongoing infrastructure upgrades that are evident throughout the neighborhood. Note the new brick sidewalks, trees, streetlights, and the resurfaced streets and alleys.

No visit to LeDroit Park would be complete without a walk through the campus of Howard University, which is located to the immediate north of the LeDroit Park neighborhood. Georgia Avenue runs almost through the center of the university complex and is the commercial hub of the campus.

Howard University is the largest and most comprehensive predominantly African American university in the United States. The university provides educational services and training to over 15,000 students from across the nation and approximately 109 countries and territories. Their varied customs, cultures, and dress give the university an international character. It is a research-oriented university founded in 1867 by members of the First Congregational Society of Washington and named for Gen. Oliver Otis Howard, head of the Freedman's Bureau. Its mission was to provide an institution that would welcome all students, including freed men and women, and today it provides an educational experience of exceptional quality to students of high academic potential, with a particular emphasis on providing educational opportunities to promising black students. The university's 89-acre main campus contains dormitories, administrative offices, classroom buildings, the athletic complex, libraries, the Howard Hospital complex, radio and television broadcasting facilities, a chapel, theater, art gallery, and several auditoria. The compact campus is very pedestrian friendly.

Many of the buildings are historic landmarks, and two of them represent the university's signature architectural style. Douglas Hall, built in 1936, and Founder's Library, built in 1937, were designed by renowned architect Albert Cassell. The university's campus was planned by Cassell as well, with extensive terracing and landscaping designed circa 1935 by a prominent African American landscape architect, David Williston.

The Shaw/Howard University Metro station is at 7th and T Streets NW, approximately three blocks from the LeDroit Park neighborhood. Exit from the station's north entrance and walk north to Florida Avenue; turn right and walk one block north to T Street NW; walk east to 2nd Street. You may also take a Metro bus along Georgia Avenue to the Howard University campus. Enter the campus "quad" and walk two blocks south to T Street; proceed east to 2nd Street. The tour begins at the intersection of 2nd and T Streets NW. Visitors will walk west along T Street, which is LeDroit Park's Main Street. Second Street was formerly known as LeDroit Avenue and T Street was formerly called Maple Avenue. Former street names are posted on all of the street signs.

■ 1 **201 T Street NW.** This was the home of Dr. Anna J. Cooper who was born a slave, graduated from Oberlin College in 1884, and came to Washington to teach in the public high school for blacks on M Street NW. She received an honorary master's degree from Oberlin and served as principal for the M Street High School from 1901 to 1906, where she became involved in the now-classic controversy between Booker T. Washington and W. E. B. DuBois as it related to the appropriate educational curriculum necessary to uplift the Negro race. She believed "colored" children needed a classical academic education and manual arts education, both of which were offered in the high school. This viewpoint got her in trouble with Booker T. Washington, a champion of the manual arts education for "colored children," and the white school board in Washington, DC, whose members were alleged to have used their influence to dismiss her from her post. She later returned to the high school to teach, and she earned her doctorate from the Sorbonne in Paris in 1925 at the age of 67, where, in the French language, she examined French attitudes toward slavery during the French Revolution. In 1906, Anna J. Cooper and Dr. Jesse Lawson founded the Frelinghuysen University to provide evening education classes for employed blacks. When the university needed a permanent home, Dr. Cooper donated her house, which remained the location of the school until it closed in the early 1960s. Dr. Cooper lived to be 105 years of age.

■ 2 **200 block of T Street NW.** In this block of T Street lived A. Kiger Savoy, assistant superintendent of colored schools; Dan Monroe, an auditor at the Government Accounting Office; and Geneva Perry, a community activist, a musician who played at the Howard Theater, and the editor of a LeDroit Park community newspaper.

■ 3 **Anna J. Cooper Circle, at 3rd (formerly known as Harewood Avenue) and T Streets NW.** In many ways, this circle is the spiritual heart of the LeDroit Park community. The developers of LeDroit Park were responsible not only for the architecture and the landscaping of the subdivision but also for designing the streets and sidewalks (which remained in private hands until 1901). The circle was part of the original street pattern, although the rationale for it is not entirely clear. The circle has been redesigned and landscaped to resemble its original appearance and is scheduled to be further landscaped and repaved as part of the continuing infrastructure improvements of the LeDroit Park Initiative.

One of the early advertisements for the part referred to Harewood Avenue as a projected main thoroughfare for trolleys from the city out to the Soldier's Home farther north. Early maps, however, show that this throughway did not develop and that 3rd Street terminated just above Elm Street. It may be that the designers wished to imitate the L'Enfant Plan with its monumental circles. Indeed, we know that the houses envisioned for Harewood Avenue were to be the most lavish and the most expensive in the park. The original vista of 3rd Street was quite different from the present view, since most of the McGill houses have disappeared. Despite this change, the circle remains a strong identification and orientation point for LeDroit Park and has been the focal point of neighborhood celebrations and Christmas caroling. Although the street has retained its relatively low scale, the openness and sense of "refined elegance" envisioned by the developers has been compromised by later construction and the disappearance of the bucolic setting with large open lawns surrounding McGill mansions. The dormitory and apartment house on the east, the row houses on the west, and the elementary school at the end of the street create a more urban streetscape as one looks north along 3rd Street from the circle.

■ 4 **1901-1903 3rd Street NW at the northeast corner of 3rd and T.** The large white-and-gray house on the northeast corner of the circle is a McGill-designed house and belonged to Gen. William Birney and Arthur Birney. It is virtually unchanged from its original state. Continue walking west on T Street beyond the circle.

1901–3 3rd Street, NW

■ 5 **326 T Street NW.** This house, also referred to by some as the "half-house," was once the home of Mary Church Terrell and Judge Robert Terrell. The other half of the house, which was burned in a fire and demolished, once belonged to Mrs. Terrell's brother, Robert Church. Their father, Robert Reed Church, a wealthy Tennessee native, purchased the two homes for his son and daughter. Robert Reed Church was once thought to be the first black millionaire in the United States. 326 T Street is the only building in the LeDroit Park neighborhood that is listed on the National Register of Historic Places. Mary Church Terrell was a woman of great importance to the black community, who was active in both the women's suffrage movement and the civil rights movement. She was the first black woman appointed to the District of Columbia Board of Education. In 1953, at the age of 89, Mrs. Terrell participated in lunch counter sit-ins that helped to desegregate public facilities in the District of Columbia. Her husband, Judge Robert Terrell, a Harvard-educated attorney, was the first black municipal judge in Washington and served for a time as the principal of the M Street School.

■ 6 **330 T Street NW.** This was once the home of Fountain Peyton, one of the first 16 black attorneys listed in the 1894 Union League directory as practicing in Washington, DC. Peyton was a graduate of Howard University Law School. This residence is the home of Frank and Windy Carson Smith. Frank Smith was a civil rights activist, former council member for Ward 1 in the District of Columbia, and founder of the African American Civil War Memorial and Museum.

■ 7 **LeDroit Park Market.** This convenience store, located on the northeast corner of 4th and T Streets NW is owned by Dr. Ella Toombs and is evidence of the revitalization that is taking place in LeDroit Park. The store has been designed to depart from what has become the norm for most urban "mom-and-pop" convenience stores in urban central cities. Instead of being completely bricked-in, with merchants who seldom venture out from behind their Plexiglas barriers, this store sports picture-window glass that provides an unimpeded view of the store's wares and creates a welcoming presence in the neighborhood.

■ 8 **Vista, 4th Street (formerly known as Linden Street) NW.** Fourth Street, the only north–south thoroughfare in LeDroit Park that was aligned with the street pattern to the north, was the first area to be subdivided. For years, Fourth Street accommodated rush hour traffic by permitting two lanes of traffic to flow south to employment centers in Washington in the morning, and two lanes to flow north away from those centers to residential neighborhoods and the suburbs in the evenings. With the revitalization that is taking place in LeDroit Park, area residents prevailed upon the Department of Public Works to reduce the volume of traffic that flowed along this street through the elimination of the reversible lane that accommodated rush hour traffic. Now there is only one lane northbound and one lane southbound, allowing for a more sedate and slower-paced volume of traffic that is more respectful of the area's historic status. Continue walking west on T Street across 4th Street to the 400 block of T Street.

■ 9 **400 T Street NW.** This is the home of the family of civil rights activist and former presidential candidate Jesse Jackson.

■ 10 **405 T Street NW.** Professor Alonzo Brown, a professor of mathematics at Howard University, once lived at this location.

■ 11 **408-410 T Street NW.** Washington's first elected mayor, Walter Washington, lived here until his death in October 2003. Washington was a graduate of Howard University, was active in the New Negro Alliance, and became the head of the

National Capital Housing Authority. Mayor Washington helped to set the stage for the development of Metrorail in the nation's capital, championed housing for lower income residents of the District of Columbia, and ushered the city through the difficult years when riots threatened to devastate many city neighborhoods. The home was the former family home of Washington's first wife, Benetta Bullock Washington, daughter of the Reverend George O. Bullock, a prominent minister, pastor of Third Baptist Church, and social worker. Benetta Bullock was educated at Dunbar High School and Howard University and later became principal of Cardozo High School and the director of US Women's Job Corps.

■ **12** **412 T Street NW.** This was the former home of Dr. Ernest E. Just, professor of zoology at Howard University for over thirty years, renowned biologist, and author of a classic biology text, *The Biology of the Cell Surface*. Dr. Just's portrait has been placed on a Black Heritage US postage stamp.

■ **13** **418 T Street NW.** Dr. Hattie Riggs, a black educator from Calais, Maine, who taught at the M Street High School, lived at this location. Although Dr. Riggs earned her medical degree, she never practiced medicine.

■ **14** **420 T Street NW.** Professor Nelson Weatherless, early advocate of equal rights, educator, and activist, once lived at this location. Currently, Dr. Bernard Richardson, dean of the Howard University Chapel, resides here with his family.

Continue walking west along T Street, crossing 5th Street (formerly known as Larch Street) to the 500 block of T Street.

■ **15** **504 T Street NW.** The first black officer to die in World War I, Maj. James E. Walker, lived at this address, as did the principal of Armstrong High School, Capt. Arthur Newman. Captain Newman's wife, Jennie, and Major Walker's wife were sisters.

■ **16** **506 T Street NW.** This was the home of Roscoe I. Vaughn, who was an architect and head of the Manual Training Department of the District of Columbia schools.

■ **17** **517 T Street NW.** Another good example of McGill's work, this finely detailed home has been well preserved.

■ **18** **525 T Street NW.** James McGill designed this home, complete with stable, and it is one of the finest remaining homes in the historic district.

■ **19** The **Howard Theater,** just across Florida Avenue from the neighborhood at 620 T Street, was built in 1910. It was the first theater built exclusively for African American entertainers and audiences, who, because public facilities were segregated, were unable to go to theaters patronized by whites. The Howard Theater anchored the eastern end of what was then known as the "Old Black Broadway," a stretch of theaters, lounges, restaurants, and other social

517 T Street, NW

and entertainment venues patronized by both blacks and whites. The theater is scheduled to be renovated as part of the LeDroit Park Initiative's cultural district development. The LeDroit Park community provided accommodation for many of the entertainers who performed at the theater, which, along with the Apollo in New York, the Uptown in Philadelphia, the Royal in Baltimore, and the Regal in Chicago, was the stage on which many of the more prominent black entertainers in the past half century made their debuts.

The Howard Theater played a very important role in the development and promotion of black talent. It not only hosted famous singers, big bands, dancers, and comedians but also introduced new talent through its amateur-night contests. Winners of these contests included Ella Fitzgerald, Billy Eckstein, and Bill "Ink Spots" Kenny. The Howard was host to stars like Pearl Bailey, Sarah Vaughn, Lena Horne, Sammy Davis Jr., Billie Holiday, and Dick Gregory. In the 1950s and 1960s, it showcased rock and roll music and the Motown sound. The Platters, Gladys Knight and the Pips, Smokey Robinson and the Miracles, James Brown, the Temptations, and the Supremes (who made their first stage appearance at the Howard) all appeared at this theater. The Howard is quiet now, after having been unsuccessfully reopened twice for very short periods of time. It now awaits the continuation of the area's renaissance.

Turn north on 6th Street (formerly known as Juniper Street): Dr. Eva B. Dykes was one of the first black women to receive a PhD. She lived on 6th Street NW.

Walk north one block on 6th Street to the 500 and 600 blocks of U Street (formerly known as Spruce Street). To the west along the U Street corridor are examples of the redevelopment that is redefining the area and making it one of the city's most desirable neighborhoods. Although a tour is not included in this publication, the 10-block area is easy to negotiate on foot and is highly recommended if time for a tour permits. Once referred to as the "Black Broadway" because of the many nightclubs, restaurants, and shops, the corridor has attracted new residential condominiums and retail shops as well as extensive restoration. Near the easternmost entrance to the U Street/Cordozo Metro station, at U Street and Vermont Avenue NW, is a memorial park dedicated to African Americans who served in the Civil War. A new four-story office building, with retail uses at street level, surrounds the westernmost entrance to the station at 13th and U Streets NW. To the north of the station are the historic Ben's Chili Bowl restaurant, the restored Lincoln Theater, and the new Ellington Plaza apartment and retail complex. Several vacant parcels along the corridor are being developed with new residential and commercial units, and many existing storefronts will be rehabilitated over the next few years. Residential restoration and new construction are taking place to the south and north of the U Street corridor as well.

■ **20 600 and 500 block of U Street.** Howard University and LeDroit Park have traditionally had a close relationship. Amzi L. Barber, one of LeDroit Park's developers, came to Washington to head the Normal Department at Howard, later served as trustee and acting president of the university. Faculty members, administrators, and students have always lived and worked in the area. The renaissance taking place in the area has continued this tradition. The 12 newly constructed and nine rehabilitated homes on the north side of U Street were completed during the first phase of the LeDroit Park Initiative. Two-thirds of these homes were sold to and occupied by Howard University employees with the other one-third occupied by municipal employees and area residents. The backdrop of the hospital serves as a visual reminder of the town–gown interface and the importance of developing harmonious relationships between the university and the community.

■ **21 621-607 and 529 U Street NW.** These are homes that have been renovated as part of the LeDroit Park Initiative. All have been sold to Howard University employees. Distinctive address plates identify these homes as part of the LeDroit Park Initiative.

■ **22 605, 603, 601 U Street NW, 535, 527, 525, 523, 521, 519, 517, 515, and 515 1/2 U Street NW.** These homes have been newly constructed on lots owned by the university and have been sold to community residents and Howard University employees. Distinctive address plates identify these homes as part of the LeDroit Park Initiative.

■ **23 512 U Street NW.** Willis Richardson, dramatist of the Harlem Renaissance and the first African American to have a serious play produced on a Broadway stage, lived in a house once sited here. Richardson was educated at the M Street High School.

The Ethiopian Art Players in Chicago, Washington, and New York performed the *Chip Woman's Fortune. The Broken Banjo* (1925) and *Bootblack Lover* (1926) were awarded the Amy Spingarn Prize.

Walk east on U Street to 5th Street.

At the northern terminus of 5th Street and visible from the intersection of 5th and U Streets is the historic **Freedmen's Hospital building,** which is now Howard University's C. B. Powell School of Communications building. Continue to walk east along U Street to the 400 block.

■ **24 400 block of U Street NW.** This is the only remaining block in LeDroit Park that is original to the 1870s development and contains no intrusions. James McGill designed all of the houses in this block.

400 Block of U Street

■ **25 419 U Street NW.** Oscar DePriest lived here while serving in Congress. When elected in 1928, DePriest was the first black to serve in Congress since 1901.

■ **26 417 U Street NW.** This was the home of Percy A. Roy, craftsman, artisan, and manual arts instructor at the District of Columbia's Armstrong High School. His flower garden was highly acclaimed and photographed in the now-defunct *Evening Star* newspaper.

■ **27 414 U Street NW.** Clara Taliaferro, a pharmacist and daughter of John Henry Smyth, lived at this address. Smyth was an attorney and graduate of Howard University's first law school class in 1871. In 1878, President Rutherford B. Hayes called upon Smyth to serve as minister and consul to Liberia in recognition of his work for the Republican Party in the 1876 election. He served in this capacity until 1885.

■ 28 **406 U Street NW.** This was once the home of Garnet C. Wilkinson, who was a graduate of the M Street High School, Oberlin College, and Howard University Law School. Wilkinson served as assistant superintendent of colored schools for 30 years until 1954 and then as assistant superintendent of the District of Columbia's integrated school system.

■ 29 **402 U Street NW.** James M. Carter, professor of English at Howard University, and his family lived at this location.

Continue walking east along U Street, crossing 4th Street to the 300 block of U Street.

■ 30 **300 block of U Street.** The northern side of this block was redeveloped in the late 1990s by Manna, a nonprofit housing developer entity, with single-family row houses for first-time homebuyers. Historically, one of the founders of the first black citizens' association, William Cochran, lived at 315 U Street. Right next door at 317 U Street lives Teresa Brown, the first African American founder of a historic preservation society in Washington, DC, the LeDroit Park Preservation Society. Ms. Brown was instrumental in securing local and national historic designation for LeDroit Park and has participated in the review of plans for the renewal of the area.

■ 31 **338 U Street NW.** This was the home of Octavius Williams, a barber at the US Capitol, who bought this home in 1893, and was one of the first blacks to buy a home in the area once the racially restrictive covenants were removed.

■ 32 **321 U Street NW.** While the current 321 U Street address is part of the redevelopment sponsored by Manna in 1996–97, the original home with that address is where the renowned poet Paul Laurence Dunbar moved with his wife, Alice (also a poet), after their marriage.

■ 33 **320 U Street NW.** Julia West Hamilton, civic leader and president of the Phillis Wheatley YWCA for 28 years, lived at this location. Ms. Hamilton was the first woman president of the board of trustees of the Metropolitan AME Church where she served for 28 years, and she served as treasurer of the predominantly white Women's Relief Corps Auxiliary of the Grand Army of the Republic. She was also a member of the National Association of Colored Women and the National Council of Negro Women.

■ 34 **319 U Street NW.** Maj. Christian A. Fleetwood and wife Sara lived at this location. Fleetwood was a Civil War hero and Medal of Honor soldier. His wife was the first black superintendent of nurses at Freedmen's Hospital.

At the end of the 300 Block of U Street, turn left onto 3rd Street and walk north to Elm Street.

■ 35 **Vista looking east on Elm Street.** See the Gage Eckington Elementary School, built in 1977 at the northern end of 3rd Street, and the Old Gage School Building at the end of Elm on 2nd Street. Also in view on the north side of Elm

Street is Carver Hall, the Howard University dormitory located at 211 Elm Street NW. This building was built in 1942 to house male Negro government workers and was acquired in 1948 by Howard University to provide off-campus housing for male students. The dormitory is named after the renowned scientist and former professor at Tuskegee Institute, Dr. George Washington Carver.

Vista looking south at the 1900 Block of 3rd Street toward the Anna J. Cooper Circle:

■ **36 1915 3rd Street NW.** The present site of the Lucy Diggs Slowe Hall, another Howard University dormitory, named after the first dean of women at Howard University. The present building was constructed in 1942 to house single female Negro government workers and was acquired by Howard University in 1948 to provide off-campus housing for female students. The dormitory site was originally the location of James McGill's home. McGill enjoyed a brief but prolific architectural career. At the age of 19, he joined the office of Henry R. Searle, a Washington architect, and during the next six years he rose from draftsman to architect. He opened his own office in 1872 and was soon associated with Amzi L. Barber, former trustee and acting president of Howard University in the development of LeDroit Park. In addition to the homes in LeDroit Park, he designed 60 other homes, five churches, two markets, a roller-skating rink, and four major office buildings, including the LeDroit Building, still a downtown Washington landmark. He moved out of the LeDroit Building in 1881, advertising both as an architect and a building supply salesman. He left architecture altogether the next year, and for the next 25 years ran a prosperous building supply business.

■ **37 1915 3rd Street NW.** Also at the site where the Lucy Diggs Slowe Hall now stands was once the residence of one of the best-known black surgeons of the day, Dr. Simeon Carson. Dr. Carson had a private hospital in the 1800 block of 4th Street.

Also on 3rd Street was the house (now demolished) of Amzi L. Barber, the builder of most of the McGill-designed houses in LeDroit Park. Amzi L. Barber, like his father, was trained for the ministry at Oberlin College. He came to Washington in 1868 to head the normal department at Howard University. He was later elected to a professorship of natural history and, at age 29, was appointed acting president of Howard University. He left the university to spend full time developing the LeDroit community. His business interests included the building and management of the LeDroit Building in the 900 block of F Street NW and other real estate interests. During the 1880s, he developed homes in Columbia Heights, north and west of LeDroit Park, constructing Belmont, which he rented to Melville Fuller, chief justice of the United States. Barber's major interest changed in the mid-1880s to the Barber Asphalt Paving Company, which made him a very wealthy man.

■ **38 1938 3rd Street NW.** This house was the boyhood home of Edward W. Brooke, who was educated at Dunbar High School, Howard University, and Boston University Law School. He was the first African American elected to statewide office in Massachusetts (attorney general, 1962). In 1963 Brooke was elected to the US Senate and served in that capacity until 1979. Brooke grew up in this house, and his family moved to Brookland while he was a student at Howard. His father, Edward Brooke II, was an attorney with the Veterans Administration for 50 years.

■ 39 **1910 3rd Street NW.** A McGill-designed house, this is the former residence of J. J. Albright, a prominent Washington businessman and a dealer in coal.

Walk north again to Elm Street, turn west on Elm Street, and walk through the 300 block of Elm to the intersection of 4th and Elm. Look to the south on 4th Street.

■ 40 **1934 4th Street NW.** This is the bachelor home of Paul Laurence Dunbar, where he stayed when he was working at the Library of Congress. Look to the north on 4th Street.

■ 41 **2030, 2034, 2038 4th Street.** These homes were completely renovated and sold to Howard University employees as part of the LeDroit Park Initiative. The distinctive address plates identify these homes. Since the rehabilitation of these homes, all of the other homes on the west side of this block have been upgraded or are scheduled for improvement.

Cross 4th Street and continue walking west in the 400 block of Elm Street.

■ 42 **406, 408, 410 and 411 Elm Street, 2022 4th Street, 414 and 416-420 Elm Street NW.** These houses were known as the 4-Elm Street Project. In the 1980s, these houses were restored by a combination of matching funds from the Department of the Interior, the homeowners, and the Department of Housing and Community Development.

■ 43 **407, 409, 415, 417, 419, 427, 429 and 431 Elm Street NW.** These homes were restored using funds from the Howard University Hospital and matching grants from the Department of the Interior.

■ 44 **407, 409, 425 and 431 Elm Street NW.** These homes were gutted completely, rehabilitated, and sold as part of the LeDroit Park Initiative.
The distinctive address plates readily identify these homes.

Walk west on Elm Street to 5th, turn north on 5th Street and walk one block to the 400 block of Oakdale Place. Walk east on Oakdale Place for one block to 4th Street.

■ 45 **400 block of Oakdale Place NW.** These houses were completely renovated by Howard University, the first rehabilitated as part of the LeDroit Park Initiative, with two exceptions, 412 and 422, which were privately owned. All of the homes were sold to Howard University employees. Note the distinctive address plates.

■ 46 **422 Oakdale Place NW.** Lillie Robinson, a baker and long-time resident of Oakdale Place, lived at this location with her husband, Thomas Boyd Robinson. The two moved to Oakdale Place in the 1950s and lived in an apartment building that was demolished prior to the construction of the Howard-owned parking lot on the north side of Oakdale Place. The couple subsequently moved into 422 and lived there for several decades. Before he passed away, Thomas Boyd told Lillie not to move, no matter how much she was encouraged to do so as other neighbors sold their properties to the university. She resolved to stay in place long after all of the other homes on the block had been purchased by the university and vacated. However, Robinson, who died in 2001 at the age of 85, lived long enough to see the entire block rehabilitated and to greet her new neighbors. She declined the university's offer to have her own home rehabilitated at no cost to herself, because her husband had paneled their home throughout and she did not want that evidence of his hard work and love demolished.

Vista on 4th Street at Oakdale Place NW. Looking east into the 300 block of Oakdale at the intersection of 4th and Oakdale, you can see a three-story apartment building, part of the Kelly Miller Public Housing development. This building is scheduled for renovation. The Kelly Miller development, which extends two blocks behind this building toward the north and east, was named for Dr. Kelly Miller. Dr. Miller was a prominent professor at Howard University who introduced the first social work curriculum to the campus. He later became dean at the university and lived in a home along 4th Street, which has been demolished.

■ 47 **2038 4th Street NW.** This was once the location of a barbershop and was renovated and sold to a university employee as part of the LeDroit Park Initiative.

Walk south along 4th Street to the 1800 block.

■ 48 **1839 4th Street NW.** This McGill home, still in excellent condition, is the home of the former president of the LeDroit Park Civic Association. Another former president of the Civic Association resides across the street from this home in one of the row houses that was later developed in the area. Both neighborhood leaders were instrumental in obtaining resident consensus around the nature and quality of the redevelopment that Howard University and Fannie Mae were implementing in the area.

At Florida Avenue and 4th Street NW, walk east on Florida Avenue around the Frazier Funeral Home for a few feet. See the vista to the north and east of the funeral home along Rhode Island Avenue and the large building on the north side of the street.

■ 49 **301 Rhode Island Avenue.** This large expansive property was once the site of the residence of David McClelland, one of the original owners and developers of LeDroit Park. The Elks Lodge now uses the site, which until 1998 was the location of a Safeway grocery store. The property has been completely adapted and rehabilitated for use as the headquarters for the United Planning Organization, the District of Columbia's antipoverty agency.

Turning back to Florida Avenue, proceed west along Florida Avenue NW. Florida Avenue was once an arterial that housed numerous black businesses and physicians' offices. Many of the physicians ran their practices out of their homes; they included Ralph Wright, Sidney Sumby, Edmund Wilson, Clarence Tignor and Algernon Jackson. Dr. Leo Williams opened the first black pharmacy on Florida Avenue NW. Frazier's Funeral Home at 4th and Florida continues to be a familiar landmark.

■ **50 455 Florida Avenue NW.** This was once the location of the popular Harrison's Café, which was owned and operated by Robert Harrison.

■ **51 463 Florida Avenue NW.** Educator, dentist, artist, and author, Dr. John E. Washington lived at this location. He wrote a book titled, *They Knew Lincoln*. His wife, Virgie, was a pharmacist and social worker.

■ **52 467 Florida Avenue NW.** Mother Dear's Community Center was established at this location in August 1987 by the Reverend Annie Woodridge to serve lower income families in the surrounding community. Rev. Woodridge had been ministering to the poor all over the city since 1958, and after running a similar facility on 14th Street for some 18 years, she was forced to move as 14th Street became redeveloped. A wealthy realtor purchased this building for Rev. Woodridge so that she might continue her ministry there. One month after moving into the building, Rev. Woodridge passed away. Today, her daughters run the center, which houses a clothes pantry, an after-school program for children, and a feeding program.

■ **53 501 Florida Avenue NW.** Dr. George Butcher opened a drug store here.

■ **54 511 Florida Avenue NW.** Dr. Ionia Whipper, who sheltered unwed girls in her home, was a descendent of William Whipper, a newspaper editor and an early advocate of nonviolent resistance.

■ **55 519 Florida Avenue NW.** This address was once the location of the LeDroit Park Preservation Society and was restored at one time with matching funds from the Department of the Interior.

Old Anacostia

(Black residential area, late-19th-century buildings,
Anacostia Neighborhood Museum)

Sam Parker, updated by Ryan Harris and Alvin R. McNeal

Distance: 1 1/2 miles
Time: 3/4 hour
Bus: 90, 92, P2, P6, and 02
Metro: Anacostia (Green Line); transfer to 90 bus

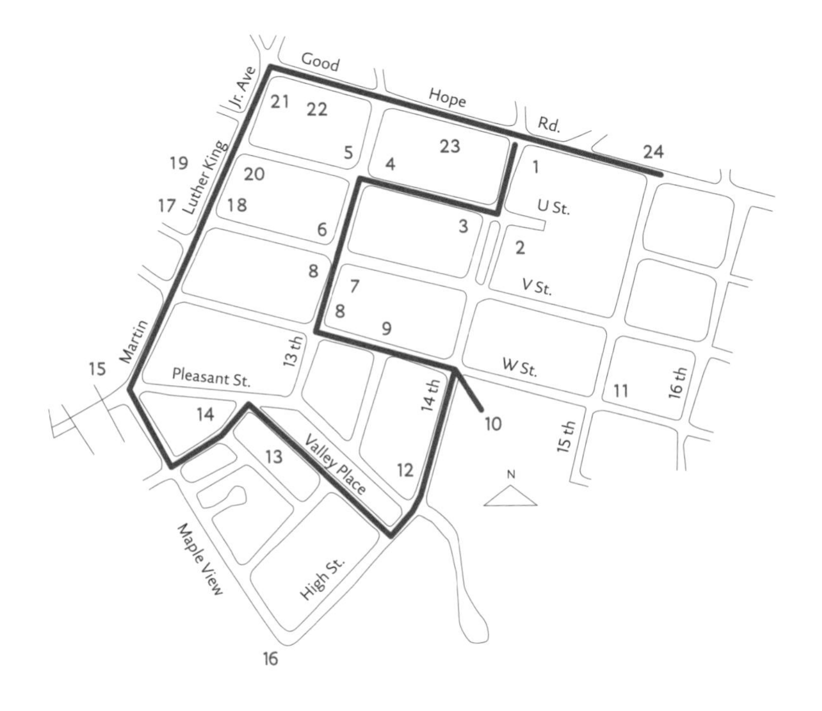

Incorporated in 1854 as one of Washington's earliest residential subdivisions, Old Anacostia retains considerable historical, architectural, and environmental appeal. The area had evolved from an ancient settlement of the Nacotchtank ("Nacostine") Indians into rich farmland. By the latter half of the 19th century, a subdivision called Uniontown developed into a working-class neighborhood and encompassed other minor subdivisions. Though the composition of its residents has changed over the years, many of its social and physical resources endure and continue to influence the community. Old Anacostia derives its distinctive sense of place from its rolling area, its views to Downtown Washington, the charm and human scale of its buildings, as well as an appealing neighborhood environment.

Old Anacostia has a positive and readily identifiable character. The cohesive quality is apparent in the physical evidence of a pleasant and remarkably intact low-density, late-19th-century neighborhood. Unfortunately, the neighborhood has become quite distressed over the years, and many boarded-up buildings and trash-strewn lots exist.

The Anacostia Neighborhood Museum is located at 1901 Fort Place SE. It is part of the Smithsonian Institution museum system and is a neighborhood landmark that should not be missed. It emphasizes art and culture by minorities.

■ 1 The tour begins at **14th Street and Good Hope Road.** Old Anacostia first began to develop as a residential community after 1854, when John W. VanHook and two other men purchased 240 acres of farmland from the Chichester Tract for development into a residential subdivision. The original grid of streets laid out by the Union Land Association has survived to the present day and is framed by Good Hope Road to the north, 15th Street to the east, W Street to the south, and Martin Luther King Jr. Avenue to the west. Known initially as Uniontown, the development was aimed at the middle-class employees of the nearby Washington Navy Yard across the Anacostia River.

■ 2 At 14th Street between U and V Streets is the striking **Old Market Square,** a block long and 40 feet wide. It was part of the original layout for Uniontown and was the prime focal point of the community.

■ 3 The belfry of **St. Philip the Evangelist Episcopal Church** provides an interesting visual reference along the square.

■ 4 The houses at **1312 and 1342 U Street SE** represent two of the early dwellings still remaining. No. 1312 features an elaborate bracket cornice, window pediments, and a handsome cubical cupola. This striking residence stands in pronounced contrast to the later houses around it.

■ 5 Though deteriorated, the houses at 1230–50 U Street SE, called **"Roses Row,"** are potentially handsome. Their form and detail are remarkably well integrated. All of the units are presently occupied. The architectural character of Old Anacostia is in many ways unique when compared to that of other communities in the Washington area. Nowhere else does there exist such a homogeneous collection of late-19th-century small-scale frame and brick buildings. The pleasant environment of Old Anacostia is less the product of outstanding architecture than the result of average buildings working together with remarkable success to create a cohesive and expressive whole.

■ 6 The Victorian Gothic is represented by two churches at diagonally opposite corners of V and 13th Streets. **St. Teresa's Catholic Church** was designed by E. Francis Baldwin, partner in the Baltimore firm of Baldwin and

Pennington, and was built by Isaac Beers in 1879. A stucco building of simple form, the church is embellished by a large rose window on the front facade, decorated with a simple circular tracery.

■ 7 **Delaware Baptist Church** (formerly Emmanuel Episcopal Church), is more irregular in form. Erected in 1891, the building employs rustic stonework with varied brown tones. Its highly picturesque massing adds considerably to the building. The massive corner belfry, with its tall spire and spreading eaves, makes the church one of the most prominent visual landmarks in Old Anacostias.

Delaware Baptist Church

■ 8 A walk along **13th Street between V and W Streets** shows an attractive streetscape with its canopy of trees, row of brick duplexes set off by white frame porches and iron fences, and picturesque churches and churchyards. The exteriors of the frame houses in Old Anacostia were embellished, often interchangeably, with varying degrees of Cottage-style, Italianate, or mansard details of the period. The decoration of these buildings was simplified from that of the more elaborate brick townhouses built elsewhere in Washington at this time. Yet these small houses, with their repetitive rhythm of regularly spaced porches, windows, and doors, succeeded in achieving great expressiveness and neighborhood homogeneity. These buildings provided the setting for lively and interesting streetscapes and a community environment of great pride and appeal.

■ 9 The duplex at **1310–12 W Street SE** is an example of the prevalent worker's cottage built after the turn of the century. Notice the rooflines, which reinforce a strong geometrical appearance.

■ **10** **Cedar Hill,** 14th and W Streets, built about 1855, was the home of Frederick Douglass, a runaway slave, abolitionist, orator, writer, civil servant, and diplomat from 1877 until his death in 1895. The handsome brick house, with its commanding view of Washington, is listed in the National Register of Historic Places. The National Park Service restored the property in the 1970s and added a museum/visitors center. This earth-covered visitors center provides an unobtrusive architectural counterpoint to the commanding presence of the Cedar Hill mansion. Hours for both Cedar Hill and the visitor center: daily 9:00 a.m.–4:00 p.m.

■ **11** From the front of the Douglass home notice the Queen Anne **house at 15th and W Streets,** built between 1887 and 1894.

■ **12** The house at **2217 14th Street SE** was remodeled with the assistance of the National Housing Services, as was the house at 1342 Valley Place SE.

■ **13/14/15** An interesting walk down **Valley Place and Mt. View Place** will take you back to Martin Luther King Jr. Avenue.

Cedar Hill

■ **16** If you are using a car, stop at Our Lady of Perpetual Help School, 1602 Morris Road SE. It offers one of the most sought-after **views of Washington** west of the Anacostia. From 1854, what are now called Martin Luther King Jr. Avenue and Good Hope Road were earmarked for commercial development. The first establishments, which included the legendary Duvall's Tavern and George Pyle's Grocery, were located at the intersection of these two streets. However, the two thoroughfares have not developed as envisioned. Today, many vacant structures abut the frontages.

■ **17/18** Two later additions include an interesting **art deco building** at 2022 Martin Luther King Jr. Avenue SE and the **colossal chair** of the old Curtis Brothers furniture store. The chair is a neighborhood landmark.

■ **19** The first home of the Anacostia Bank, **2021 Martin Luther King Jr. Avenue SE,** was built between 1903 and 1913 and is a marvelous expression of the Georgian Revival mode. The building currently houses the Anacostia Economic Development Agency.

■ **20** The monumental building at **Martin Luther King Jr. Avenue and U Street** is an example of neoclassical revival style and was built between 1913 and 1927 as the second home of the Anacostia Bank. This building presently houses a branch of Riggs Bank.

■ **21** Three storefronts at **1918–22 Martin Luther King Jr. Avenue SE** highlight a new treatment of commercial buildings that appeared between 1936 and 1943. Notice the pediments over each store. The unit at no. 1922 retains evidence of the original window-sash panels, revealing the richness of the initial composition.

■ **22** Several of the two-story commercial buildings, such as **1227 Good Hope Road SE,** have been converted to residences. Though it was heavily modified on the first floor, the upper portion of the building remains substantially intact, revealing handsomely proportioned brick detailing in the corners and arches crowning the windows.

Notoriety was brought to Good Hope Road in 1865, when John Wilkes Booth used it as an escape route after he assassinated President Lincoln.

Although new structures have been built in Old Anacostia over the past decade, the commercial area has been subject to changes of varying scope, sometimes as minor as an addition of updated and often tasteless signs, at other times as major as the replacement of existing buildings with new ones. Many of the new buildings, unfortunately, are unarticulated structures that add nothing positive either to the streetscape or to the community. Some of them at least make an effort to maintain the scale and setback of the surrounding buildings.

■ **23** The **Verizon Telephone Building,** one of the new additions to the area, cuts a hole in the residential block of U Street.

■ **24** At 1522 Good Hope Road SE is **Neighborhood Housing Services,** a private nonprofit organization made up of area residents and representatives of financial institutions, businesses, and the District of Columbia government, working together for neighborhood improvement. NHS provides long-term, low-interest loans to property owners to repair code violations. Visitors are welcome at the NHS office.

Georgetown—West and Waterfront

(Historical residential district, new mixed-use infill developments, shops and restaurants, C&O Canal, Potomac River waterfront, Georgetown University)

Robert H. Cousins, expanded by Marilyn (Mickey) Klein, updated by James Troy

Distance: 2 1/2 miles
Time: 1 1/2 hours
Bus: 32, 34, 35, 36, 32B, and G2
Metro: Foggy Bottom/GWU (Blue and Orange Lines)

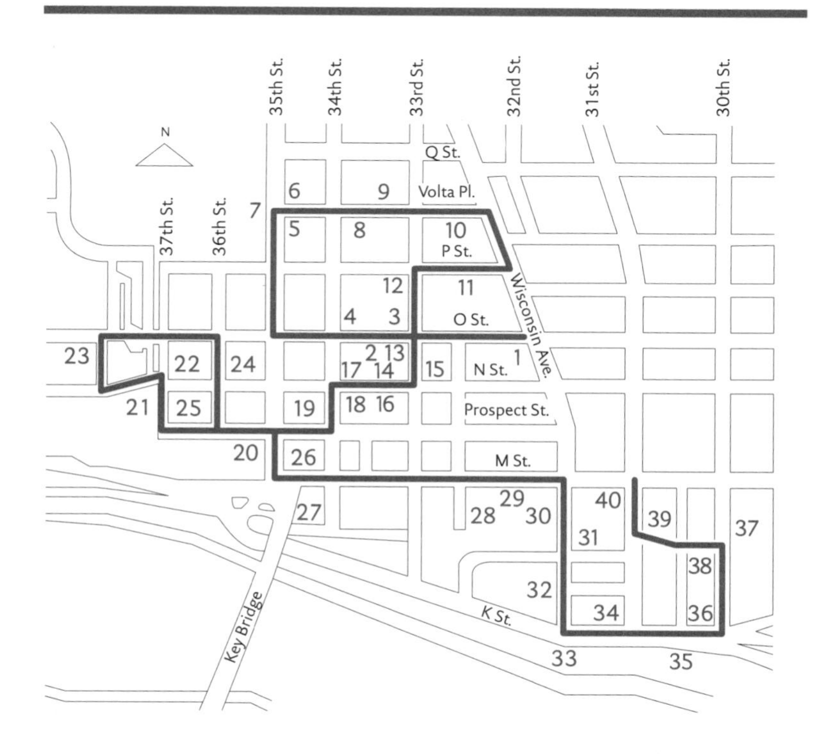

In 1751 the Maryland Assembly founded what it called Georgetown and drew up a plat for the land south of present-day N Street, to the river. However, there is evidence that a grant of land, comprising what is now known as Georgetown, was awarded much earlier to Ninian Beall in 1703. In the 1740s, tobacco from nearby Maryland growers was being inspected, crated, and shipped from warehouses along the Potomac River at Georgetown. Then, in 1791, Georgetown was included in the area selected by President Washington to be the seat of government. Work had already started on the Chesapeake and Ohio (C&O) Canal, much farther west, in 1875, even though this important artery was not completed through Georgetown itself until the 1830s.

By the beginning of the 19th century, the people who were successful in commerce and government were building their fine residences in the area north of N Street. (Dumbarton Oaks and Evermay were built in 1801, and more modest but handsome Federal houses still standing in the 3300 block, the 3100 block, and the 2800 block of N Street were built in the period between 1813 and 1820.)

Georgetown declined in importance as a major tobacco port in the early part of the 19th century, as steam navigation made deeper ports more desirable. In 1871 Georgetown was joined with the City of Washington and became part of the District of Columbia. For the next 50 years it was not the fashionable place to live that it is today, but speculators continued to add Victorian row houses next to formal Federal mansions, on their gardens or on subdivided land, and Georgetown took on its urban village character. Bounded by Georgetown University on the west; Rock Creek on the east; large houses along R and S Streets as well as Montrose Park, Dumbarton Oaks, and Oak Hill Cemetery on the north; and the Potomac River on the south, Georgetown today has grown within its "borders." Because of its proximity to Downtown, its village and pedestrian scale, the beauty of its neighborhood streets filled with historic houses of all sizes, and its convenient shopping area, it is at the top of the list of desirable places in Washington in which to live. In fact, it is so desirable and such an economic magnet that it is constantly in danger of being overbuilt and overrun with traffic.

Georgetown today is an urban, cosmopolitan neighborhood of contrasts. On relatively quiet, tree-shaded residential streets, with brick sidewalks, fine old Federal homes with walled gardens are set next to Victorian workers' houses, only 12 to 14 feet wide. Entrances and setbacks vary; facades, doors, and trim are painted in subtle colors to blend with the architecture and neighboring houses. Montrose Park and Dumbarton Oaks on the north offer landscaped breathing space, as does the peaceful C&O Canal on the south, edged with a brick path for strollers and galleries, shops, and historic houses. Along the commercial streets of Wisconsin Avenue and M Street, on the other hand, there is continual bustling activity. Restaurants of all nationalities, shops, vendors, and movie theaters vie for attention from pedestrians on crowded sidewalks.

Within this historic neighborhood, the battle of preservation and compatible development is never ending. As new shops, hotels, townhouses, and apartments have been added on old parking lots, former gas station sites, and subdivided large lots, and as the waterfront has been developed, traffic congestion and citizen concern have become increasingly intense. There is no Metro stop in the area, although there is Metrobus service along the major thoroughfares.

The "Old Georgetown Act," passed by Congress in 1950, defined the historic district, which was added to the National Register of Historic Places as a National Landmark in 1967. The Old Georgetown Act also calls for Commission of Fine

Arts review of all new development and of exterior modifications to existing developments. In most cases, the review has helped to maintain a harmony of materials, architecture, and scale and has restrained commercialism. No neon signs are allowed in Georgetown, for example. However, the Fine Arts Commission review is only advisory and can be overruled by the city.

With the redevelopment of the waterfront, the area below M Street is densely developed with townhouses, apartments, restaurants, shops, and offices. It is as if a new community has been added to the old, yet Georgetown continues to hold its charm and to be one of the most fascinating parts of Washington.

The Georgetown Waterfront is planned for additional redevelopment, including a new boathouse for Georgetown University. Take the Foggy Bottom Metrorail and then walk west along Pennsylvania Avenue across Rock Creek Park or take the Georgetown Metro Connection van to Wisconsin Avenue and O Street.

■ **1** The tour of Georgetown begins at Wisconsin and O Streets NW, in the heart of the commercial area. Take a few steps down O Street to **St. John's Episcopal Church** (1809) at the corner of O and Potomac Streets. This lovely old church is attributed to William Thornton, the original architect of the Capitol, and of Tudor Place in Georgetown and the Octagon House, headquarters for the American Institute of Architects Foundation. Like the Capitol, this church has undergone many modifications. Thornton was a friend of Presidents Washington, Jefferson, Adams, Madison, and Monroe. Notice the old trolley tracks and brick street, a reminder of earlier days—and a way to slow the traffic moving through the neighborhood.

■ **2** 3322 O Street NW, the **Bodisco House** (1822), is a fine example of the Federal style of architecture. Notice the graceful wrought-iron stair rails, the elliptical fan-shaped window over the front door, and the slender sidelights. In the mid-19th century, the house was the elegant home of the Russian minister to the United States. In the 1930s, in the midst of the Depression, it was converted into 10 apartments. Now beautifully restored, it was home to Sen. John Heinz of Pennsylvania until his death in 1991.

■ **3/4** At **3325 O Street NW,** across the street from the Bodisco House, is a projecting-bay, conical-roofed Queen Anne row house. Built in the 1890s for about $3,500, it is one of many houses of this type in Georgetown and in other Washington neighborhoods. At **3331 O Street** is a Georgian Revival house with a mansard roof. Note the elaborate entry and the broken pediment.

■ **5** At 35th Street, turn right, noticing no. 1404, built about 1800. **1525 35th Street NW** was a home of Alexander Graham Bell's parents.

■ **6** On the opposite side of the street, across from the Georgetown Visitation School (1537 35th Street NW) is the **Volta Bureau** (1893). Alexander Graham

St. John's Episcopal Church

Bell used his prize money for inventing the telephone to found the bureau to study the problems of the deaf.

■ 7 At 1500 35th Street NW is the **Georgetown Visitation Preparatory School and Monastery (Convent),** the first Catholic school for girls in the original 13 colonies. The white Gothic Revival chapel was designed by a French chaplain and built in 1821. The corner red brick building on 35th Street was built in the 1830s, and the part facing P Street was built in the 1850s. The Academy Building, designed by Norris K. Starkweather and built in 1873, has Italianate features and a mansard roof. Notice the hood moldings around the tall windows and the elaborate molding over the front door. Much of the school burned down in early 2000 but has been nicely rebuilt. Here, you can turn right on Volta Place (no street signs are visible here so it might get confusing—please refer to the map often), or take a short detour several blocks north on 35th Street to walk past the Cloisters, a residential development between Winfield Street and Reservoir Road. Built in the early 1980s, the row houses were designed to blend into Georgetown's brick vernacular architecture. At 35th and Reservoir is **Duke Ellington High School** (originally Western High School). Built in 1898 in Classic Revival style, it is now a city-wide school for the arts. Theater groups for public performances use its modern theater, designed by Keyes Condon Florance. Proceed back down to Volta Place for the next stop on the tour.

■ 8 **Pomader Walk** (1885), on Volta Place between 33rd and 34th Streets. Once in sorry disrepair and called "Bedlam, DC," these 10 small houses, first restored in 1950, are now choice places to live.

■ **9** Across the street on Volta Place, you will pass the **Volta Playground.** Its tennis courts, playground, and pool are actively used by nearby residents.

■ **10** At **3230–16 Volta Place NW** you will see a former police station converted by Robert Bell, Architects and Associates, into an attractive residential enclave, with a rear communal courtyard. The architect terms the results "Fantasy Federal." The buildings relate to Federal-style architecture with Palladian windows, French doors, and dormers, but with the updated, over-scaled windows, oriels, skylights, and two-story spaces inside, the interiors are bathed in light.

Turn right on Wisconsin Avenue, walking past the Georgetown Club at no. 1530. Its facade dates from the late 1790s. President Reagan dined here the night before he was shot and on his first night out after recovery. Turn right on P Street.

3230–16 Volta Place NW

■ **11** At **3264 P Street NW** you will see a surprisingly simple pink and tan frame house set in a country garden.

■ **12** **1430 33rd Street NW,** the lovely yellow house on the southwest corner of 33rd and P was built in 1807 on the site of the oldest house in Georgetown, built in 1733. Turn left on 33rd Street.

■ **13** At **1316 33rd Street NW** is an unusual former carriage house that combines Tudor Revival architecture in the back with its half-timbering, and Gothic Revival stained glass windows in the front.

■ **14** You may have noticed that many of the mid-19th-century houses in Georgetown retain on their facades **fire marks,** labels of the various fire assurance companies, which showed that the homeowner had sound credit with the company. Until 1871, volunteer firefighters served the community. Notice the symbols at **1312 and 1310 33rd Street NW,** for example.

■ **15** N Street, between 33rd and Potomac Streets, has a row of **six Federal houses** built by Walter Clement Smith in 1815 that have remained essentially unchanged. Notice the wrought-iron stairway and graceful fan light over the door at no. 3259 and the Flemish bond pattern of the bricks (laid in alternating headers and stretchers).

■ **16 3307 N Street NW** (1811). John F. Kennedy and his wife lived here at the time he was elected president. William Marbury built this Federal house.

■ **17 3327–39 N Street NW.** This group of five houses, known as **Cox's Row,** named after the owner-builder, a former mayor of Georgetown, was built in 1817. The handsome doorways, dormers, and garland decorations on the facade are characteristics of the Federal period. One, no. 3333, has been converted into condominiums.

Cox's Row

■ **18 3334 N Street NW** (about 1860). This Italianate house is typical of many built in American cities from pattern books between 1840 and 1880. Its bracketed cornice and long hooded windows are characteristic features. Turn left on 35th Street to Prospect Street.

■ **19 3425 Prospect Street NW.** This handsome house is known as **Quality Hill** and was built in 1798 by a general in the Revolutionary War. Sen. Claiborne Pell has lived here for many years.

■ **20** 3508 Prospect Street NW—**Prospect House.** Erected in 1788, this house in the late 1940s was the home of James V. Forrestal, the first secretary of defense. The first two owners were friends of George Washington.

3334 N Street NW

■ **21** At 37th and N Streets, the **Lauinger Memorial Library,** Georgetown University, was the subject of prolonged debate among the Fine Arts Commission, the Citizens Association of Georgetown, the National Capital Planning Commission, the university, and others. The result, designed by John Carl Warnecke Associates and completed in 1970, now seems to fit comfortably into the campus and the community. The rhythm of its projecting bays and its sympathetic color, texture, and massing combine to add interest to, but not a sharp intrusion on, its surroundings.

■ **22** A **housing complex** for 360 students on the right side of 37th Street, taking a half block between N and O, was designed by the internationally known architect Hugh Newell Jacobsen, a Georgetown resident. The U-shaped dormitory grouping surrounding an interior park resembles small townhouses, each with its own entrance. By following the natural slope and including English basements, the architect was able to maintain the scale and character of the nearby small residential buildings.

■ **23** At 37th and O Streets is the pedestrian entrance to **Georgetown University,** established in 1789 as Georgetown College. The university is the oldest Catholic and Jesuit institution of higher education in the United States. Straight ahead is the impressive Healy Hall, built in 1879 in the Flemish Romanesque style and designed by Smithmeyer and Pelz, who also designed the Library of Congress. Its central clock spire can be seen from many places around the city. Inside, Gaston Hall hosts concerts and lectures open to the public. Behind Healy Hall is Old North, which dates from 1795. Notice the mix of contemporary and traditional architecture on the campus.

■ **24** Walk up O Street, turning right on 36th Street, where you will see the **Holy Trinity Church,** where President Kennedy worshiped. The church was originally built in 1851 and restored in 1979. The original church to the rear, entered at 3513 N Street NW, was dedicated in 1792 and remains the oldest standing church in the District of Columbia.

■ **25** Across 36th Street the **mix of shops and restaurants** is convenient for residents and students. Evening extension courses are offered to the community in classroom buildings on 36th Street. The 1789 restaurant is a favorite watering hole for Georgetown students in the basement bar called the Tombs.

■ **26** At Prospect walk to 35th Street. You are sure to see the high rises of Rosslyn, Virginia, across the Potomac River. Without historic district protection, the character of Georgetown might have been threatened or destroyed by the intense development pressures that shaped Rosslyn. Just a few short steps from here is the steep staircase to M Street where *The Exorcist* was filmed. The **"Old Georgetown Falls Street,"** 35th Street from Prospect to M Streets, has cobblestone paving. Its topography is similar to that of a San Francisco street.

■ **27** Notice across M Street the **Francis Scott Key Park** near the Key Bridge to Virginia. Francis Scott Key, author of the "The Star-Spangled Banner," was a resident of Georgetown for many years. His house (now torn down) overlooked the river at 3516–18 M Street NW.

At this point, you may wish to stop for a snack on M Street, continue another day, or continue along M Street and down to the waterfront.

■ **28** The **Market House** at 3276 M Street was restored in the late 1970s by Clark, Tribble, and Li as a miniature food emporium and is now Dean & DeLuca, a highly successful food store. Originally built as a public market in 1864 and used for that purpose until the late 1930s, it later was used as an auto parts store.

■ **29** On M Street between the Market House and Wisconsin Avenue, where a tobacco warehouse once stood, is now **The Shops at Georgetown Park.** Part of the building that houses the shops was built in the 1800s; this historic site once accommodated horse-drawn omnibuses. Later it was used to service electric streetcars and trolleys. In the 1960s the site was selected by the White House as the location of the "Situation Room" and housed equipment for the first hotline to Moscow. During the excavation process in transforming the site into its current Victorian style, multilevel shopping center, archaeologists unearthed and cataloged thousands of artifacts that can be seen in the Georgetown Park Museum. The Georgetown Park Mall was designed by Lockman Associates. The first part opened in 1981. It is an intriguing preservation project, which retains the exterior facades and scale of 19th-century buildings, while containing a multilevel neo-Victorian sky-lit shopping center. Enter through the main doorway, and you will find an array of elegant shops, small cafes and restaurants, and a central plaza with a fountain, benches, and plants. The Georgetown Park Mall development includes apartments above the stores.

■ **30** You should leave Georgetown Park from one of the two south exits on Level 2. These exits lead to bridges that cross the C&O Canal. Pause on the bridge in summer and you may see one of the mule-drawn barges, operated for tourists by the National Park Service, on the canal. The bridge will then lead you to Canal House, a **mixture of offices and residential condominiums** in a beautifully restored warehouse. The building first served as a stable, built in 1878, for the Georgetown Railroad Company. A welcoming public courtyard has been created at the east end of the building. Lockman Associates restored the warehouse in 1979.

You may proceed down Wisconsin Avenue to the next sight or you may want to wander a little around this area, taking a look down Cecil Place to Cherry Hill Lane, where you will find a group of well-restored townhouses. Across Cecil Lane is the Peppermill, a large residential project that combines rehabilitation with newly constructed "mews houses"—and this is worth a look, too.

Georgetown Park

■ **31** Walk down Wisconsin Avenue toward the river. On your left, you will notice **Grace Church,** set back from the street on its raised courtyard. Built about 1866 in the Gothic Revival style, it originally served as a mission church for boatmen plying the C&O Canal.

■ **32** **Waterfront Center.** Near the corner of Wisconsin Avenue and K (Water) Street is Waterfront Center, a 90-foot-high office/retail building, designed by Hartman Cox Architects. The rebuilding of the waterfront area has been the subject of bitter debate about height, density, and uses for several decades. The permit for this structure was obtained before new zoning took effect and reflects what the old industrial zoning would allow. Integral to its design is the preservation of the **Old Dodge Warehouse Company Buildings** (about 1813). The Center for Community Change owns the warehouses and has its headquarters here.

■ **33 Whitehurst Freeway.** The elevated Whitehurst Freeway, constructed in 1949 over K Street along the Potomac River, has been a cause for debate within the community for the past 20 years. When it was built, to relieve congestion on M Street and to serve as a commuter bypass, the waterfront area was industrial, with a lumberyard, sand and gravel operation, a flourmill, and a rendering plant, as well as a rail line used to haul coal. As these activities disappeared and the waterfront began to be redeveloped, the freeway was seen by many as a visual barrier to the river. In the late 1980s, the District government studied alternatives to the elevated structure, including a ground-level parkway that would improve its relationship with its surroundings. The District government's plan is for a $48-million rehabilitation of the elevated freeway, which will include road widening, new lighting, replacing the existing deck and parapets, and painting the structure in shades of gray. The National Park Service plans to develop a park with shade trees along the waterfront.

Waterfront Center

■ **34** The **Old Georgetown Incinerator** (about 1930) is a four-story art deco industrial structure with a towering smokestack. It sits on an acre of land that has been recently developed into a movie-theater complex, residential condominiums, and an 86-room Ritz Carlton Hotel. A plaque on the side attests to its history. Suter's tavern is believed to have stood here from 1783 to 1795. On March 30, 1791, George Washington is said to have met neighboring landowners in

Suter's Tavern and negotiated the purchase of lands required for the Federal City, later called Washington. Pierre Charles L'Enfant, who reputedly completed the original plan for the capital city there in 1791, also used Suter's Tavern.

■ **35** Across K Street, between 31st and 29th Streets, is the **Washington Harbour,** a 1-million-square-foot office and residential development designed by Arthur Cotton Moore Associates. The development includes a new east–west pedestrian boardwalk at the river's edge, as well as an adjacent small riverside park—public amenities that the city required that the developer provide. The design allows the river to be seen from all entrances, as well as from the restaurants and cafes that line the plaza. Although the scale and design of the major structures have been controversial, the plaza and boardwalk have created a lively public space that welcomes strollers, bikers, boaters, residents, workers, sunbathers, and restaurant patrons. To protect against flooding, a state-of-the-art system of adjustable floodgates around the project has eliminated the need for permanent barriers.

■ **36** New red brick offices and residences: Leaving Washington Harbour through the main entrance, cross K Street and walk along (or through the courtyard of) **Jefferson Court,** 1025 Thomas Jefferson Street NW, an office building designed by Skidmore, Owings & Merrill and completed in 1984. It can be entered on Thomas Jefferson, K, and 30th Streets. As you walk up 30th Street, notice recent red brick residential developments at **1001 and 1111 30th Street NW (James Place).**

■ **37** **CFC Square** is a contemporary red brick building designed by architect Arthur Cotton Moore. Located at the northeast corner of 30th Street and the C&O Canal and extending through to 29th Street, it was completed in stages between 1975 and 1983. The project includes offices and a residential apartment hotel, Georgetown Mews.

■ **38** 1055 Thomas Jefferson Street NW. Designed by Arthur Cotton Moore, **The Foundry** combines its new red brick construction with the preservation and adaptation of a landmark structure (an old foundry) and is oriented to the C&O Canal. The building now houses a restaurant, some shops, and galleries. The landscaped areas on both sides of the canal, maintained by the National Park Service, offer pleasant sites for summer concerts and the terminal for canal boat tours.

■ **39** **1058 Thomas Jefferson Street NW.** The current office use is an example of the continuing uses of old structures for changing purposes over a period of time. This little structure was built originally as a Masonic Hall about 1810. Between Thomas Jefferson and 31st Streets, along the canal's towpath, is a **group of small houses** built on speculation in 1870. Artisans and workers originally used them. Since that time they have been converted into shops, offices, and residences.

■ **40** **Canal Square,** 1054 31st Street NW, is an innovative office and specialty shop complex that successfully incorporates some old warehouses along the

C&O Canal into the project and is built around an inner court. It was designed by Arthur Cotton Moore and completed in 1971. Leave the complex and head for 31st Street, turn into the small courtyard, and then go up through the stairs into the alley ahead. Then turn left and notice "Blues Alley" on your left as you leave the alley. Blues Alley is a long-established place to hear fine jazz—it now has a branch in Tokyo.

Note the new construction at Bank Street and M Streets opposite Market Square. It is a mixed-use project being constructed by Kadon Construction.

Back on M Street, you can take any bus on the 30 Route to the George Washington University Hospital stop and walk down 23rd Street to the Foggy Bottom Metro station at I Street NW.

Georgetown—East

(Historic residential district, specialty shops, restaurants, C&O Canal)

Robert H. Cousins, updated by James Troy

Distance: 2 miles
Time: 1 hour
Bus: On Pennsylvania Avenue: 32, 34, 35, 36 and 38B
Metro: Foggy Bottom/GWU (Blue and Orange Lines)

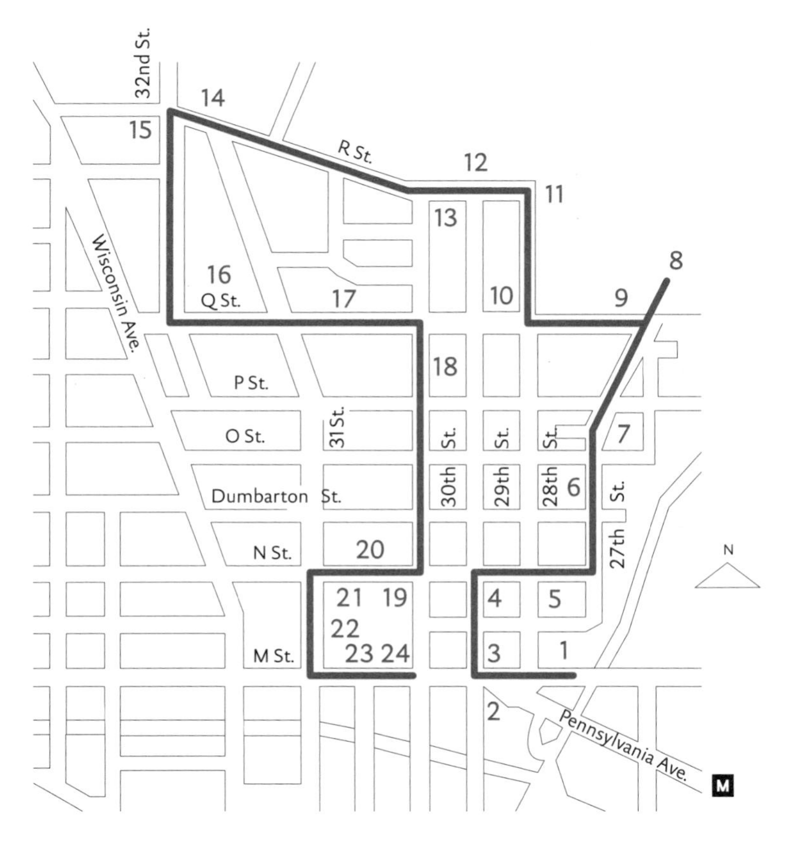

Start your tour on M Street, just west of the M Street Bridge over Rock Creek Park. This point corresponds to one of the eastern entrances to Georgetown. Take the Metrorail to the Foggy Bottom/GWU stop and walk west to M Street NW.

■ 1 On your right is a **mixed-used complex** that was created out of the old Corcoran School (facing 28th Street) and its former playground. The project, designed by Arthur Cotton Moore, is intended to reflect its gateway location by siting a new four-story building (2715 M Street NW) containing a pointed tower at its east end and making a connection, by means of a three-story wing, with the smaller-scale existing structures on the west. The new building contains retail and office space along M Street and apartments in the rear, looking into the courtyard. The carefully restored **Corcoran School Building** (now containing offices) and five new townhouses complete this small-scale but interesting project.

■ 2 Across M Street between 28th and 29th Streets is the **Four Seasons Hotel and office complex,** designed by the Washington office of Skidmore, Owings & Merrill. The rectangular brick structure includes hotel, office, and retail space. This contemporary building also celebrates its gateway location with a dramatic clock tower rising from its midst and facing Pennsylvania Avenue. The new building wraps around the 19th-century row of shops at the corner of 29th Street known as Diamond Row, and its back doors connect to the Chesapeake and Ohio Canal and its towpath.

■ 3 On the northern side of the intersection of 29th and M Streets are two relatively new and successful infill office buildings. The **Embassy of Mongolia** is located on the east at 2833 M Street NW, and the **First Union Bank Building** is located on the west at 2901 M Street NW. The Citicorp Building was built in the early 1970s, imitating the Federal style. Reflecting a different approach, the whimsical Signet Bank, designed by Martin and Jones and built in 1981, is a good example of postmodern contextual architecture. Its multipaned windows with their round tops are similar to those on the First Union Bank building across 29th Street; its classical columns relate to the decorative columns of the art deco drug store next door to the east. The Embassy of Mongolia building won an AIA preservation award in 1982.

■ 4 **2806, 2808, and 2812 N Street NW** make one of the most outstanding groups of fine Federal architecture in the Georgetown area. They were all built between about 1813 and 1817. Nos. 2806 and 2808 are almost identical, except that they are opposite-handed. No. 2812 is larger and has symmetry. It is referred to as the Decatur House because it is said that Commodore Stephen Decatur's widow lived here after his death.

■ 5 In the rear yard of the corner house at **2726 N Street NW,** on a brick wall against the neighboring house on 28th Street is a large colored mosaic designed by Marc Chagall. The artist had reportedly been a friend of the owners and, on a visit there, had observed that the site was perfect for some alfresco art. The best view of the mosaic used to be at the northwest corner of the intersection (in front of the synagogue), but the shrubbery along the inside of the wall has succeeded in blocking the view almost entirely. Now it is recommended that the mosaic be viewed from the sidewalk alongside the wall on 28th Street.

■ 6 **1350 27th Street NW,** built in 1968, was designed by Hugh Newell Jacobsen, a prominent Washington architect. The house represents an excellent alterna-

2806 N Street NW: The Gannt-Williams House

tive to the "fake Federal" style found elsewhere throughout Georgetown as new infill houses were added in the 1950s and 1960s. Its scale and materials fit in well with the Victorian neighborhood.

■ 7 **1411–19 27th Street NW.** These townhouses were built in 1954 after a revision to the zoning regulations required off-street parking at the rate of one parking space for each dwelling unit. Although parking space is required to be shown on building plans and the buildings then built accordingly, it is not ultimately required to be used for that purpose. (Note the subsequent conversions of the garages to other uses.)

■ 8 Across Q Street and located down an extension of 27th Street is **Mount Zion Cemetery,** a site rich in local history. For the burial of its members, both white and black, the Dumbarton Street Methodist Church acquired the eastern half of the cemetery in 1808, although in 1816 the black members of Dumbarton Church withdrew to form the Mount Zion AME Church (located at 1334 29th Street NW). The western half of the cemetery was purchased in 1842 by the Female Band Society, a cooperative benevolent society of free black women, for the burial of free blacks. With the opening of Oak Hill Cemetery in 1849, however, white members of Dumbarton Church began to favor that newly fashionable "garden cemetery," and eventually they leased the eastern half of Mount Zion Cemetery to Mount Zion Church.

Although maintenance of the combined cemetery over the years has been sadly lacking, the Afro-American Bicentennial Corporation, in the early 1970s, directed a clearing of debris and overgrowth from the cemetery. In 1975 the cemetery was designated a Historic Landmark and was recommended for nomination to the National Register of Historic Places. Also fortunate for the cemetery's future maintenance was its inclusion in 1988 in a Black History National Recreation Trail directed by the National Park Service.

■ **9** **Dumbarton House,** at 2715 Q Street NW, now the headquarters of the National Society of Colonial Dames, was built between 1799 and 1804. Though described as Federal architecture on the plaque set into the mansion's wall, it has decidedly Georgian characteristics (the central pedimented pavilion, which projects very slightly, and the keystone lintels). It was moved from its original location on what is now Q Street to its present location in 1915. It is open to the public weekdays 2:00–5:00 p.m.

■ **10** At **2813 Q Street NW** is a Victorian house that was redone and doubled in size by Hugh Jacobsen in 1959. It was one of the first attempts in Georgetown to renovate in a manner that combines contemporary ideas and materials with more traditional themes.

■ **11** **Evermay,** at 1623 28th Street NW, is one of the showplaces of Georgetown and is the scene each year of a tea at the end of the Georgetown Garden Tour. It was built between 1792 and 1794, greatly modified over the years, and finally carefully restored to its original Georgian splendor. The original owner purchased the ground for this building with money he made from proceeds of sale of the land where the White House and Lafayette Square now stand.

■ **12** Inside Oak Hill Cemetery, at 29th and R Streets, stands the **Oak Hill Chapel,** designed by James Renwick. It was erected in 1850 and is one of only four structures designed by Renwick still standing in the District. This strong and dignified little Gothic Revival building is based on much earlier rural English chapels of the 13th and 14th centuries, though the materials used were acquired locally: Potomac gneiss and red Seneca sandstone. Oak Hill Cemetery, approached through the handsome gates next to its fanciful gatehouse (1849), is open weekdays by request; consult the sign at the cemetery's entrance.

■ **13** Across the street at **2920 R Street NW** was the home of former Katherine Meyer Graham, the late chairman of the board of the Washington Post Company. After Ms. Graham's death, the home was sold to a private individual.

■ **14** **Dumbarton Oaks,** at R and 31st Streets, is worth an afternoon visit all by itself. This magnificent 16-acre estate is now owned by Harvard University but reflects the generosity and interests of its benefactors, the late Robert and Mildred Bliss. Mrs. Bliss was a very accomplished horticulturalist and landscape architect. If you visit at the right time of the year, you can see extensive gardens, ranging from a formal pebble mosaic pool to a romantic rustic pool shaded by lindens. Mr. Bliss was a foreign

Oak Hill Chapel

service officer and ambassador to Argentina. He collected pre-Columbian works of art, which are now housed in a handsome museum designed by Philip Johnson. It is open to the public during designated hours and is reached from the 32nd Street side of the property. Not to be overlooked is the great Georgian mansion, which was the original house at The Oaks and was built in 1801. Telephone (202) 339-6401 for information about hours and fees for touring the gardens.

■ **15** The **Scott-Grant House,** at 3238 R Street NW, was built in 1858, and was once occupied by President Ulysses S. Grant as a summer White House. The property, quite large for Georgetown, has had some additional houses built on it, though the original mansion still has an appropriate setting.

■ **16** **Tudor Place,** which has its main entrance at 1644 31st Street NW, occupies nearly the entire large block created by Q, R, 31st, and 32nd Streets. It was built in 1815 and was designed by William Thornton, the winner of the original competition for the design of the US Capitol. This important building, its style unique in Georgetown, provides an interesting contrast between its severe Federal north facade and its south facade with its generous and finely detailed windows and its classical domed two-story Greek temple. Quite remarkably, this great house, until sometime in the last decade, has housed only one family descending from Thomas Peter and his bride, a granddaughter of Martha Washington. The house and gardens are open to the public, but by appointment only.

■ **17** **Cooke's Row** consists of four double detached houses (3007–29 Q Street NW) built in 1868. These basically Victorian structures appear to derive from the design for an Italian villa, though their heavier sculptural effect and prominent mansard roofs (on the two end buildings) reflect a Second Empire French influence. The houses, set back from the street in little green parks and separate from each other, create a pleasant precinct that is unlike most of Georgetown.

■ **18** The house at **1527 30th Street NW** is one of two Italianate villas designed by Andrew Jackson Downing and Calvert Vaux in the 1850s. (The second villa, greatly altered, is located at 28th and Q Streets.) The house at 1527 30th Street NW (which has now been converted into condominiums) has been extensively added to on the south along 30th Street and on the east along Q Street. The original building at no. 1527, however, retains much of the flat-walled and asymmetrical massing of an Italianate villa.

1527 30th Street NW

■ **19** The central portion of this large house at **3014 N Street NW** was built in 1799, though obvious additions were added later. It is notable for its nicely detailed round-top windows on the first floor, and for that reason is thought to be the work of William Thornton. In 1915 it was acquired by Abraham Lincoln's son, Robert Todd Lincoln, who served as secretary of war and ambassador to England.

■ **20** The house at **3017 N Street NW** was acquired by Jacqueline Kennedy after the assassination of her husband in 1963. She didn't stay there very long, however, since hordes of sightseers caused her to complain of the invasion of her privacy. She subsequently moved to a high-rise apartment building in New York.

■ **21** The fine old Federal house at **3038 N Street NW** was built in 1816 and was occupied by W. Averell Harriman up to his death. It has typical Federal details: bull's-eye lintels over the windows and a modest but finely detailed fanlight over the door.

■ **22** Though the building at **1221 31st Street NW** now houses the Georgetown branch of the US Postal Service, this Renaissance Revival building, designed in the manner of an Italian palace, was originally a customs house for the bustling port of Georgetown. It was designed by Ammi B. Young and constructed in 1857–58.

■ **23** The **Old Stone House,** at 3051 M Street NW, is believed to date back to about 1766. In any event, it is generally accepted as the oldest building in the District of Columbia and is now the property of the National Park Service, which maintains it as a public museum. The ample grounds to the right and behind the house contain beautiful gardens and attract, in their own right, weary tourists and local office workers at lunchtime.

■ **24** The row of four houses at **3001–3009 M Street NW** (now with retail space on the ground floor) show the common three-bay facade typical of the Federal period. The two houses on the right are dated about 1790, the two on the left a little later. The group was carefully restored in 1955.

You are now in the heart of the retail section of Georgetown, so you may want to finish your tour at a local bar or step into any of the nearby specialty shops along M Street and Wisconsin Avenue.

3001–9 M Street NW

Nearby Historic Suburban Areas

Old Town Alexandria, Virginia

(18th-century port city, specialty shops and restaurants, high-demand residential neighborhoods and infill condominiums, Torpedo Factory Art Center)

Andrea Lubershane and James L. Wilson, updated by James L. Wilson

Distance: 1 1/3 miles

Time: 1 1/4 hours

Bus: Alexandria DASH System

Metro: King Street (Blue and Yellow Lines)

Driving: Go south from Washington, DC, on the George Washington Memorial Parkway toward historic Mount Vernon. In Alexandria the GW Parkway becomes Washington Street. Pass the statue of a Confederate soldier at Prince Street then turn left at the next intersection onto Duke Street. Park on the street in the 500 block of Duke Street, then walk north two blocks to the fountain at Market Square to begin the tour.

Founded by John Alexander, a Scottish merchant, Alexandria was incorporated in 1749 by an act of the Virginia General Assembly. It became a flourishing seaport and trading center, surpassing the port of New York and rivaling Boston in shipping activity. George Washington was intimately involved with Alexandria, from his days as a teenage surveyor to his becoming first president of the United States. Many colonial sites still exist here in excellent condition and most are open to the public. Waterfront improvements and development have occurred during the past two decades, making Alexandria both a historical and a modern city.

From 1791 to 1847 Alexandria was part of the District of Columbia and was once considered as a site for the US Capitol. During the Civil War, Union soldiers occupied this Confederate city. But with the advent of railroads, the economy of Alexandria declined. Warehouses and wharves along the Potomac deteriorated. Housing also became dilapidated.

A six-block commercial urban renewal program called the Gadsby Project was completed in 1981, 20 years after it had begun. Gadsby rekindled the spirits of Alexandrians and led to renovations throughout much of Old Town. Formerly dilapidated warehouses were transformed into fashionable shops and warehouses. Three Metro stations, which opened during the 1970s, added further impetus to the redevelopment. A decade-long policy by the city council has also revived the once-dilapidated and neglected eyesore of a 3-mile-long waterfront. Today the Alexandria waterfront has become a successful model of urban waterfront planning. Be sure to see this now glamorous and lively showplace.

■ 1 **Market Square Fountain and City Hall.** Begin your tour at the fountain in front of City Hall at 301 King Street. During the French and Indian War, British troops paraded in front of this historic block. The reenactment of this event is held in front of Gadsby's Tavern every November. Market Square was the first block in the Gadsby's urban renewal area.

■ 2 The **Carlyle House** was built in 1752 by John Carlyle, a wealthy Scottish merchant. This historic house served as the meeting place for General Braddock and five British governors when they proposed the Stamp Act of 1765, an incidence of "Taxation without Representation" that served as the spark that ignited the American Revolution. The Northern Virginia Regional Park Authority restored the Carlyle House in 1976, making it one of its few urban parks in Northern Virginia. Springtime blooms beautifully in the public gardens behind the house. Open Tuesday–Sunday 10:00 a.m.–4:00 p.m.; closed on Monday.

■ 3 The **Ramsay House,** Alexandria's oldest house, was built in 1724 as a home for the city's first lord mayor, William Ramsey, another Scottish merchant and city founder. The colorful yellow house has been restored and serves as the tourist information center, open daily 9:00 a.m.–5:00 p.m. Dozens of free flyers and a short movie about Alexandria are available there.

■ 4 The **Stabler-Leadbeater Apothecary Shop,** founded in 1792, served continuously as a drug store from 1792 until 1933. Martha and George Washington and other early countrymen ordered medications here.

The bronze plaque on the outside wall states that during the colonial era, "manufacturing, wholesaling, and dispensing of medicines were combined as a single enterprise of pharmacists in urban centers." The authentic furnishing includes a remarkable collection of early medical ware and hand-blown glass. Open Monday–Saturday 10:00 a.m.–4:00 p.m. and Sunday 1:00–5:00 p.m.

■ 5 The former **Green Steam Furniture Works** at 200 South Fairfax Street was a garage for the repair of Mercedes-Benz automobiles until the late 1970s. It has been converted to condominiums. This building typifies reuse of old buildings in Alexandria.

■ 6 The restored residence at **215 South Fairfax Street** further typifies the private improvements to Alexandria during the past decades. Public amenities such as brick sidewalks, underground wiring, colonial-style lampposts, and street trees spurred private investments in restoration and new infill townhouses.

■ 7 The **Old Presbyterian Meeting House** was built in 1774 by Scottish founders of Alexandria. The interior is well preserved. The slate roof was removed in 1989 and replaced with a copper roof, which was deemed more authentic. A cemetery behind the church holds the Tomb of the Unknown Soldier of the American Revolution. Push the button at the fenced grave for a detailed audio narration.

Funeral services for George Washington were held here in December 1799 and are periodically reenacted with great accuracy. The church is on the National Register of Historic Places. Attend a Sunday church service at 8:30 or 11:00 a.m.

■ 8 **Gentry Row,** left of Lee Street, the brick-paved street, is lined with homes of early merchants and many important Alexandria patriots of the American Revolution. Cobblestone **Captains Row,** the 100 block of Prince Street, contains homes of colonial sea captains. Most of the early streets in Alexandria were either dirt or paved with cobblestones that had been rounded by centuries of wear by river water.

■ 9 The **Athenaeum** is one of Alexandria's two surviving examples of Greek Revival architecture. Built 1852 as a bank, the structure later served as a Methodist church and as an exhibition hall for the Northern Virginia Fine Arts Association. Yes, the original color was pumpkin orange! Unless there is a special exhibit, the hours are Wednesday–Saturday 11:00 a.m.–4:00 p.m. and Sunday 1:00–3:00 p.m.

■ 10 **Lower King Street,** the 100 and 200 blocks, includes many interesting shops and an unusual variety of restaurants. This highly successful commercial area was made even more successful by the 1983 restoration and opening of the Torpedo Factory Art Center, and by the modern waterfront piers. The small park at the waterfront end of King Street typifies city council's long-term philosophy of public acquisition of the waterfront, changing the land from private industrial to public uses. Upper King Street, looking toward the Masonic Temple, has been redeveloped. The King Street Metro station, which opened in 1983, gave impetus to extensive redevelopment of upper King Street.

■ **11** The **Torpedo Factory complex** was built during World War I and employed over 5,000 people during the war. Later used as a federal records center for many years, the four main buildings in the complex were purchased in 1971 by the City of Alexandria. In 1982 building no. 10 was demolished and replaced by an enclosed public parking lot and by more than a hundred private residences. Buildings no. 1 and no. 3 along the waterfront were renovated and converted into offices, retail shops, and a permanent home for the Torpedo Factory Arts Center and Alexandria Archaeology Museum. The Market Building and the Chart House Restaurant, located behind the Torpedo Factory, opened for business in 1990. The center is open everyday 10:00 a.m.–5:00 p.m. Now walk through the Torpedo Factory Arts Center to the boardwalk overlooking the Potomac River. The wonderful mix of restaurants and private boating as well as public sightseeing boating was accomplished less than a decade ago.

■ **12** **Founders Park** was created by the city during the 1970s after the site was rescued from Watergate Developers, who had planned to construct four 12-story condominiums on it. This is one of several parks designated to provide public access to the Potomac River.

■ **13** The **Alexandria Bank** opened in 1807 at this location. Renovation of this historic building, the oldest bank building in the state of Virginia and the second oldest in the United States, was completed in 1980. Today the building is occupied by the Oxford Finance Corporation.

■ **14** The exterior of **City Hall,** along Cameron Street, remains unchanged from the early 1800s. Interior renovations were completed in 1982, after city courtrooms were moved into a new courthouse at 510 King Street. Step inside the Cameron Street entrance to view an exhibit about historic City Hall, which has served continuously as the seat of Alexandria's local government for nearly two centuries.

■ **15** **Gadsby's Tavern** was originally a small coffee house, built in 1752. Because it was so popular, a larger addition known as the City Hotel was built in 1792. A jewel of Georgian architecture, Gadsby's Tavern was the site of the preparation of the Fairfax Resolves of George Mason, predecessor document to the Bill of Rights. The tavern was popular with George Washington throughout his life. It also served as a theater. Traveling troupes of actors came frequently and presented their plays there. Gadsby's Tavern has been restored for use as a working restaurant, serving colonial foods.

■ **16** **Tavern Square** takes its name from Gadsby's Tavern. The city purchased the properties in the block, razed all structures except Gadsby's Tavern, relocated the former tenants, and resold the cleared land to a private developer. Sit down on one of the benches, and enjoy the sights and sounds. The small fountain next to Gadsby's Tavern is made from one of General Braddock's original Revolutionary War cannons.

Gadsby's House

■ **17** **Banker's Square** was one of the four remaining blocks of Gadsby Project Phase II. This block, named after the building that currently houses the SunTrust Bank, also contains retail businesses and offices.

■ **18** **Courthouse Square** was dedicated in May 1981, marking the completion of the Gadsby Project. The courthouse utilizes a large bay of solar heating panels atop the rear roof, combining modern technology with historic fabric.

■ **19** **Christ Church** was completed by John Carlyle in 1773 and served as a place of worship for George Washington and Robert E. Lee. It is an English country–style church with panels inscribed by James Wren with the Lord's Prayer and the Ten Commandments. The brick addition to the parish hall was designed to look like the original. In the old churchyard are many graves of Confederate soldiers. Nearly every president of the United States has attended Christ Church. The most recent brick pillars on Columbus Street were completed in 2002.

■ **20** The **Friendship Engine House** was originally manned by the Friendship Fire Company, a volunteer corps of citizens organized in 1774, which included George Washington as an early member. In 1900 the constitution and bylaws of Friendship Fire Company were rewritten to say that one of the main goals of the fire company was to perpetuate the memory of George Washington. Come in and see original artifacts such as the horse drawn fire engine purchased in 1851. Open Friday and Saturday 10:00 a.m.–4:00 p.m. and Sunday 1:00–4:00 p.m.

This block, labeled Firehouse Square, was privately redeveloped in the same manner as the earlier block of Gadsby's urban renewal area.

■ 21 **The Dip,** named after a natural topographic feature, is defined as a 13-block area bounded by Duke, Washington, Henry, and Franklin Streets. It was originally characterized by dilapidated houses, incompatible land uses, and undeveloped land. In 1970 the city council approved the Dip Urban Renewal Project for the low-income area. Groundbreaking occurred in 1975, with completion in 1980. The intention was to build new housing that longtime residents of the area could afford. The project did more than double the number of housing units, to more than 400 units, many of them subsidized. But with a changing economy, the project shifted from one intended principally to foster home ownership to one creating largely rental housing.

■ 22 **The Lyceum & Statue** was constructed in the 1830s. It later became a public meeting place and was nearly razed during the early 1970s. Following restoration in 1973, the Lyceum was designated as the Virginia Bicentennial Center for more than 10 years, beginning in 1976. Today it serves as a museum that emphasizes the history of Alexandria and includes a souvenir shop. Admission is free. Open Monday through Saturday 10:00 a.m.–5:00 p.m.

The statue in the middle of Washington Street is titled *Appomattox*. It was erected in 1889 to mark the spot where, in May 1961, many of Alexandria's sons left to join the Confederate army. The statue faces south and the text on the plaque refers to "The War between the States." Loyal Alexandrians of the 1860s did not consider the conflict to be a "civil war." The statue has become controversial, representing to some people the respect for those who defended their beloved state of Virginia and to others a symbol of slavery.

■ 23 Robert Young built the **"Franklin & Armfield" house at** 1315 Duke Street about 1812. Robert Young was brigadier general of the Second Militia of the District of Columbia. (Alexandria was then part of the District.) As a captain, Young commanded the cavalry in George Washington's funeral procession. Due to financial difficulties, Young sold the site to Franklin and Armfield in 1876 prior to the completion of the house. The firm operated a large slave auction house and trading market on the site for more than 33 years. The house has undergone several alterations. The "slave pens" that surrounded the house were torn down in 1870 and the six houses at 1301–1311 Duke Street were built on the site. By the 1830s, the city of Alexandria had become the largest slave-trading center in the United States. It is reported that Franklin and Armfield shipped 100 or more slaves to New Orleans every two weeks, and approximately 3,750 slaves passed through the auction house. Currently the house is owned and occupied by the Northern Virginia chapter of the National Urban League.

For information on other interesting sites in Alexandria, inquire at the Ramsey House tourist center or look online at www.funside.com.

Takoma Park, Maryland

(First planned commuter suburb, established residential areas, restored Victorian buildings, commercial corridors)

Lisa Schwartz from material contributed by Caroline Alderson and Historic Takoma, Inc., updated by Suzanne Ludlow and Sherry Mauck

Distance: 2 3/4 miles
Time: 2 hours
Bus: K2, K8, 50, 52, 54, P2, F4, and F6
Metro: Takoma (Red Line)

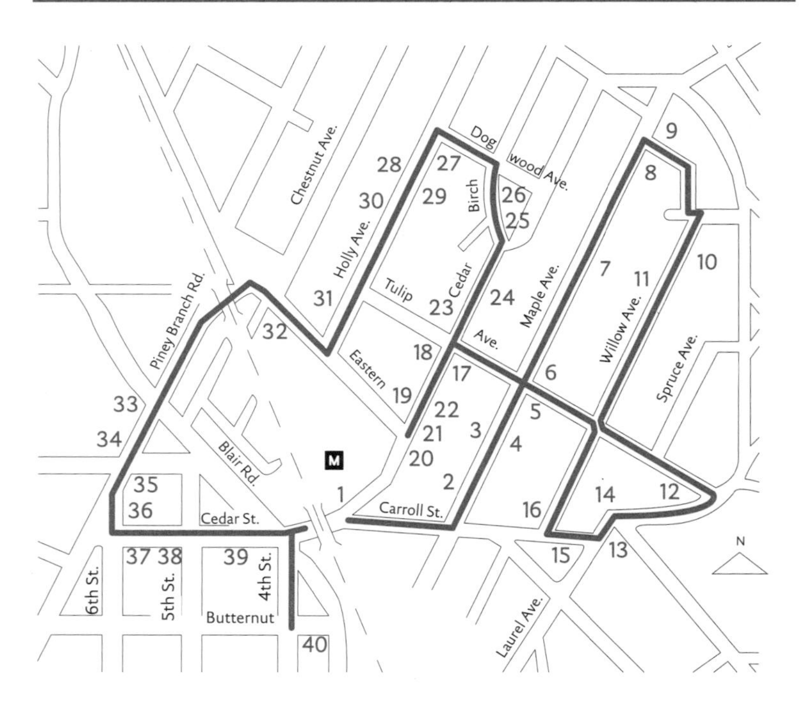

Takoma Park was founded in 1833 when real estate promoter and developer Benjamin Franklin Gilbert bought 90 acres of farmland spanned by the Baltimore and Ohio (B&O) railroad tracks on the Maryland/District of Columbia boundary line. As the first planned commuter suburb in Montgomery County, Takoma Park was part of a national trend in the 1880s—a movement from urban areas to open green suburbs along railroad and trolley lines.

The founding of Takoma Park came in the wake of the post–Civil War expansion and growth of Washington, which led to a housing shortage for federal workers. Gilbert geared his promotions to these workers and other members of the middle class, emphasizing the many amenities of his new town—space, pure spring water, sylvan glades, natural beauty, and a healthful environment free from the "noxious airs" and malarial swamps of Washington—all of which could be had for the same price as renting a flat in Washington. Gilbert took a strong personal interest in Takoma Park—he built a house for himself in the community; he donated land for churches, schools, and parks; and he served as the first mayor when the town incorporated on the Maryland side in 1890. He also promoted the town as a healthful resort and developed one of three resort hotels built in the 1890s, all of which eventually failed.

In more recent years, Takoma Park has become known for its progressive politics and the many battles that its citizens have waged to maintain its special character. These have included opposition to freeways, institutional expansion, demolition linked to expansion of the Metro system, and the development plans of neighboring jurisdictions. Today, Takoma Park boasts of its status as Tree City, as Azalea City, and as a nuclear-free zone. Yet the portion of the town near the Takoma Metro retains its late-19th-century suburban quality, and many of its original homes remain.

Because Gilbert developed without regard to jurisdictional lines, this tour includes both Maryland and the District of Columbia. Most of the area traversed on the tour is designated as a historic district on the National Register of Historic Places.

■ 1 The tour begins at the **Takoma Metro station,** near the former site of Takoma Park's B&O railroad station. This is the historic center of Takoma Park.

The Metropolitan Branch of the B&O Railroad was completed from Washington to Point of Rocks, Maryland, in 1873. The railroad tracks were originally at grade level—the Cedar Street underpass was constructed in 1912. The original Victorian B&O Railroad station, built in 1886, was burned by arsonists in 1967. It was the center of an early commercial area that included two general stores, a drugstore, a carriage factory, coal and wood yards, a blacksmith shop, a social club, a meeting hall, and a hotel. The Takoma Metro station was opened in 1978. At the community's insistence, it included only a small parking lot to discourage all-day commuter parking. In the late 1990s, a proposal was made to develop the station property into a mixed-use site with 90 high-end townhouses, some live-work townhouses, and a park area. The townhouses would be near the bus bays, parking consolidated in a garage, and buses in between. The proposal was controversial in part because the Metro property was more attractive than the surrounding area, which was dominated by parking lots, vacant lots and buildings, and marginal businesses. Although the development project was slowed, developers became interested. Across the street from the Metro entrance is Elevation 314, a development with 52 apartments and three retail shops, scheduled to open in spring 2004. Environmentally sensitive design aspects are included in the building plans. Directly across the tracks from the station entrance is the Cedar Crossing condominium development scheduled to open in late 2004.

■ **2** Walk east on Carroll Avenue, toward and past the 7-11 store, and turn left onto Maple Street. On the left, next to the Maplewood Apartments, you will find the **DC/Maryland Marker** (about 1798), surrounded by white grating. This marker predates the subdivision of the area by many years. It helps to illustrate the extent to which Gilbert ignored jurisdictional lines in laying out Takoma Park. Gilbert had always hoped that the town would be incorporated in both Maryland and the District of Columbia, but when the Maryland side was incorporated in 1890, the District Commissioners took charge of the District of Columbia side. Nevertheless, the District side of the line continues to be known as Takoma, and the ties between the two jurisdictions remain close.

■ **3** The **Dr. E. B. Bliss House** at 7116 Maple Avenue, built in 1886, is an Italianate villa from the Picturesque movement, popularized by Andrew Jackson Downing in his pattern books of the 1840s and 1850s. Its characteristic features are the square tower or campanile projecting well above the roofline as the central element of an L-shaped plan with gabled wings, the tall and narrow paired windows, the square porch supports with beveled corners, and the quoins or blocks at the corners. Note also the windows with central panes surrounded by many smaller panes at the building entrance, and the jigsaw-cut porch railings. One of the most fascinating features of the house is that it appears to be made of brick and stone but is actually constructed of wood. The wood facade is scored to imitate brickwork. It was originally painted a brick color, with the joints painted white, which further enhanced the illusion. E. B. Bliss was President Garfield's doctor after he was shot. Bliss used his fee to build the house.

■ **4** Look down the driveway of **7129 Maple Avenue,** across the street from the Bliss house. You will see a large, two-story carriage house with a loft, with an automobile garage directly in front of it built about 1910. The original house is no longer extant.

■ **5** The double-fronted **Ford Brothers House** at 7137–39 Maple Avenue was built in 1885 for brothers Byron and Seth Ford. It is among the most notable of the stick-style houses in Takoma Park. Typical of this style are the gable-framing details, the thin and Stick-like porch supports and balustrades, and the diagonal bracing and brackets. The house has been painted in an authentic Victorian color scheme.

■ **6** The **Takoma Park Presbyterian Church** at Maple and Tulip Avenues was built in 1923, but this corner has been a site of worship since Takoma Park was founded. The earliest religious services on this site were held in a tent. The non-denominational Union Chapel, a frame structure, was built here in 1888 on land donated by Gilbert. The property was sold to the Presbyterians in 1893, the same year that the Episcopalians built Trinity Episcopal Church at Dahlia Street

Dr. E. B. Bliss House

and Piney Branch Road. The town's first public school was located where the Presbyterian Church's Fellowship Hall now stands, next to the church building on Tulip Avenue.

■ 7 The **Porter House,** at 7305 Maple Avenue, built in 1886-87, is a fine example of the Queen Anne style but also incorporates elements of the Stick and Shingle styles. Typical Queen Anne features include the asymmetrical plan, the wide wraparound porch, and the half-round tower. Note also the decorative stickwork in the gables and the fishscale shingles combined with clapboard siding. The porch originally had turned supports and a geometric patterned frieze.

■ 8/9 The houses at **1 Valley View Avenue** and **7417 Maple Avenue,** both built in the 1920s, are notable for their freestanding automobile garages built in the same style as the houses. The similarity of the houses and garages extends to the roof overhang and pitch and trim detailing.

Turn right up Valley View Avenue, and then make your next right onto Willow Avenue, a street featuring several types of bungalows. "Bungalow" was a term used by the British in India around 1825 to signify a low house surrounded by a veranda and used as a "rest house" by travelers. In this country, bungalows were a vernacular, one- to one-and-a-half-story subcategory of the Craftsman style, popular from about 1905 to the early 1920s. This style was inspired primarily by the work of the Greene brothers of California, who were influenced by the English Arts and Crafts movement and oriental wooden architecture. It was an economizing development in house construction that opened up home ownership to a broader spectrum of the population. The style featured a low-pitched, gabled roof (occasionally "hipped," or four-sided) with a wide unenclosed overhang, exposed roof rafters, false beams or braces added under the gables, and a full or partial porch often supported by "battered" or slanted columns or pedestals, often extending down to the ground.

Most of the homes on Willow Avenue were built in 1913 and 1914 by the Morgan brothers, who were also the owners. The bungalow styles on this street include Colonial, Mission, Japanese, Swiss chalet, English cottage, and Spanish styles. Bungalows became very popular in Takoma Park as streetcar lines spread to new sections of the city.

■ **10** **7315 Willow Avenue,** built in 1913, has a very modern appearance that was highly unusual for structures in Takoma Park during this period. Built of stucco, its smooth, rectilinear surfaces, streamlined appearance, and horizontal emphasis reflect Spanish-style architecture popular in California at the time, as well as the Prairie style of Frank Lloyd Wright and the art moderne style.

■ **11** **7306 Willow Avenue,** built in the Tudor revival style, has a steep gable that is stuccoed and decorated with patterned wood bracing. The woodwork demonstrates the use of false half-timbering, imitating medieval infilled timber framing. Note the multipaned windows, another Tudor Revival feature.

■ **12** Turn left onto Tulip Avenue. At 7060 Carroll Avenue, at the intersection of Carroll Avenue and Tulip Avenue, you will find the **Takoma Old Town Auto Service Center,** formerly Glickman's Service Station. Built in 1933, this Tudor Revival–style garage demonstrates the domestic influence in early roadside commercial architecture. It is comparable in style with the Little Tavern restaurants throughout the Washington area. Note the stucco gables with diagonal stickwork to suggest half-timbering, similar to those at 7306 Willow Avenue. The steeply pitched slate roof with flared gable ends supported by heavy eave brackets and the arched door and window openings trimmed in randomly cut fieldstone are reminiscent of English cottage architecture. The black bricks are overfired to provide texture. The building is listed on the Maryland Inventory of Historic Sites.

As you turn the corner onto Carroll Avenue, you will enter **Takoma Old Town,** a commercial district with stores featuring many unusual products and services. This district was the site of an extensive public and private commercial revitalization effort in the early 1980s. Public amenities—such as curb and gutter replacement, new streetlights, brick sidewalks, a clock, and a new park featuring a Victorian-style gazebo at Carroll and Westmoreland Avenues—were combined with private improvements to storefront facades, which adhered to design standards defined and enforced by city ordinance. A farmers market takes place along Laurel Avenue every Sunday from April to November.

Most of the buildings along this stretch of Carroll Avenue and Laurel Avenue were constructed in the 1920s or later, during the streetcar era in Takoma Park. The introduction of streetcar service along Carroll Avenue in

1897, with subsequent service improvements and extensions in 1900, 1910, and 1918, led to the transformation of this area from a residential street to a commercial strip, a development typical of streetcar corridors.

■ **13 6931–37 Laurel Avenue** was built in the Spanish Colonial style during the 1920s or 1930s. Note the clay tile roof and black and red tilework at the base of the building. The three-sided projecting bays of the storefronts are typical of early-20th-century retail architecture.

The building is the former site of a log cabin built in 1888 by Gilbert as a meeting place for elections and political rallies by both the Democratic and Republican parties. It later served as a town meeting place, a chapel, a garage for fire engines, a jail, and finally a tool shed. The cabin was destroyed by fire on Halloween night in 1915. An adjacent 60-foot wood tower, built in 1889, provided views of the surrounding countryside until it was judged unsafe and dismantled in 1893.

■ **14 7000–2 Carroll Avenue** is a fine example of the art deco style. The building is streamlined, and demonstrates the unabashed use of modern materials such as concrete and pressed aluminum. Note the concrete accents on the piers, the concentric zigzag cornice decoration, the black tile base, and the awning and original lamp sconces, which repeat the zigzag building motif.

7000–2 Carroll Avenue

■ **15** The **Takoma Park Seventh-Day Adventist Church** (1953), at Laurel and Carroll Avenues, is built in the Gothic Revival style, with cut fieldstone, rose windows, and arched windows and entrances. The Seventh-Day Adventists became the most significant religious group in Takoma Park after they were persuaded by Gilbert to move their headquarters to Takoma Park from Battle Creek, Michigan, in 1904. The Adventists brought a conservative, family-oriented lifestyle with them, in which vegetarianism was required and drinking, gambling, and dancing were banned. Ironically, this conservatism contributed to the failure of Takoma Park's resort hotels, which Gilbert had tried to foster.

Until 1989, when it moved to Silver Spring, the Adventist headquarters was located in several buildings in this area in both Maryland and the District of Columbia, including the modern 10-story tower visible across Carroll Avenue.

However, several institutions built by the Adventists have remained in Takoma Park. The Washington Sanitarium, built in 1907, was demolished in 1982 to make way for the expansion of the Washington Adventist Hospital. Columbia Union College, originally a school for missionaries known as the Washington Training Center, is another important local institution and is celebrating its centennial in 2004. The Review and Herald publishing house moved to Hagerstown, Maryland, in 1982, but the original building remains at Eastern Avenue and Willow Street.

■ **16** The limestone-faced **Suburban Trust Building** at 6950 Carroll Avenue is now a branch of Bank of America. It was built in 1927 in the Renaissance Revival style. The building is formal, symmetrical, and monumental, with Renaissance-derived features, including tall multipaned arched windows, well-proportioned cornices with tooth-like dentils, and door and window trim.

■ **17** Turn right onto Willow Avenue, and then left onto Tulip Avenue. On the corner of Tulip Avenue and Cedar Avenue is the **Thomas-Siegler House and Gardens,** perhaps the most significant historic property in Takoma Park.

The home of Horace and Amanda Thomas, built in 1884, was the first house to be completed in Takoma Park. The house, carriage house, and spacious garden illustrate life as it was in the first years of Takoma Park's history. Mr. Thomas was Takoma Park's first postmaster, storekeeper, and stationmaster. Soon after he died in 1889, Amanda Thomas added a two-story addition to the house on the Cedar Avenue side with a wraparound porch and turret. The Thomas house was originally covered with wood clapboards similar to those on the carriage house.

In 1919, Franklin and Catherine Siegler purchased the property from the Thomas family. Their sons, E. Horace Siegler and Eugene Siegler, were noted Department of Agriculture scientists. Their botanical interest is reflected in the extensive landscaping of the one-acre property. The wraparound porch was removed and the house was covered with stucco in the 1920s or 1930s.

The property was threatened with development in 1984. Through the efforts of local citizens, the Trust for Public Land, the Maryland Open Space Program, and the City of Takoma Park, the landscaped grounds and carriage house were purchased, restored, and preserved as a city park.

■ **18** Turn left onto Cedar Avenue, originally named Oak Avenue. At 7112 Cedar Avenue is the **Ben Davis House,** built in 1888. Davis, a former mayor and town clerk, lived here with his large family for many years. This Queen Anne house features an asymmetrical design and highly textured surface; a steeply pitched, multigabled roof with decorative elements on the gables; a full-width porch with matching railing and porch frieze; a tall, patterned chimney; and single-pane windows combined with smaller panes. The main gable contains a pulpit balconet, fishscale shingles, and ornamental bargeboard that are echoed in the dormers. The chimney on the left goes right through the dormer—note the triangular, multipaned windows on either side of the dormer.

■ 19 **7100 Cedar Avenue** was built in 1890 in the Shingle style. Houses built in this style were swathed in a continuous layer of shingles, with no interruption of the shingles at the corners. In some examples of the style, such as this one, the lower floor was covered with clapboard and only the upper stories were covered with shingles. Like Queen Anne houses, Shingle-style houses have irregular outlines, but plans are simpler, fewer decorations are employed, and towers are usually half rather than full.

The hipped roof of the house has an eyebrow dormer containing circular openings, and the second story features an oval stained-glass window. The two-story circular tower intersects the curving wraparound porch, which has classical, not turned, supports.

■ 20 **202 Cedar Avenue NW,** built in 1908, is just over the Maryland/District of Columbia line (hence the change in street numbering systems). Designed by architect Fred G. Atkinson, it is a distinctive hybrid of the one-story bungalow with Colonial revival elements, most notable of which are round instead of battered (slanted) columns. Note the beveled clapboard siding, the hipped roof with gambrel center dormer (a Dutch Colonial Revival feature), the broad front porch with six classical columns, the diamond pane windows, and the original tin shingles. The original cost of the house was $3,740. Two identical houses are located in North Takoma, near Montgomery College.

■ 21 The **Ida Summy House** at 7101 Cedar Avenue, built in 1886, is next door to 202 Cedar Avenue NW but is inside the Maryland border. It is named for its first owner, who suggested the name *Tacoma,* an Indian word meaning "high up, near heaven," to Gilbert over a game of bridge. Gilbert changed the *c* to a *k* to avoid confusion with Tacoma, Washington; he later added "Park" to emphasize the town's natural beauty from its sylvan atmosphere.

The house typifies vernacular suburban architecture of the late 19th century. It has retained its original slate roof, but the porch lattice and brackets have been removed.

■ 22 **7103–5 Cedar Avenue** was built in 1907 as apartments for railroad workers but was converted into a duplex in the 1970s. The building is in the Second Empire style and features a dual sloped mansard roof with gabled dormers on the steep lower slope and a molded cornice; arched head windows; and classical columns. (The mansard roof is named for François Mansart, the 17th-century French architect who invented it. This roof style was revived during the Napoleonic era of 1852–70, France's Second Empire.)

■ 23 **7204 Cedar Avenue** is the former site of the home of B. F. Gilbert, which was built in 1885 and burned about 1913.

Born in 1841 in Madison County, New York, Gilbert came to Washington as a hotel clerk in 1862. He began his career as a real estate promoter and developer in 1867. In 1883, he bought and subdivided the Grammar Farm, which became Takoma Park. In 1886 and 1889, Gilbert bought additional farmland to expand Takoma Park. In 1890, when the town was incorporated, he was elected the first mayor of Takoma Park, but he resigned in 1892 to supervise the development of the Takoma Park Loan and Trust addition. The 1893 panic and national depression ruined Gilbert financially. He suffered a paralytic stroke in 1901 and died of uremic poisoning in 1907 at the age of 66.

The current house was built in 1913 in the neoclassical style, a reaction to the perceived excesses of the historic period of the late 19th century. The building demonstrates the Jeffersonian ideal in architectural design, which was strongly influenced by Roman architecture. Note the Roman temple front and Italian Renaissance motifs such as the Palladian window (an arched window surrounded by sidelights) facing Cedar Avenue, partially obscured by vines.

■ **24** 7209 Cedar Avenue, known as the **"Boat House,"** was built in the 1890s. It was designed by Harvey Page, a well-known Washington architect who also designed the now-demolished Palais Royale, Woodward and Lothrop's old north building. It is one of the few architect-designed homes in Takoma Park, and is an outstanding example of the Shingle style, with the simplified massing and absence of applied decoration typical of the style. Note the side-facing gambrel roof and curved central tower. The porch, like the rest of the house, was originally covered with shingles but was altered in the early 1980s.

■ **25** The **Burrows House,** at Cedar and Birch Avenues, presents a commanding facade to the street. Originally built in the 1890s as a high-style Victorian house, it underwent a neocolonial rehabilitation in the late 1930s. The two-story portico replaced a one-story porch and balcony with a Mount Vernon–style Colonial porch railing. All front doors and windows were replaced, and an 18th-century-style entrance with elliptical fanlight and sidelights was added. The three Victorian features remaining are the multipatterned slate roof, the medieval-style patterned chimneys, and the original narrow windows on the side of the house facing Birch Avenue.

■ **26** Continue down Birch Avenue to the **Price House** at no. 7303. The house was built in 1987 on a small infill lot by architects Jeanne and Travis Price and received an AIA award for design excellence.

The architects combined two major themes in their design. The first was a contextual interpretation of the neighborhood. Elements of high-pitched dormers, bold colors, and classical columns echoing neighborhood houses are blended with "imported" modernist materials such as glass block and curving metal railings. The second design determinant was a large glass southern exposure to provide passive solar heating and natural lighting. The facade on the south side was also carefully treated with an arbor for shading.

The house was placed on the site to preserve the existing tulip magnolia trees, which were the inspiration for the colors of the stucco-like material on the house.

■ **27** Turn left onto Dogwood Avenue, and left again onto Holly Avenue. At **7305 Holly Avenue,** you will find a classic, one-story bungalow with offset gables facing the street. The heavy squared piers, the multipaned windows, and the false beams projecting from the gable ends are all typical Craftsman features.

This bungalow is a Sears kit house, a mail-order house shipped in pieces and assembled on site. Sears offered these kit houses by catalog from 1908 to 1940. Over the years, 450 different house models were made available to buyers. The quality of the materials offered and the company's generous credit terms were strong selling points for the Sears houses. Kit houses manufactured by Sears and other companies made home construction more economical and therefore more affordable to a wider range of the population. A number of these houses in a variety of styles may be found in Takoma Park.

■ **28** **7300 Holly Avenue** is a Dutch Colonial Revival house, built about 1915–25, with a cross gambrel roof and clipped front gable and side dormers. The house has original pressed-tin shingles on the roof and the second floor, a stucco first floor, classical porch columns, and triple front windows on the first and second floors. Note the patterned panes in the second-story windows.

The Dutch Colonial Revival style was dominant during the first half of the 20th century. The gambrel roof is borrowed from houses built by New World colonists from the Netherlands, which were in turn modeled after English and Dutch houses of the Atlantic seaboard.

■ **29** The Stick-style house at **7219 Holly Avenue** is articulated by its paint scheme. Built in the 1880s, the house is typically angular, in contrast to the Queen Anne style, with the primary decorative feature being the diagonal stickwork on the wall, meant to suggest half-timbering. Note the jigsaw porch brackets and the beveled clapboard.

■ **30** Dramatically poised on an incline, **7216 Holly Avenue,** a Victorian Picturesque / Queen Anne house, is a wonderful example of the spatial play of the Victorian era. The variation in the roofline and massing is achieved by cutting away niches on the second floor. The porches and front gable feature matching decorative detail. The brick red and mustard paint scheme is typically Victorian. The house was built about 1885–95.

■ **31** **7106 Holly Avenue,** built in 1987, won an award from Montgomery Preservation, Inc., for new construction in a historic neighborhood. This new house is compatible with its surrounding neighborhood in scale, massing, roofline, materials, and detail. The open porch with its substantial columns and the steep pitch of the roof with intersecting gables are reflective of the architectural elements found in the late-19th- and early-20th-century houses of the area. The overall scheme shows a strong debt to vernacular architecture of that period without being a superficial replication.

The project architects were David Rinn (preliminary design) and Paul Treseder (final design), and the structure was built by Presidential Associates.

■ **32** Turn right on Eastern Avenue, which forms the DC–Maryland boundary. At the corner of Eastern Avenue and Chestnut Avenue is the **Cady Lee Mansion,** a magnificent high-style Queen Anne house built in 1887. Perhaps the best-known house in Takoma Park, it is a DC Landmark and is listed on the National Register of Historic Places. It was designed by Leon E. Dessez, a prominent turn-of-the-century architect, who also designed the Admiralty House, now the vice presidential residence. It is the lone survivor of a group of splendid Victorian residences built along the railroad tracks, now replaced by garden apartments and Metro parking, which were planned by Gilbert to provide conspicuous proof to the passerby of the affordable elegance of Takoma Park.

Cady Lee Mansion

The house features a typically Queen Anne asymmetrical design with irregular massing, multiple gables with finials, an elaborate curved wraparound porch with turned supports, a three-story tower with third-story porch that repeats the first-story porch pattern, and a slate roof with tall, patterned, medieval-style chimneys. The fishscale shingles on the second and third stories and the elaborate detail of the trim give the house an extremely varied texture.

The house was threatened with demolition in 1974 when the heirs of Mary Cady Lee planned to sell the house to a developer who intended to construct garden apartments on the site. These plans were canceled when the house was placed on the National Register and designated a DC Landmark. A buyer interested in restoring the house was found, and it became a private residence. However, renovation of the house was not possible until it was purchased in the 1990s by Frances Phipps, a Takoma Park resident and developer, carefully restored, and then sold in 2002 to be used as the organizational headquarters for the Forum for Youth Involvement.

■ **33** Turn left onto Piney Branch Road and continue past the railroad underpass to **7124 Piney Branch Road NW** at the intersection of Piney Branch Road and Blair Road. Built about 1900, this eclectic house has medieval English influences and is closely related to the Tudor Revival style. The house is of stucco and frame construction, with a wide front porch, slate roof, and tall, patterned chimneys. The most notable element is the Old World stepped gable with diamond-paned windows.

■ **34** The **Knox House** at 7106 Piney Branch Road NW, built in 1910, is a one-and-a-half-story cottage bungalow with a Swiss chalet influence. The porch is supported by double square columns with curving white brackets, and the lower story and porch base are a light-colored stucco. The white double triangular brackets and window trim contrast with the dark brown shingles. The many small panes in the upper windows and the overhanging eaves with exposed rafter ends are Craftsman touches.

■ **35** The **Trinity Church and Rectory,** located at Piney Branch Road and Dahlia Street, were designed by Philip Hubert Frohman, the main architect of the National Cathedral, and built in 1937 and 1941, respectively. The congregation's original church, built on this site in 1893, is no longer extant. The present church, built in the late Gothic Revival style, is constructed of native rubble stone and trimmed with cast stone. With its stained-glass windows, it looks like a 13th-century English country church. The rectory was built to resemble the chapter house at the National Cathedral.

■ **36** Turn left onto Cedar Street. **At 535 Cedar Street NW** you will find a late Queen Anne house featuring the finest spindlework in Takoma Park. Built in 1908, the house is a very late example of this style, sometimes called "free classic" because of its liberal incorporation of classical elements.

The house features repetitive patterns in an asymmetrical plan. The spindlework of the first-floor porch balusters is repeated in the smaller pattern of the porch frieze, and the porch balusters, supports, and brackets are also repeated in the smaller second-floor porch. The curved arch framing the porch entrance is surrounded with dramatic beaded spindlework. The classical elements include the arched windows in the third-floor gables and the Palladian window of the main gable. Note also the two-story, three-sided bay and the latticework windows facing 6th Street.

■ **37** The American Four-Square architectural style, as typified in the **Innis House** at 532 Cedar Street NW, was developed as a reaction to the typically ornate Victorian styles. The boxy, simplified massing, the limited decoration, and the hipped roof with matching hipped front dormer are characteristic of the Four

Square style. Constructed in 1911, the house was originally owned by the first registered pharmacist in the United States.

■ **38** The **Takoma Branch of the District of Columbia Library,** at 5th and Cedar Streets, was built in 1911 with money donated by Andrew Carnegie, with the stipulation that Takoma Park citizens would purchase the site. Angus Lamond, a Takoma Park resident and fellow Scot, knew Carnegie and had asked him for help. Residents in both Maryland and the District raised money for this project, the first library branch in the DC system.

The Renaissance Revival brick structure with wood trim is one massive story with a simplified entablature, composed of a frieze and dentils at the roofline, with a hipped slate roof. The arched windows with keystones and quoins at the corners are typical features of this style.

■ **39** The **Watkins Apartment House,** a brick, six-unit building at 406 Cedar Street NW, was built by coal merchant William Watkins in 1908 for his six daughters and their families. The structure has a flat roof and rectangular form, with five-windowed bays resembling fortress towers at each corner, and one over one window topped by concrete lintels. The three-tiered front porch features four prominent columns filled in with molded concrete. The center double-panel entrance door with transom overlooks a steeply terraced lawn, and the multipaned glass front doors on the upper floors open onto the second- and third-story porches. The house is similar to the earlier hotel Watkins built on the other side of the railroad tracks in 1892, which burned in the following year. The building was completely renovated in 1981, and is now condominiums.

■ **40** Turn right onto 4th Street, an early-20th-century commercial strip. The brick sidewalks and crosswalks and the uniform facade treatments were completed as part of a commercial revitalization effort in this area by the District government.

At the intersection of 4th Street and Butternut Street is the **Takoma Theater,** built in 1923 as a 500-seat motion picture theater. Constructed of brick, steel, and reinforced concrete at a cost of $55,000 to $60,000, it was designed by John J. Zink, a prominent Washington theater architect. The theater featured a classical interior at a time when the predominant style of movie theaters was eclectic and exotic. The design incorporates two first-floor retail storefronts.

A Lutheran congregation held their first services here in 1924 until they constructed their own church at 7th and Dahlia Streets in 1927. The building has been owned by playwright Milton McGinty since 1983. Recently the Takoma Theater Arts Project formed to help renovate and program the theater.

Next door is the Takoma Village Cohousing development, completed in 2001. It is made up of 43 self-sufficient housing units as well as shared space for cooking, dining, and community activities. This project has won awards for its energy-efficient design features.

Retrace your steps on 4th Street to Cedar Street and turn right to return to the Metro station.

About the Authors and Contributors

The following individuals contributed to this edition of *Washington on Foot*.

Christopher Alleva is a senior associate with the Fraser Forbes Company, specializing in real estate markets in the state of Maryland. He holds a bachelor's degree in accounting from Villanova University.

Maybelle Bennett, a native Washingtonian, is director of the Howard University Community Association. She holds a master's degree in planning. She coordinates the planning, development, and community service activities of the university's revitalization efforts known as the LeDroit Park Initiative. Ms. Bennett also oversees the university's AmeriCorps program. She was a member of the District of Columbia Zoning Commission and the District of Columbia Board of Zoning Adjustment for 16 years.

Paul Douglass, a transplanted Californian, is a lawyer, writer, and urban land broker who has resided in Washington, DC, with his wife, Cheryl, since 1973.

John Fondersmith, AICP, is a development review specialist in the District of Columbia's Office of Planning. He has been a planner and planning consultant in the public and private sectors for over 30 years.

Ryan Harris, AICP, holds a master's degree in regional planning from Cornell University and is employed as a regional planner with the Metropolitan Washington Council of Governments. He is an active member with the local APA Chapter and is responsible for the chapter's Web site.

Dan Hessman is a retired professional engineer. For the past 13 years, he has been an active participant in the American Volksport Association, completing 650 sanctioned 10-km walks covering 46 states.

Suzanne Ludlow, AICP, is community and government liaison in the City of Takoma Park, Maryland. She has held this position for 10 years.

Sherry Mauck holds degrees in linguistics and library science from Georgetown University and the University of Maryland. She is a career employee of the Central Intelligence Agency.

Stephanie Protopappas is a senior at Foxcroft High School in Middleburg, Virginia. She is an avid walker.

James Troy is the editor of various newsletters that focus on real estate developments throughout the Washington metropolitan area.

Carol Truppi, AICP, has nearly 20 years of experience in planning and landscape architecture. She holds a master's degree in landscape architecture from Harvard University and a bachelor's degree in environmental design from the University of Massachusetts.

James Wilson holds a master's degree in city planning from The Catholic University of America. He worked for the City of Alexandria for 31 years as a city planner and retired in 2000.

The following individuals contributed to previous editions of *Washington on Foot*; their contributions range from writing and expanding, to rewriting and updating. Lin Brown, Pierre Paul Childs, Robert H. Cousins, Charity Vanderbilt Davidson, John Fondersmith, Peter Fuchs, Suzanne Ganschinietz, Alan A. Hodges, Carol Hodges, Marilyn (Mickey) Klein, Antoinette J. Lee, Alvin R. McNeal, Julia Pastor, Ruth Polan, Frederic Protopappas, John J. Protopappas, Berry Steeves, Charles Szoradi, William Washburn, Lindsley Williams, James L. Wilson, and Kathleen Sinclair Wood.

Many artists have contributed to the artwork included in *Washington on Foot*, most notably Brian Barth, Fred Greenberg, Reena Racki, and Leo Schmittel.

A special thank-you is extended to David F. Erion in the Operations Planning and Administrative Support Branch of the Washington Metropolitan Area Transit Authority (WMATA) for providing information on bus and rail schedules. Additionally, Jo Ann Harrison, secretary to Alvin R. McNeal, provided invaluable clerical and support services throughout the preparation of this publication.